Designing and Evaluating Public Health Interventions

Sutapa Bandyopadhyay Neogi
Anuj Kumar Pandey
Editors

Designing and Evaluating Public Health Interventions

Unwrapping the key concepts using case studies from India

Springer

Editors
Sutapa Bandyopadhyay Neogi
Department of Health Systems and Implementation Research
International Institute of Health Management Research (IIHMR)
New Delhi India

Anuj Kumar Pandey
Department of Health Systems and Implementation Research
International Institute of Health Management Research (IIHMR)
New Delhi India

ISBN 978-981-97-9573-4 ISBN 978-981-97-9574-1 (eBook)
https://doi.org/10.1007/978-981-97-9574-1

This Springer imprint is published by the registered company Springer Nature Singapore Pte Ltd.
The registered company address is: 152 Beach Road, #21-01/04 Gateway East, Singapore 189721, Singapore

Preface

Public health is the backbone of a thriving society, underpinning the well-being and prosperity of communities worldwide. Effective public health interventions can significantly reduce the disease burden, improve the quality of life, and enhance health equity. This book, *Designing and Evaluating Public Health Interventions: Unwrapping the Key Concepts Using Case Studies from India*, aims to serve as a comprehensive guide for health professionals, researchers, and students dedicated to this critical field.

India, with its diverse population and unique health challenges, provides a rich tapestry for examining public health strategies. Through detailed case studies, we explore the complexities of designing and evaluating interventions that address a wide spectrum of health issues, from infectious diseases to chronic conditions and from maternal and child health to mental health. Each chapter merged with case studies offers practical insights and evidence-based approaches, drawing from real-world experiences in Indian contexts.

Public health interventions should not be viewed as a one-time solution to address perpetual problems. It is a dynamic process that continuously evolves based on the problem statement, the changing burden of diseases, the maturity of health systems, emerging evidence on interventions, the cost-effectiveness of interventions, their scalability, and above all, national priorities. There have been instances where an intervention, apparently successful in a limited geographical area, could not yield similar results when scaled up. It therefore requires careful consideration while designing research keeping the end result of scalability and cost-effectiveness in mind. Unbiased evidence that informs polices is eventually more sustained in any populace.

Case-based teaching emulates real-time problems with probable solutions. Those that are based on problems emanating from field-level situations provide an opportunity to discuss, contemplate, and critique for common good. This sort of participatory and engaging pedagogical method links theory with practice and vice versa. It is increasingly being recognized that case studies should strongly complement lecture-based classroom teaching to enhance the grasp of the subject and instil critical thinking.

This work is intricately linked with the disciplines of health and hospital management. Effective public health interventions require not only robust design and evaluation frameworks but also efficient management and administration within healthcare settings. Hospitals and healthcare institutions play a pivotal role in implementing and sustaining these interventions, making the integration of health management principles essential.

Our inspiration and foundation stem from the ongoing research and activities conducted by the International Institute of Health Management Research (IIHMR), Delhi. IIHMR Delhi has been at the forefront of advancing health management education, research, and practice. Their projects and collaborations have contributed significantly to our understanding of public health dynamics in India and beyond. By incorporating their findings and methodologies, we aim to bridge the gap between theory and practice, providing a pragmatic approach to public health challenges.

We hope this book will be a valuable resource for those involved in public health, offering guidance and inspiration for designing impactful interventions. It is our aspiration that readers will be equipped with the knowledge and tools necessary to create and evaluate public health strategies that are both effective and sustainable.

Thank you!

New Delhi, Delhi, India

Sutapa Bandyopadhyay Neogi
Anuj Kumar Pandey

Overview: Case Studies

The use of case studies is widely acknowledged as being a good tool for comprehending how different interventions may affect the ever-evolving and complicated health system. A well-documented case study might ease the task of understanding what, where, when, and how an intervention might be successfully implemented and later scaled as a national policy. These case studies also help readers understand the length and breadth of a public health intervention in order to achieve and endure the anticipated effects.

The available literature[1] suggests that public health case studies have capabilities to address various objectives such as

(a) To provide an understanding to improve the relevance of the development of a context-specific intervention.
(b) It strengthens the understanding of 'how' an intervention works.
(c) It simplifies the comprehension of 'how' and 'why' intervention impacts vary across diverse scenarios.
(d) It also ensures robust, evidence-based decision-making.

Thus, these case studies would introduce readers to the concept of public health interventions. These would be discussed in the context of some real-time interventions which later became a part of the national policy. These case studies from diverse disease situations and interventions backed up with robust evidence aim to build the capacity of the reader to conceptualize, conduct, and analyse a research work to understand the 'what', 'where', 'when', and 'how' of designing and evaluating a public health intervention.

[1] Paparini S, Green J, Papoutsi C, Murdoch J, Petticrew M, Greenhalgh T, Hanckel B, Shaw S. Case study research for better evaluations of complex interventions: rationale and challenges. BMC Med. 2020;18(1):301. https://doi.org/10.1186/s12916-020-01777-6. PMID: 33167974; PMCID: PMC7652677.

Acknowledgements

Health Management Research aims to continually build up the evidence base to influence implementation science. Case study teaching method is an active form of learning by analysing cases that are real or invented stories.

This book, *Designing and Evaluating Public Health Interventions: Unwrapping the Key Concepts Using Case Studies from India*, synthesizes the evidence from well documented and acclaimed interventions to address pertinent public health issues. It aims to orient learners on how to justify the implementation of any intervention in a given context and finally bridging the gap between laboratory to bedside and community and between research and policy.

We thank all the authors whose research papers have been synthesized into case studies for the purpose of our learning. The rigour of their research finally culminates into publications that reflect their global standing.

We acknowledge the contributions of our esteemed co-authors: Prof. Preetha GS, Dr. Siddharth Sekhar Mishra, Dr. Rupsa Banerjee, Dr. Vinay Tripathi, and Dr. Samraj Sahay. Their dedication, expertise, and collaborative spirit have enriched the content and quality of this book. We thank Prof. Preetha GS and Dr Vinay Tripathi for their constructive feedback while reviewing the contents.

We owe our gratitude to all the staff and faculty members of IIHMR Delhi who supported us in every way to help us complete this task. Special credit goes to our library, whose extensive resources have been indispensable to our research and writing process. The access to comprehensive literature and data has greatly facilitated our work. We thank Mr. Jagdish Prasad, Ms. Meenakshi, and Mr. Ashok Kumar for their patience and commitment all along.

We are indebted to our senior management and Prof. SD Gupta in particular for his constant guidance and encouragement to fulfil the mission and vision of IIHMR, which is to generate knowledge for budding health professionals. His visionary leadership and passion for health management research and commitment to improving public health outcomes have been a constant source of inspiration.

We are profoundly grateful to Springer for accepting our work, especially to Ms. Vandana Joshi and Ms. Neeraja Padmanabhan from Springer, for their unwavering support and assistance throughout the publishing process. Their professionalism and guidance have been invaluable in bringing this book to its completion.

We extend our heartfelt gratitude to our parents, friends, and family for their unwavering support and encouragement throughout this journey. Their love and understanding have been our greatest source of strength.

This book is a testament to the importance of rigorous research and thoughtful design in public health interventions, and it is our sincere hope that it will contribute meaningfully to the field. Like any other author, we too derive strength and motivation from our esteemed readers who, in all their wisdom, might find this book beneficial for their students and public health practitioners. We strongly encourage you to provide us with constructive critique and guidance that will help us enhance the quality of its contents. Your contribution will extend beyond the realms of this book.

We do hope that you find this book useful. Wishing you a Happy Reading!

Contents

Abbreviations

AFP	Acute flaccid paralysis
AOR	Adjusted odds ratio
ASHA	Accredited Social Health Activist
AWW	Anganwadi workers
BCG	Bacillus Calmette–Guérin vaccine
BPL	Below poverty line
BSID-III	Bayley Scales of Infant Development
CCT	Conditional cash transfer
CDC	Centers for Disease Control and Prevention
CDSAG	Child Deaths Study and Action Group
CEA	Cost-effectiveness analysis
CI	Confidence interval
ciKMC	Community-initiated kangaroo mother care
CMA	Cost-minimization analysis
CTRI	Clinical Trials Registry-India
CUA	Cost-utility analysis
DALYs	Disability-adjusted life years
DHR	Department of Health Research
DMHP	District Mental Health Programme
DPT	Diphtheria–pertussis–tetanus vaccine
EBM	Evidence-based medicine
EBPH	Evidence-based public health
ENDS	Electronic nicotine delivery systems
EPI	Expanded Programme on Immunization
EUA	Emergency Use Authorization
FAQ	Frequently asked questions
FDA	Food and Drug Administration
FGDs	Focus group discussions
GCP	Good clinical research practice
GNI	Gross national income
GOI	Government of India
GP	General practitioners
Hb	Haemoglobin
HBNC	Home-based newborn care
HCQ	Hydroxychloroquine
HPS	High-performing states
HYE	Healthy-years equivalent

ICER	Incremental cost-effectiveness ratio
ICMR	Indian Council of Medical Research
ICTRP	International Clinical Trials Registry Platform
IDIs	In-depth interviews
IEAG	India Expert Advisory Group
IMNCI	Integrated Management of Neonatal and Childhood Illnesses
IMR	Infant mortality rate
IPPI	Intensified Pulse Polio Immunization
IPV	Inactivated polio vaccine
IV	Intravenous
IV iron	Intravenous iron
JSY	Janani Suraksha Yojana
KMC	Kangaroo mother care
LAR	Legally acceptable/authorized representative
LPS	Low-performing states
LYS	Life-years saved
M&E	Monitoring and evaluation
MDG	Millennium development goals
MMR	Maternal mortality ratio
MOHR	My Own Health Report
MRC	Medical Research Council
NABH	National Accreditation Board for Hospitals & Healthcare Providers
NFBS	National Family Benefit Scheme
NFHS	National Family Health Surveys
NGOs	Non-governmental organizations
NHP	National Health Policy
NIH	National Institutes of Health
NMBS	National Maternity Benefit Scheme
NMR	Neonatal mortality rate
NOAPS	National Old Age Pension Scheme
NPP	National Population Policy
NPSP	National Polio Surveillance Project
NRHM	National Rural Health Mission
NSAP	National Social Assistance Programme
NSSO	National Sample Survey Organization
O	Observation
OPD	Outpatient department
OPV	Oral polio vaccine
OR	Operational research
ORS	Oral rehydration solution
PAR	Participatory action research
PCPNDT	Pre-Conception and Pre-Natal Diagnostic Techniques
PHI	Public health interventions
PN	Practising nurses
RCTs	Randomized controlled trials
RQ	Research question
SC/ST	Scheduled caste and Schedule tribe

SDGs	Sustainable Development Goals
SO	Strategic objectives
SOTs	Special outreach teams
SR	Shishu Rakshak
SRS	Sample Registration System
SSD	Sex selection drugs
UTs	Union territories
VDPV	Vaccine-derived polio virus
WHO	World Health Organization
WPVs	Wild polioviruses
X	Intervention

1 Introduction

Anuj Kumar Pandey

In 1997, M. Jenicek discussed the linkage concerning epidemiology, evidence-based medicine (EBM), and evidence-based public health (EBPH). Later, he defined EBPH as "conscientious, explicit, and judicious use of current best evidence in making decisions about the care of communities and populations in the domain of health protection, disease prevention, health maintenance and improvement (health promotion)" [1, 2]. Practicing evidence-based public health indicates incorporating research with evidence from implementation in programmatic or health systems settings. The overall aim is to increase research-based evidences for policy-level decision-making [3].

Brownson et al. expanded upon the concept of EBPH, defining it as "the development, implementation, and evaluation of effective programs and policies in public health through application of principles of scientific reasoning, including systematic uses of data and information systems and appropriate use of program planning models" [4, 5].

The implementation of evidence-based medicine (EBM) has brought significant advancements to medical practice. However, challenges arise with the unplanned application of EBM, reaching a point for some that resembles dogmatic adherence [6]. Properly designed and well-conducted research can offer the best evidence to determine the safety and effectiveness of any intervention [7, 8]. A health intervention encompasses any action conducted to evaluate, enhance, sustain, encourage, or alter health or health-related conditions. Approaching public health evaluation with a comprehensive systems perspective has the potential to amplify the significance and robustness of evidence, contributing to the reduction of health disparities and the enhancement of overall health outcomes [9].

"Interventions" are activities to improve or protect the health status of population/community at large [10]. Public health (PH) interventions are aimed at communities rather than individuals and are essential for ensuring sustainable healthcare services [11]. These interventions play an important role in not only improving overall health and longevity but also in enhancing quality of life, thereby boosting overall productivity.

Several interventions are introduced, tried, and tested on a limited scale by a range of implementing bodies, including government and non-governmental development partners. However, only a few are successfully scaled up and ultimately integrated into state or national programs [12]. Unfortunately, some successful interventions have failed to produce the desired results when scaled up.

A. K. Pandey (✉)
Department of Health Systems and Implementation Research, International Institute of Health Management Research (IIHMR), New Delhi, India
e-mail: anuj@iihmrdelhi.edu.in

S. Bandyopadhyay Neogi, A. K. Pandey (eds.), *Designing and Evaluating Public Health Interventions*, https://doi.org/10.1007/978-981-97-9574-1_1

There is a huge deficit of competent personnel, who can design and implement research relevant to programs and policies in public health space. Therefore, there is a need to sensitize public health professionals on the relevance of research in policy/decision-making. It is essential to train people managing health programs on the importance of research for better decision-making [13].

The ultimate goal of any public health intervention is to assess if the intervention achieved the expected outcomes like improved quality of life, reduced mortality, decreased risk factor, etc. As awareness of the necessity for evidence-based public health continues to increase, this book, *Designing and Evaluating Public Health Interventions*, will assist in designing and analyzing interventions to improve practice.

This book is a fine amalgamation of theoretical concepts and practical dimensions illustrated through case studies. These case studies from India demonstrate the efforts to bridge the gap between "what should be done" and "what has been done." Each one brings with it years of experience and efforts to address burning public health issues. These would serve as food for thought for discussions during any academic or research program.

The contents of this book will equip readers to:

- Describe the different types of public health interventions.
- Frame an appropriate research question on a public health intervention, including relevance and expected outcome.
- Describe approaches to designing a public health intervention.
- Formulate the implementation plan of an intervention.
- Develop a monitoring and evaluation framework of a public health intervention.
- Choose the most appropriate study design to test the effectiveness of an intervention.
- Assess scalability of an intervention.

References

1. Jenicek M. Epidemiology, evidenced-based medicine, and evidence-based public health. J Epidemiol. 1997;7(4):187–97.
2. Komatsu RS. Evidence based medicine is the conscientious, explicit, and judicious use of current evidence in making decisions about the care of individual patients. Sao Paulo Med J. 1996;114(3):1190–1.
3. Masic I, Miokovic M, Muhamedagic B. Evidence based medicine—new approaches and challenges. Acta Inform Med. 2008;16(4):219–25.
4. Brownson RC, Gurney JG, Land GH. Evidence-based decision making in public health. J Public Health Manag Pract. 1999;5(5):86–97.
5. Brownson RC, Baker EA, Deshpande AD, Gillespie KN. Evidence-based public health. Oxford University Press. [Internet]. [cited 2021 Nov 29]. Available from:https://global.oup.com/academic/product/evidence-based-public-health-9780190620936?cc=in&lang=en&.
6. Spence JD. The need for clinical judgement in the application of evidence-based medicine. BMJ Evid Based Med. 2020;25(5):172–7.
7. gcp1.pdf [Internet]. [cited 2021 Nov 29]. Available from: https://www.who.int/medicines/areas/quality_safety/safety_efficacy/gcp1.pdf.
8. Balakumar P, Inamdar MN, Jagadeesh G. The critical steps for successful research: the research proposal and scientific writing: (a report on the pre-conference workshop held in conjunction with the 64th annual conference of the Indian Pharmaceutical Congress-2012). J Pharmacol Pharmacother. 2013;4(2):130–8.
9. McGill E, Er V, Penney T, Egan M, White M, Meier P, et al. Evaluation of public health interventions from a complex systems perspective: a research methods review. Soc Sci Med. 2021;272:113697.
10. Schaffer MA, Anderson LJW, Rising S. Public health interventions for school nursing practice. J Sch Nurs. 2016;32(3):195–208.
11. Stojanovic J, Wübbeler M, Geis S, Reviriego E, Gutiérrez-Ibarluzea I, Lenoir-Wijnkoop I. Evaluating public health interventions: a neglected area in health technology assessment. Front Public Health. 2020;8:106.
12. Morris ZS, Wooding S, Grant J. The answer is 17 years, what is the question: understanding time lags in translational research. J R Soc Med. 2011;104(12):510–20.
13. Hanney SR, Gonzalez-Block MA, Buxton MJ, Kogan M. The utilisation of health research in policy-making: concepts, examples and methods of assessment. Health Res Policy Syst. 2003;1(1):2.

Concept of Public Health Interventions

2

Rupsa Banerjee

Learning Objectives

After going through this section, participants will be able to:

- Define public health interventions and explain with examples.
- List the types and levels of practice of public health interventions.
- Explain the process of selection of public health interventions.
- Explain intervention delivery strategies.
- Explain integration of public health interventions.

2.1 Definition of Public Health Intervention

A health intervention is any action or set of actions undertaken for improvement, maintenance, and promotion of health and assessment, prevention, treatment, and rehabilitation of disease conditions. Public health interventions focus on communities or the population at large and are intended to promote well-being and prevent disease, disability, or death. Public health interventions play an important role in the overall health, longevity, and productivity of a community as they help improve quality of living of communities and health of vulnerable sections of the population, reduce health costs, and improve health outcomes of populations. These interventions take into consideration the various determinants of health and are applied across multiple levels of prevention, though they are mainly aimed at health promotion and primary prevention.

It is important to note that public health interventions focus on entire populations and are not limited to only those individuals who seek care. Some examples of public health interventions would include home-based newborn care to reduce neonatal and infant mortality, regular screening of school children for early identification of vision and hearing disorders, social marketing to improve public awareness and utilization of health programs, enforcement of laws related to speed limit to prevent road traffic accidents, etc.

2.2 Types of Public Health Interventions

Public health interventions can be designed at various levels depending on the target population and level of prevention. A Public Intervention Wheel was originally proposed in 1998 by Keller et al. [1], to demonstrate the scope of interventions

R. Banerjee (✉)
Department of Health Systems and Implementation Research, International Institute of Health Management Research, New Delhi, India
e-mail: rupsa@iihmrdelhi.edu.in

S. Bandyopadhyay Neogi, A. K. Pandey (eds.), *Designing and Evaluating Public Health Interventions*, https://doi.org/10.1007/978-981-97-9574-1_2

as a model for population-based public health practice in nursing. The Wheel defines public health interventions across three levels of delivery: individual, community, and health systems level. Interventions can be grouped across five domains, as illustrated in Fig. 2.1.

There are three levels of practice of public health interventions [3]:

1. *Systems-focused practice* is that which is not directly implemented on individuals or communities but targets the systems that impact health. It includes changes in organizations, policies, and laws.

   Examples are "maternity benefit" of 6-month paid leave given to women during pregnancy and childbirth to take care of her child, the Janani Suraksha Yojana which provides cash incentive to mothers for institutional delivery, etc.
2. *Community-focused practice* aims either at entire communities/populations or at target (high-risk) groups within the population. It brings about changes in community norms, awareness, attitudes, and practice. Campaigns targeted toward improving practices related to safe water, sanitation and hygiene, participatory rural appraisals, pulse polio campaign, etc. are examples of community-focused population-based practice.
3. *Individual/family-focused practice* is directed at individuals as part of families or high-risk groups. It aims at changing knowledge, attitude, and practice at individual level, especially of those who are identified as being part of the population at risk.

   Examples are Integrated Management of Neonatal and Childhood Illnesses (IMNCI), targeted interventions to prevent HIV/AIDS transmission in high-risk groups, opportunistic screening of non-communicable diseases, etc.

Q.2.1 *Kindly refer to case studies on Janani Suraksha Yojana (JSY), Home-Based Newborn Care (HBNC), and IV Iron Sucrose. Identify the levels of practice of these public health interventions.*

Public health interventions are assumed to be population-based and are grounded in an assessment of the population's health status. Though aimed at three different levels of practice, individual and family level, community level and health systems level, each intervention can be practiced at all levels with the exceptions of case finding (individual level) and coalition building and organizing communities (community and system level).

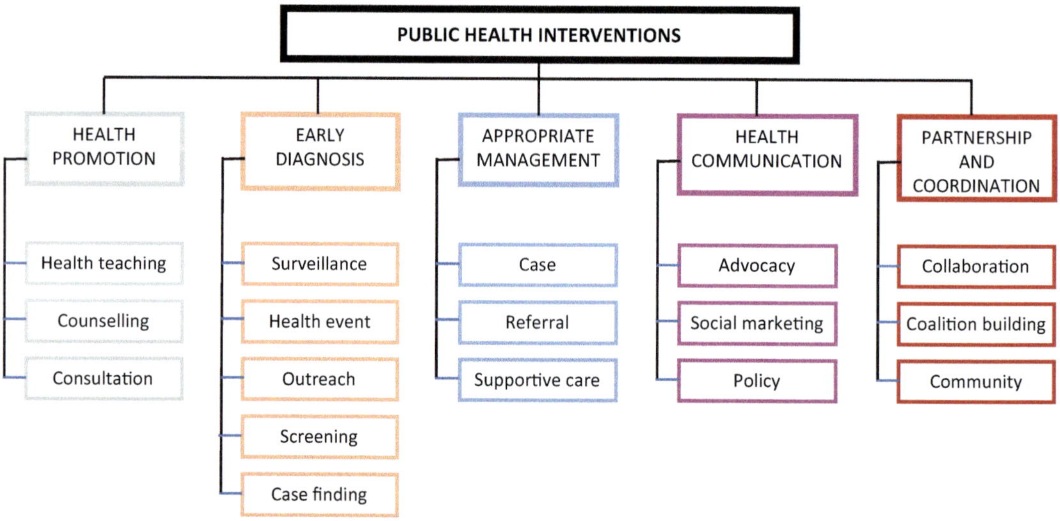

Fig. 2.1 Types of public health interventions (Adapted from The Intervention Wheel) [2]

2.3 Selection of Intervention

Health problems are often complex and multifactorial and there are several solutions to a health problem. For example, malnutrition among children can be reduced by a number of preventive, supportive, and therapeutic interventions like exclusive breastfeeding, appropriate complementary feeding, micronutrient supplementation, maternal nutrition, safe water and sanitation, screening and early diagnosis of SAM, nutritional rehabilitation, school lunch program, etc. Conversely, there are several causes of under-five deaths including diarrhea. It becomes necessary to identify interventions which are effective in reducing under-five deaths from one or multiple causes. Once the best intervention is identified (based on multiple factors as discussed below), it can be implemented among the population to reduce under-five mortality.

Evidence-based public health practice relies on integration of research which generates evidence with policy and program implementation. Any public health intervention which is considered for implementation should be backed by strong evidence supporting the effectiveness of the intervention in addressing the health problem. Figure 2.2 depicts the process of selection of a public health intervention. The following steps may be adopted for selecting public health interventions as shown in Fig. 2.2.

2.3.1 Determining a Public Health Problem

The first step of selection of an intervention for implementation in public health practice is to identify the burden of the disease/health condition and ascertain that it is a significant public health problem for which the intervention is planned. This is done by gathering evidence through secondary research, if available, or by collection and analysis of primary data.

Several criteria can be used to judge whether a disease or condition is a public health problem. These criteria are used for prioritizing the diseases based on which intervention measures are adopted.

Criteria for judging the public health importance of the problem:

- Incidence and prevalence of the disease compared to existing thresholds
- Severity and sequelae of the disease
- Disability caused by the disease
- Mortality caused by disease
- Socioeconomic impact of the disease
- Communicability of the disease
- Potential of the disease for causing an outbreak
- Public perception and concern regarding the disease
- International requirements (public health emergencies of international concern)

Criteria for judging the ability to prevent or control health problems:

- Availability of control measures
- Availability of treatment
- Capacity of the health system to implement control measures (availability of resources and health systems readiness).

A health problem is regarded as a significant public health problem based on existing disease prevalence thresholds, severity of disease, mortality and disability caused by the disease, socioeconomic impact, communicability, potential for outbreak, and public concern. These are often decided based on the goals and targets laid down. Targets enlisted under Sustainable Development Goals (SDGs) could be the starting point for most public health interventions.

> **Q.2.2** *Kindly refer to Raipur Rani project case study. What was the public health concern? Justify your answer.*

2.3.2 Sources of Data

Data on health can be obtained from primary or secondary sources:

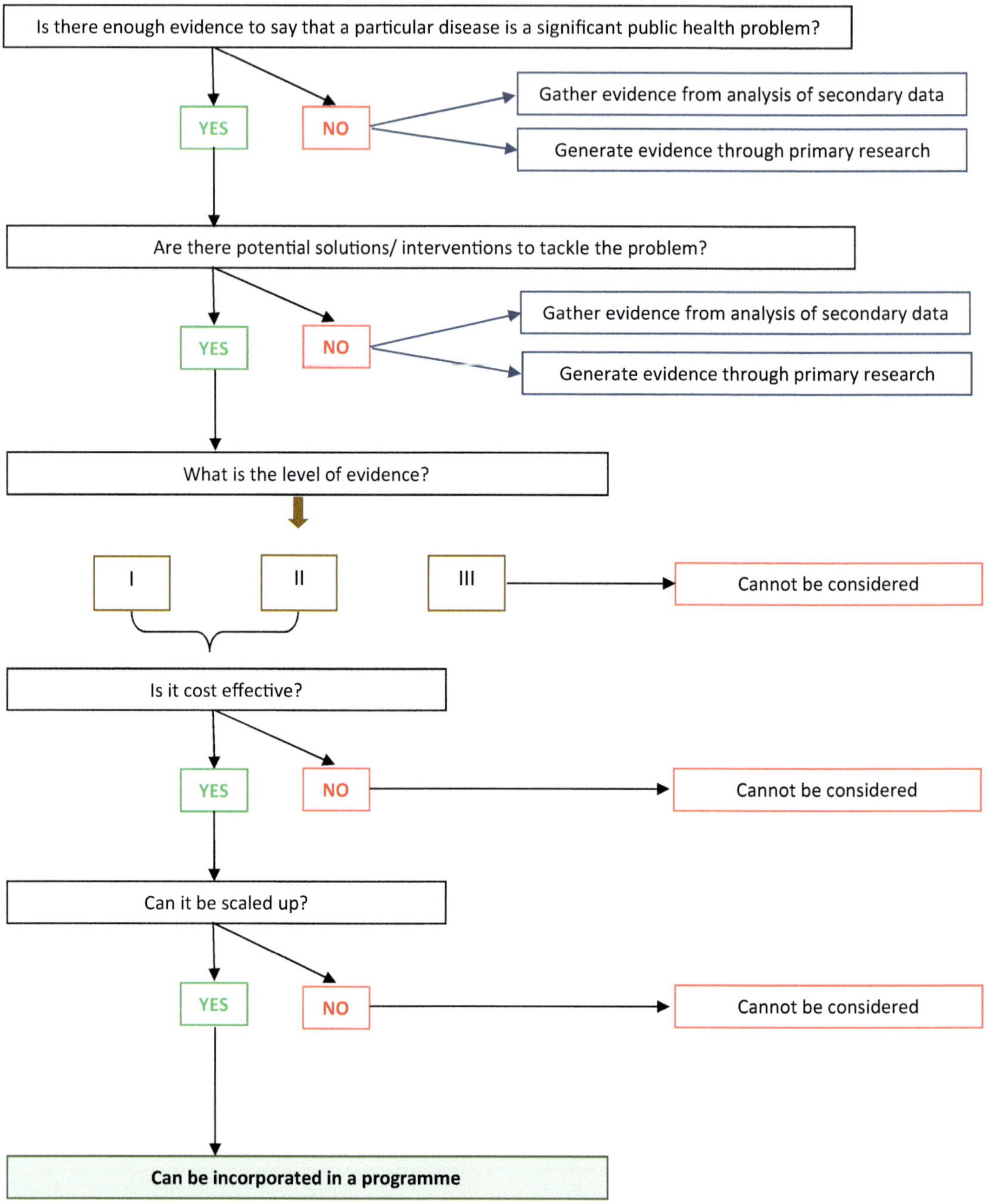

Fig. 2.2 Selection of public health intervention

- *Primary health data* are those that are obtained directly from an individual by the researcher or by hiring some agencies. Primary data can consist of interviews, measurements, and investigations. You can collect primary data through community surveys (house-to-house) or from individuals in an organization like hospitals, schools, offices, industries, etc. It is to be noted that validity of results yielded from analysis of the primary data depends upon the robustness of methodology of the primary research study.

- *Secondary health data* are those which are already collected and published by others. When this published data is used by a researcher, it is known as secondary data. There are several secondary sources of health data like Census, Sample Registration System, disease notification, hospital records, disease registers, epidemiological surveillance data, population surveys (National Family Health Surveys and District Level Health Surveys), and rural health statistics publications.

Q.2.3 *There were some anecdotal reports stating that women in certain parts of the country consumed medicines during pregnancy for a male child. Based on this report, discuss whether an intervention is required. What additional information is needed to plan for an intervention. Refer to case study on Sex Selection Drugs.*

2.3.3 Assessment of Level of Evidence

The second step is to identify whether there are any potential solutions or interventions to tackle the problem. Interventions may have been piloted in various settings, as experimental research studies or as part of health programs. If there are available population-based interventions which have already been tested, they are examined for level of evidence of effect.

Evidence-based public health relies on finding adequate good-quality evidence and using that evidence to make public health decisions. There is a hierarchical system of classifying the quality of evidence which are known as levels of evidence. These levels are based on the design and strength of the research studies which have been undertaken to generate evidence. In general, the level of evidence is assumed to improve from observational studies (case series, case-control, and cohort studies) to experimental studies (randomized controlled trials) to systematic reviews and meta-analysis.

For the purpose of selecting a public health intervention, there are several classifications of levels of evidence based on the magnitude of effect of the intervention against the disease/public health problem of interest. Even though, keeping in mind the complexity of public health interventions, a "classic" RCT may not always be possible, clinical trials and systematic reviews of clinical trials are still considered the best level of evidence [4].

We have classified degree of evidence broadly into three levels [5]:

- **Level I**: Sufficient evidence of effect is available, i.e., a causal relationship has been established between the intervention and reduction in cause-specific mortality in developing countries (systematic reviews of RCTs/good quality individual RCTs).
- **Level II**: Limited evidence of effect is available, i.e., an effect is possible, but available data is not sufficient to establish a causal relationship. This could be because of conflicting evidence from several studies or inadequate representation of low- and middle-income countries (systematic reviews of cohort or case-control studies/individual cohort studies).
- **Level III**: Inadequate evidence of effect is available, i.e., available data do not show a presence or absence of an effect or major qualitative or quantitative limitations (individual case-control studies/case series/poor-quality case-control and cohort studies).

Q.2.4 *Refer to Janani Suraksha Yojana and Solidarity Trial for the level of evidence. Discuss why there was an exception in case of Solidarity Trial'.*

If no interventions have been tested yet, evidence needs to be generated regarding its effect. This is done by conducting primary research. Well-designed research studies with sound methodology should be planned to test the effect of interventions. Evidence generated is then examined for level of evidence of effect.

Only those interventions with available evidence of effect (Level I and Level II evidence) can be considered for further evaluation and implementation.

2.3.4 Assessment of Cost-Effectiveness

The next step is to evaluate the cost-effectiveness [6] of the selected interventions which have shown adequate effectiveness (Level I and Level II) in reducing cause-specific morbidity and mortality against the public health problem under question. Cost-effectiveness analysis estimates and quantifies the costs of alternative interventions against their health gains. This helps identify intervention(s) which have the potential to yield greater positive health outcomes by utilizing less resources. Health gains are calculated in terms of lives saved or death/disability averted. A common measure for health gain is disability adjusted life years (DALYs), which represents a weighted combination of mortality and morbidity due to a disease. Cost-effectiveness analysis is done to either compare multiple interventions or to compare an intervention against the status quo. Cost-effectiveness is also calculated for different levels of population coverage, e.g., 50%, 75%, 90%, etc.

Selection of intervention is done based on the cost-effectiveness ratio. When two or more interventions are compared, the intervention with the least cost-effectiveness ratio is selected. Another approach is to use a cut-off value of cost-effectiveness ratio beyond which an intervention is not used. This is especially useful when comparative interventions are not available, or a single intervention is being evaluated. Yet another method is to identify the threshold based on gross national income (GNI). Multiples of GNI per capita have been commonly used to interpret results of economic evaluations [7]. The use of such thresholds has been criticized for being too high to represent actual willingness to pay [8]. The use of country-level league tables comparing incremental cost-effectiveness ratios is therefore suggested. Economic evaluation of public health interventions is dealt with in detail in subsequent chapters.

2.3.5 Assessment of Scalability

The final consideration is assessment of the intervention for scalability. Scalability is the ability of a health intervention, which has been proved to be effective on a small scale or under controlled conditions or specific context, to be expanded to reach a greater population and/or in different context while retaining its effectiveness. Scalability largely depends upon the context and design of the intervention. Assessment of scalability of a health intervention requires looking into various factors like political context, dissemination and advocacy, user organizations, type of intervention, feasibility factors, costs/resource mobilization, training, monitoring, and evaluation. If the intervention is shown to be scalable to a larger population, it can be then incorporated into a program. Scalability assessment of a public health intervention will be explained in detail in a subsequent chapter.

Example 1 [5]

As discussed, the first step in selecting an intervention is to identify a public health problem. We know that the under-five mortality rate in India is high with almost 35 out of 1000 children dying before they reach 5 years of age. With this information, let's say, our aim is to find out an appropriate intervention which will contribute to reducing child mortality in India. We would need to start by identifying the leading causes of deaths among children aged 0–5 years in India. A literature search and review of national survey records would help us list out the causes of death of under-five children and the proportion of deaths due to each cause. We find that the causes of childhood morbidity and mortality in decreasing order of importance are diarrhea, pneumonia, malaria, HIV, vaccine preventable diseases, congenital malformation, and injuries.

We then decided to focus on reducing diarrhea-related deaths among under-five children.

The next question is whether there are any potential solutions/interventions to tackle the problem. For this, we would first need to gather data on available interventions to reduce diarrheal deaths through a thorough review of avail-

able evidence. By conducting a literature search, we can identify the possible interventions.

– *Exclusive breastfeeding, appropriate complementary feeding, oral rehydration therapy (ORT), zinc supplementation, vitamin A supplementation, rotavirus vaccine, measles vaccine, cholera vaccine, safe water, and sanitation.*

With multiple interventions available, we would then need to examine each intervention for the level of evidence. This is done by referring to clinical trials which have studied the effectiveness of each of these interventions separately. To supplement this information, we can also refer to systematic reviews and meta-analysis which provide the strongest level of evidence.

We find level 1 evidence for six of these interventions: breastfeeding promotion, rotavirus vaccination, measles vaccination, cholera vaccination, oral rehydration therapy, and safe water and sanitation. In order to select one or more of these interventions for implementation under a health program, the next question we would have to answer is how cost-effective are these interventions. This can once again be answered by secondary research or through collecting primary data. We would need information regarding the median cost of intervention per child against the median mortality reduction.

Intervention	*Median cost/child (USD)*	*Median diarrheal mortality reduction (%)*
Breastfeeding promotion	*9*	*10.5*
Rotavirus vaccination	*104*	*24.1*
Cholera vaccination	*4*	*1.5*
Measles vaccination	*13*	*16*
Water supply and sanitation	*25 (rural), 81(urban)*	*65*
Oral rehydration therapy (ORT)	*3*	*95*

Source: Disease Control Priority Project

From the above table, we can conclude that ORT is the most cost-effective among the interventions. We then need to examine ORT (1965–1969) as an intervention to reduce childhood diarrheal deaths for scalability. If it is amenable to scale-up, it can be incorporated into a health program.

2.4 Intervention Delivery Strategies

After selecting the appropriate intervention, the next important step is to decide how to deliver the intervention to the target group/beneficiaries. The approaches used to introduce the intervention such that they reach the beneficiaries effectively are collectively known as delivery strategies. Delivery strategy includes the intervention, target group, and means of distribution.

An intervention can be delivered in two ways:

- **Delivery as *vertical programs* (*disease-focused*)**:
  This refers to focused, active, disease-specific intervention delivery on a massive scale in the community. Vertical programs have their own financing, management structures, and staff and service delivery which are not integrated with other health programs. Since the introduction of these programs does not depend upon the existing health system, they can generally be implemented relatively quickly. For example, leprosy control activities were launched under a vertical program.
- **Delivery as *horizontal programs* (*systems-focused*)**:
  This refers to more integrated implementation through the general health system utilizing a resource-sharing process. A number of health services are delivered simultaneously under the same management structure. An intervention introduced through a horizontal mechanism might take longer to implement but has a greater chance of success. For example, routine immunization is implemented as a horizontal program.

Vertical and horizontal delivery mechanisms have distinct advantages. While vertical health programs are more specific and measurable, horizontal approaches offer the advantage of addressing a wide range of problems at the same time and therefore prove to be more cost-effective. A horizontal mode of intervention delivery is useful when the intervention is intended to reach a large population (all under-five children in routine immunization) and in places which have sound infrastructure and functioning health systems. Horizontal programs have also shown to be sustainable and cost-effective when services are fully integrated into health systems.

A newer delivery mechanism is the *diagonal approach* which combines the strength of both vertical and horizontal approaches. In a diagonal approach, disease-specific interventions or programs are integrated across the health system. A classic example is that of Intensified Pulse Polio Immunization (IPPI). It was initiated as a vertical program since there was separate funding, separate manpower to implement and separate monitoring system. Eventually it encompassed the entire health systems machinery, resulting in strengthening of health systems that supported the routine immunization program as well.

It is always a good idea to integrate several interventions into one single package with common service delivery mode rather than implement each intervention separately. For example, integration of women's cancer prevention and screening and prevention of parent to child transmission of HIV/AIDS in maternal and child health programs.

Q.2.5 *Refer to case study on Pulse Polio Program. Discuss the approach that was followed to deliver the intervention.*

2.5 Integration of Interventions

Integration of interventions refers to [5]:

- The delivery of more than one intervention using the same service delivery platform (e.g., ASHAs conducting population-based screening for NCDs and home-based newborn care)
- Addition of two or more interventions at one point of service delivery (e.g., utilization of immunization visits to promote and provide family planning services), or
- Ensuring coordination of activities between different levels of service delivery like community, primary, and referral levels (e.g., expanded package of services delivered in the community, health and wellness centers, and referral centers).

The best strategy for delivering public health interventions is to implement several interventions together "packages." This helps reduce program costs as well as increase program effectiveness.

Packaging interventions help *reduce program costs* in the following ways:

- It reduces program start-up costs by linking new interventions with existing programs. The existing staff and systems are used to deliver the intervention; therefore, no extra cost is incurred in the same. For example, management of sexually transmitted illnesses and abortion by manual vacuum aspiration were added to clinical care services at facilities along with other interventions in reproductive child health program.
- In limited resource settings, it can utilize the same staff and communication channels for delivering several related interventions. For example, health workers in peripheral health facilities giving immunizations can also give micronutrient supplements or conduct simple counseling on feeding.
- If some health staff deliver multiple interventions, training for all interventions can be provided at the same time, thus reducing the cost of training. For example, training on skilled birth attendance for health workers can include essential elements of delivery care along with provision of essential care at birth, postpartum contraception, and breastfeeding.
- Integration of interventions can also reduce program costs by improving efficiency of monitoring, supervision, and disease surveillance. For example, integrated supervisory

checklists, which use the same supervisors to review several program activities at one time, can save staff and travel expenses. Similarly, integrated health information systems for surveillance of several diseases at the same time avoid duplication of work.

Packaging interventions help *increase program effectiveness* in the following ways:

- It ensures that multiple causes of morbidity/mortality are addressed at the same time. For example, a skilled birth attendant can be simultaneously trained on using a partograph, conducting a clean delivery, warming the newborn, initiating early breastfeeding, recognizing when to refer the newborn for illnesses, and giving counseling to the mother on breastfeeding and recognition of danger signs. Integrating these interventions can potentially limit neonatal mortality from hypothermia, neonatal tetanus, sepsis, and birth complications. It is important to provide training on all these areas to effectively address all causes of mortality and bring down neonatal deaths.
- Combining interventions and delivering them simultaneously can lead to a greater reduction in mortality and produce a greater impact as compared to each intervention alone. The advantage of complex public health interventions is that they act by different mechanisms, independently and interdependently, which can maximize health impact. These act through multiple pathways to improve health outcomes. For example, conditional cash incentive for institutional delivery, baby friendly hospital initiative, and childhood immunization all act together through various mechanisms to reduce neonatal mortality.

References

1. Keller LO, Strohschein S, Lia-Hoagberg B, Schaffer MA. Population-based public health interventions: practice-based and evidence-supported. Part I. Public Health Nurs. 2004;21(5):453–68.
2. Minnesota Dept. of Health. Public health interventions: applications for nursing practice 2nd ed. ("The Wheel Manual"). St. Paul: Minnesota Department of Health; 2019. Available from: https://www.health.state.mn.us/communities/practice/research/phncouncil/wheel.html.
3. Keller LO, Strohschein S, Schaffer MA, Lia-Hoagberg B. Population-based public health interventions: innovations in practice, teaching, and management. Part II. Public Health Nurs. 2004;21(5):469–87.
4. Rychetnik L, Frommer M, Hawe P, Shiell A. Criteria for evaluating evidence on public health interventions. J Epidemiol Community Health. 2002;56(2):119–27.
5. Jamison DT, Breman JG, Measham AR, Alleyne G, Claeson M, Evans DB, et al., editors. Disease control priorities in developing countries [Internet]. 2nd ed. Washington, DC: World Bank; 2006. Available from: http://www.ncbi.nlm.nih.gov/books/NBK11728/.
6. Rabarison KM, Bish CL, Massoudi MS, Giles WH. Economic evaluation enhances public health decision making. Front Public Health. 2015;3:164. https://doi.org/10.3389/fpubh.2015.00164.
7. Robinson LA, Hammitt JK, Chang AY, Resch S. Understanding and improving the one and three times GDP per capita cost-effectiveness thresholds. Health Policy Plan. 2017;32(1):141–5.
8. Brownson RC, Fielding JE, Maylahn CM. Evidence-based public health: a fundamental concept for public health practice. Annu Rev Public Health. 2009;30:175–201.

3 Principles and Science of Implementation Research

Sutapa Bandyopadhyay Neogi

Learning Objectives
After going through this section, participants will be able to:

- Explain comprehensive and working definitions of implementation, operational, and health systems research.
- Describe the ways in which implementation research is being executed and specific measures to improve the quality of research.
- Develop project design, performance indicators, assignment of responsibilities, and ways to communicate effectively.

3.1 Research Domains

"A health system comprises of all organizations, people, and actions whose primary intention is to promote, restore or maintain health." This caters to the efforts to impact determinants of Health as well as direct health-improving activities [1]. It is apparent to note that ineffective health systems are hampering achievement of the Sustainment Development Goals in low-income countries [2–4] and therefore, understanding the most effective method for strengthening health systems and determining suitable actions for diverse contexts is crucial.

Literature states that a lot is being identified and known about the barriers or constraints in health system strengthening; however, there is limited knowledge on the optimal ways to alleviate these constraints [5]. Research plays a crucial role to enhance our understanding about health systems and policies especially when to remove a context-based constraint by formulating clear and empirically verifiable hypothesis [5, 6].

To begin with the basics, it is essential to know types of research domains and major criteria they differ. The primary characteristics that define these research domains are [7]:

- The focus of research, i.e., the core issues addressed in the research question.
- The users of the research output, i.e., the ways and methods they are organized and,
- Utility of research output, i.e., How do they interface with health systems?

As shown in Fig. 3.1, these research domains could broadly be defined as:

1. **Operational research** (**OR**): It is defined as "the search for knowledge on interventions, strategies, or tools that can enhance the quality, effectiveness, or coverage of program in which the research is being done" [8]. It is defined as a systematic study of the working

S. Bandyopadhyay Neogi (✉)
Department of Health Systems and Implementation Research, International Institute of Health Management Research (IIHMR), New Delhi, India
e-mail: sutapa@iihmrdelhi.edu.in

S. Bandyopadhyay Neogi, A. K. Pandey (eds.), *Designing and Evaluating Public Health Interventions*, https://doi.org/10.1007/978-981-97-9574-1_3

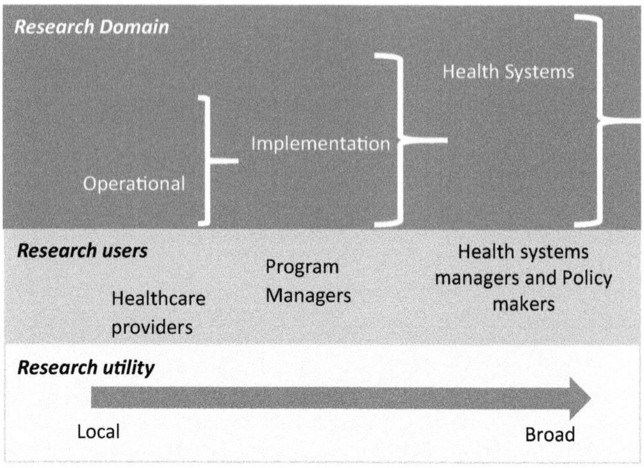

Fig. 3.1 Research to improve Health Systems

of a system with the aim of improving it [9]. Another way to define it is that any research generating practically applicable knowledge capable of enhancing program implementation, irrespective of the research design [10].

OR can be used majorly by the health care providers to improve the outcome of programs with respect to the medical care or prevention strategies, to assess the feasibility of new intervention, and also to encourage policy change. Its objective is to devise answers for existing operational challenges within particular health programs or specific service delivery elements of the health system. This begins with exploratory studies aimed at defining a problem and identifying potential solutions.

2. **Implementation research**: It is defined as "the scientific inquiry into questions concerning implementation, i.e., the act of carrying an intention into effect, which in health research can be policies, programs, or individual practices (collectively called interventions) [5]."

   Implementation research encompasses a range of elements influencing the execution of a program, including the implementation processes and outcomes. It involves proposing viable solutions for scaling, encouraging adoption, and ensuring long-term sustainability. The research initiates with an existing intervention or a proven effective package from prior studies, focusing on the challenge of expanding the intervention and seamlessly integrating it into the health system. Formative research is also integral in this process, aiding in a deeper comprehension of primary implementation obstacles and the formulation of potential implementation approaches.

3. **Health Systems Research**: It is defined as "a field that seeks to understand and improve how societies organize themselves in achieving collective health goals, and how different stakeholders interact in the policy and implementation processes to contribute to policy outcomes" [11].

   Health systems research is highly multidisciplinary and focuses on health systems. These are usually not disease-specific but concern systems problems [7]. It usually emphasizes more on social sciences, economics, and anthropological investigations.

3.2 Principles of Implementation Research

Challenges in implementation emerged due to a variety of factors, particularly those associated with the practical aspects, i.e., implementing the research activities. Unlike other research disciplines that may overlook or insufficiently address these factors, this research field serves as a foundation for decision-making based on context-specific information and evidence. This is essential for translating theory into practical reality.

Conducting implementation research involves a wide range of stakeholders from different disciplines to tackle the intricate challenges of implementation (Fig. 3.1). This type of research encompasses decision-makers responsible for policy design and program management, shaping the framework for implementation and scaling processes. The core team consists of public health practitioners and frontline workers, who are responsible for executing these decisions, collaborating with researchers from various fields.

It requires a strong foundation of the social, economic, political, and legal context. Along with these interdisciplinary collaborations portrays a vital role in implementation research. It is crucial that these stakeholders are closely involved from the inception of the study until final execution and scaling the intervention for the benefit of people at large.

The methodology for implementation research is consistently multidisciplinary and demands a convergence of various perspectives. Bammer (2003) [12] have suggested to deal with the challenges by collaborations with stakeholders of different expertise. In the same way, the conceptual model as adopted from Proctor et al. 2009 [13] provides a description of implementation research methods by classifying multi-level implementation strategies and their outcomes.

3.3 Outcome Variables in Implementation Research

Implementation studies use various methods to assess effectiveness of program implementation. Some researchers refer to attainment of outcomes by evaluating clinical outcomes of patients. Others assess the outcomes in context of the improvement in overall healthcare service delivery. Thus, researchers have defined three major functions of implementation outcome [14] as-

- Those indicators that represent success of the implementation process.
- Proximal indicators.
- Indicators representing intermediate outcomes.

Conceptual Framework for Implementation Outcomes by Proctor et al. 2009 [13], distinguishes three diverse but connected types of outcomes. The variables which can serve as indicators of good implementation are elaborated in the Box 3.1 (adapted from reference [14, 15].

Box 3.1

(a) *Acceptability*: The perception among stakeholders that an intervention is agreeable.
(b) *Adoption*: The intent to try to employ a new intervention.
(c) *Appropriateness*: Relevance of an intervention.
(d) *Feasibility*: The magnitude to which an intervention can be carried out.
(e) *Fidelity*: The extent to which an intervention is implemented as compared to its originality.
(f) *Implementation cost*: The cost being incurred in implementing the intervention.
(g) *Coverage*: The extent to which an eligible population gets benefited from the intervention or receives intervention.
(h) *Sustainability*: The extent to which an intervention is retained or established in a given setting.

Implementation research utilizes these variables to evaluate the effectiveness of the implementation process or to gain insights into how it influences an individual's health status or other significant health outcomes.

3.4 Strategies to Implement an Intervention

Figure 3.2 shows a visual representation of the planning and implementation logic models guiding the design and implementation of a program or policy, which can be used as a tool for developing an appropriate evaluation design. This

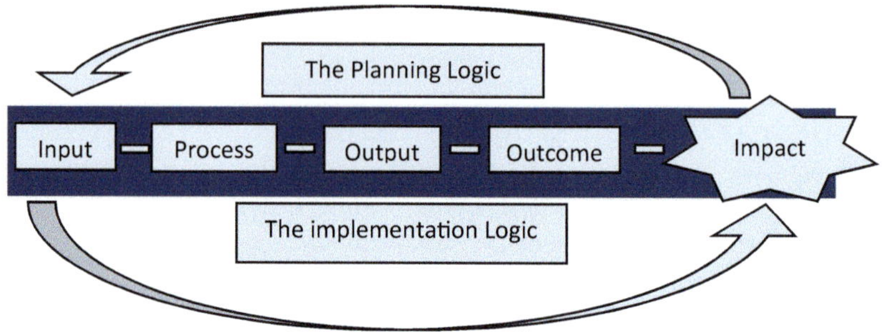

Fig. 3.2 Figure depicting the basis of Implementation and planning logic models

concept can be expanded to various strategies that are designed to support public health intervention.

> **Q.3.1** *Refer to the case studies on HBNC and Ekjut trial- both the case studies focus on high burden of neonatal mortality—Discussion on the approaches involved—Preventive v/s therapeutic aspect*

The components of Logic model are as under [16]:

- **Impact:** These are the anticipated results of long-term execution of strategies and activities. The long-term outcomes are the Impacts. These depend upon various factors beyond the program's scope of activities and strategies. Impacts are generally long term and observed usually after several years, e.g., 7–10 years.
- **Outcome**: Outcomes are a logical next step to discuss while investigating the elements of the planning model. While planning an intervention, outcomes should be thought of next because knowing the impact or the goal in context to solving the problem will help in robust plan development for achieving the outcomes.
  - Outcomes enquiries- "What change does it make?" or in other words, what difference will the inputs in terms of resources, activities or various processes have on the long-term goal.
  - Having a clear understanding of the outcomes is essential for both intensive program implementation and successful evaluation. Researchers have identified various steps for planning by asking-
    - Who is the target?
    - What is the desired change?
    - In what category is the change expected and by when the change is expected?
  - Outcomes are usually measured as mid-term achievements that take almost 3–5 years.

There are three types of outcomes which are measured at various phases of Intervention (Fig. 3.3).

- **Short-term Outcome**: Most immediate and quantifiable results.
- **Mid-term Outcome**: medium-term, intermediate, midpoint.
- **Long-term Outcome/Impact**: long-term, final, ultimate, distal outcome.

Example
Let us understand it by considering the example of Home-based newborn care as shown in Fig. 3.4. The ultimate impact that we wish to achieve is improved neonatal survival or reduction in neonatal mortality. In this example, the outcomes could be increased coverage of home visits and early identification of sick newborns.

- **Outputs:** Outputs are different from outcomes as they determine what is done as a substitute of measuring what is likely to be achieved as a consequence of what is being done. Outputs are best described as activity data and are suitable for tracking the implementation.
  - They provide an input on how well the strategies and input deployed have worked.

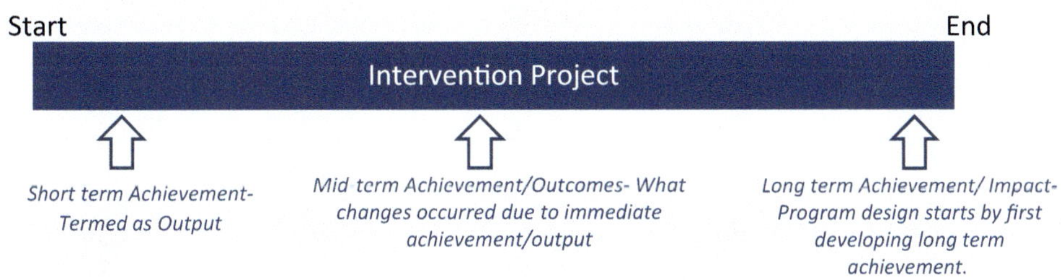

Fig. 3.3 Explaining phasewise outcomes to be measured in implementation research

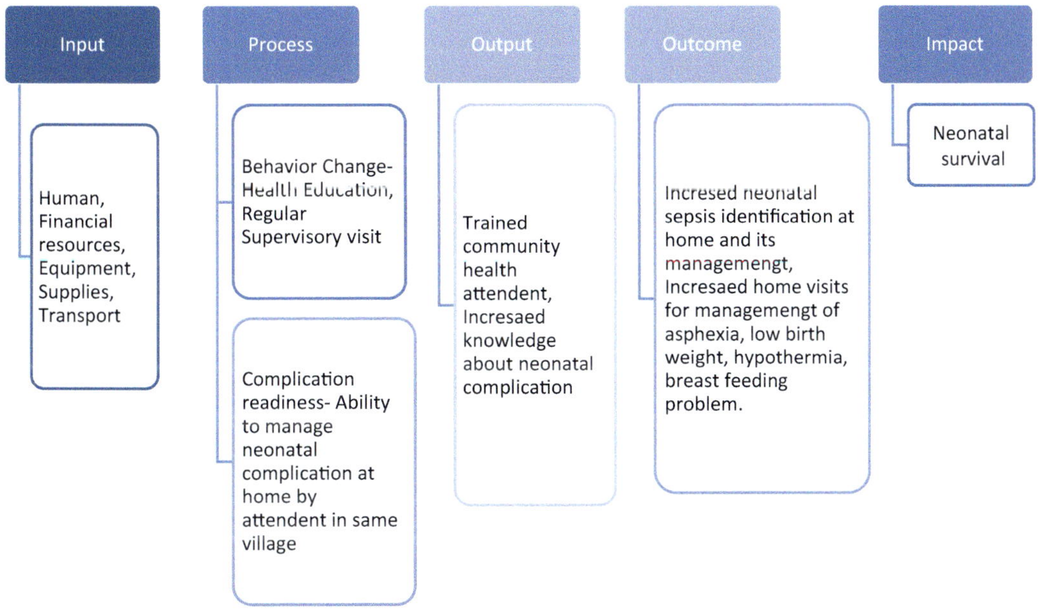

Fig. 3.4 Explaining the terms used in implementation logic model using home-based neonatal care as an example

  - They also provide an insight on projects' short-term outcomes.
- **Inputs and Process Resources (inputs):** These are some of the essential components or planned strategies and activities to achieve the goal. This is a list of all the strategies and activities devised to achieve the outcomes.
  - This includes—what needs to be to be provided for doing each process, e.g.,
    - Human Resource—trained staff
    - Money—financial resources
    - Material—medicines, reagents, supplies, etc.
    - Managerial skills
    - Infrastructure
    - Time

Please note that impact and outcome indicators are always measured at the population level. For output, process, and input indicators, these may be at the facility or the population level.

3.5 Variables Influencing the Implementation Process

There are various contextual factors which influence the implementation process. These factors change at various stages of implementation. It is essential to identify variables that influence the implementation process; thus, the monitoring and evaluation roles need to be divided at-

- The planning phase and Implementation phase (***Explained in Chap. 10 on Evaluation of Public Health Interventions***).

Sabatier, 1986 has identified factors influencing policy implementation, namely—Clarity of objectives, Causal theory, etc. [17]. These considerations should be considered during the planning phase. These methods can offer feedback to important stakeholders and facilitate learning and adjustment for implementing agencies and beneficiary groups.

References

1. Araujo de Carvalho I, Epping-Jordan J, Pot AM, Kelley E, Toro N, Thiyagarajan JA, et al. Organizing integrated health-care services to meet older people's needs. Bull World Health Organ. 2017;95(11):756–63.
2. Fryatt R, Mills A, Nordstrom A. Financing of health systems to achieve the health Millennium Development Goals in low-income countries. Lancet. 2010;375(9712):419–26.
3. Glass LM, Newig J. Governance for achieving the Sustainable Development Goals: how important are participation, policy coherence, reflexivity, adaptation and democratic institutions? Earth Syst Govern. 2019;2:100031.
4. Madon T, Hofman KJ, Kupfer L, Glass RI. Implementation Science. Science [Internet]. 2007;318(5857):1728–9. [cited 2021 Dec 27]; Available from: https://www.science.org/doi/abs/10.1126/science.1150009.
5. Alliance for Health Policy and Systems Research. Strengthening health systems: the role and promise of policy and systems research. Geneva: Alliance for Health Policy and Systems Research; 2004.
6. Travis P, Bennett S, Haines A, Pang T, Bhutta Z, Hyder AA, et al. Overcoming health-systems constraints to achieve the Millennium Development Goals. Lancet. 2004;364(9437):900–6.
7. Remme JHF, Adam T, Becerra-Posada F, D'Arcangues C, Devlin M, Gardner C, et al. Defining research to improve health systems. PLoS Med. 2010;7(11):e1001000.
8. Zachariah R, Harries AD, Ishikawa N, Rieder HL, Bissell K, Laserson K, et al. Operational research in low-income countries: what, why, and how? Lancet Infect Dis. 2009;9(11):711–7.
9. Porta M. A dictionary of epidemiology. Oxford: Oxford University Press; 2014. p. 377.
10. Kunwar R, Srivastava VK. Operational research in health-care settings. Indian J Community Med. 2019;44(4):295–8.
11. What is health policy and systems research [Internet]. Geneva: Alliance for Health Policy and Systems Research. [cited 2021 Dec 29]. Available from: https://ahpsr.who.int/what-we-do/what-is-health-policy-and-systems-research-(hpsr).
12. Bammer G. Integration and implementation sciences: building a new specialization. Ecol Soc [Internet]. 2005;10(2):6. Available from: https://www.ecologyandsociety.org/vol10/iss2/art6/.
13. Proctor EK, Landsverk J, Aarons G, Chambers D, Glisson C, Mittman B. Implementation research in mental health services: an emerging science with conceptual, methodological, and training challenges. Admin Pol Ment Health. 2009;36(1):24–34.
14. Proctor E, Silmere H, Raghavan R, Hovmand P, Aarons G, Bunger A, Griffey R, Hensley M. Outcomes for implementation research: conceptual distinctions, measurement challenges, and research agenda. Admin Pol Ment Health. 2011;38(2):65–76. https://doi.org/10.1007/s10488-010-0319-7.
15. Peters D, Tran N, Adam T, Alliance for Health Policy and Systems Research, World Health Organization. Implementation research in health: a practical guide / edited by David Peters … [et al] [Internet]. Geneva: World Health Organization; 2013. [cited 2021 Dec 30]. 67 p. Available from: https://apps.who.int/iris/handle/10665/91758.
16. Shakman K, Rodriguez SM. Logic models for program design, implementation, and evaluation: workshop toolkit (REL 2015–057). Washington, DC. Retrieved from http://ies.ed.gov/ncee/edlabs.: U.S. Department of Education, Institute of Education Sciences, National Center for Education Evaluation and Regional Assistance, Regional Educational Laboratory Northeast & Islands; 2015.
17. Sabatier PA. Top-down and bottom-up approaches to implementation research: a critical analysis and suggested synthesis. J Publ Policy. 1986;6(1):21–48.

4 Framing Research Question

Anuj Kumar Pandey

Learning Objectives
After going through this section, participants will be able to:

- Define features of research question.
- Define how to generate the objectives for research questions.
- Define validity and reliability.
- Compare measures of reliability.

4.1 Research Question

A research question (RQ) is the base of a good study essential for solving research-related problems [1]. The research question (RQ) identifies the problem requiring investigation, guides the methodology, and leads to the formulation of an appropriate hypothesis. It aims to explore an existing uncertainty in a specific area of concern, underlining the need for targeted research. A well-crafted RQ contributes to the development of a focused, debatable topic and a coherent argument.

Thus, making a robust research question is undeniably one of the crucial initial stages [1–3]. Research is an essential part in developing new clinical management protocols or evaluating an intervention and later guiding the policymakers in establishing a new health policy. Thus, it becomes crucial to understand the scientific methodologies that need to be adopted while developing research questions.

4.2 Characteristics of Good Research Question

Well written research questions are focused, well defined and cover a broad-range complex problem. A good RQ [4]:

- Specifies the problem statement
- Illustrates the issues under the study
- Increases focus on the problem statement
- Guides data collection and analysis

Thus, it is essential to explore if the planned RQ is relevant to the available time frame.

Example
Does exposure to mifepristone in pregnancy result in greater number of adverse outcomes for the woman compared with women who have not been exposed to mifepristone [5]?

A. K. Pandey (✉)
Department of Health Systems and Implementation Research, International Institute of Health Management Research (IIHMR), New Delhi, India
e-mail: anuj@iihmrdelhi.edu.in

S. Bandyopadhyay Neogi, A. K. Pandey (eds.), *Designing and Evaluating Public Health Interventions*, https://doi.org/10.1007/978-981-97-9574-1_4

4.3 Steps Involved in Designing a Research Question

Following steps [6, 7] needs to be considered:

- The first step is to identify a problem before planning can begin. Identifying a problem can be done by performing an in-depth literature review to increase familiarity with the subject topic and get acquainted with existing evidence.
- Seeking advice and guidance from other subject matter experts.
- Using FINER criteria: for developing the research question.
- Ensuring research question following PICOT format.
- Ascertaining that the research question is answerable, feasible and relevant.

4.3.1 Understanding FINER Criteria

Researcher Hulley et al. [8] recommended FINER criteria for developing research question (Table 4.1). This criterion highlights the essential points that should be included while writing a research question. An effective research question ought to specify the target audience, be pertinent to the clinical context, contribute to the advancement of field knowledge, and be of interest to both the scientific community and, possibly, the public (while adhering to ethical board standards and national research guidelines).

On one side, this criterion summarizes the essential parts of a RQ in general. Another useful format is named PICOT format which stands for Population, Intervention, Comparison, outcome, and time as shown in Fig. 4.1.

As given by *Riva J John et.al* [9] *for different study designs PICOT format may differ*. As explained in Table 4.2**,** each study designs might follow a different PICOT format.

Table 4.1 FINER Criteria for developing research question

F	Feasible	• Indicates if it is feasible to undertake the research activity within the time duration, with available resources, manpower etc. • Realistic planning for research.
I	Interesting	• It is crucial that one has a genuine interest in their RQ, can research it, and can support it with scholarly and intellectual discussion.
N	Novel	• RQ seek to establish new facts or uncover new facets of previously existing facts, as well as to support or contradict previously established conclusions. • Concepts that are incongruent or irrelevant may be concealed by an extremely elaborate RQ. • This must be concise and well-considered. Your study will be guided by one main question with multiple supporting elements.
E	Ethical	• The initial requirement for any research question is to secure approval from the appropriate authorities. • Furthermore, RQ should be formulated in a manner that minimizes the potential for harm to research participants, safeguards their privacy and confidentiality, and provides them the choice to discontinue participation in the study. • It ought to serve as a guidance for not undertaking unethical research work.
R	Relevant	• RQ should be intellectually/academically interesting. • Ideally, the inquiry should be grounded in issues that have been deliberated in the literature, in practice, or in the current context. • It should explicitly articulate the research's objectives in relation to the field of study.

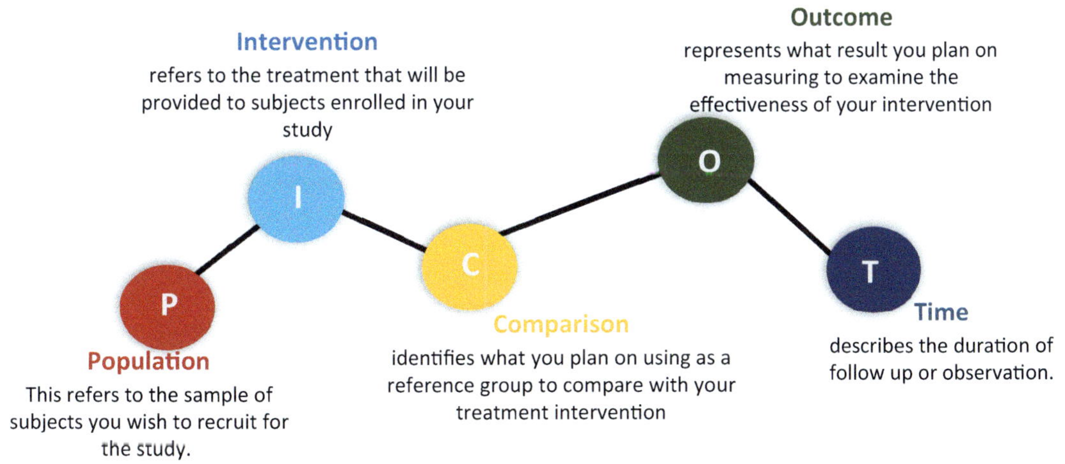

Fig. 4.1 Research question's PICOT format. (Author developed)

Table 4.2 Study designs PICOT format

PICOT format	Cohort/analytical cross sectional	Case control	Descriptive cross sectional	Interventional Study design
Population	Group of individuals, or units that meet criteria for inclusion in a study			
Intervention	Named as—Exposed: Exposed subjects enrolled in the study	Named as—outcome—refers to the subjects enrolled in the study.	X	Refers to treatment: Treatment/ intervention delivered to enrolled study participants.
Comparison	Reference group for comparison.	Without outcome identifies reference group	X	Reference (usually control arm) group for comparison
Outcome	Expected result.	Exposure: Represents those who had the exposure under study	Represents what result you plan on measuring	Expected result for examining effectiveness of intervention/s.
Time	Duration of study/follow-up/observation.			

4.3.2 Example of PICOT

- ***<u>Research question</u>***: In newborn babies, does a cesarean birth (compared with being born "normal vaginal delivery"), increase the risk of morbidity or mortality?
  - **<u>P</u>**: Newborn
  - **<u>I</u>**: Cesarean section
  - **<u>C</u>**: Normal vaginal delivery
  - **<u>O</u>**: Assessing the risk of morbidity or mortality
  - **<u>T</u>**: Time

> *Q.4.1 Ref to case studies on IV iron sucrose and Pulse polio. Frame good research questions to test effectiveness of the interventions.*

4.4 Research Hypothesis, Aim and Objectives

The hypothesis of the study should align with the primary objective [7]. The research protocol must clearly articulate the study objectives, delineating the distinct goals of the research. The objective of a study should follow the criteria of SMART which stand for specific, measurable, achievable, relevant, and time bound.

- ***Specific***: *This implies to Clearly defining what will be improved in a specific patient population by a specific date, along with the responsibility assigned.*
- ***Measurable***: *Objective should include a specific numerical target for measuring progress.*
- ***Achievable***: *Objective of the study should be realistic but challenging and must allow enough time and resources.*
- ***Relevant***: *Objective should be relevant to specific research areas.*
- ***Time***: *Objective should also have a set out realistic and clear timeframe.*

Some of the examples of SMART objectives are:

Example 1 Reduce **adverse birth outcomes** during delivery by **75%** within **1 year**.

- *What*—Adverse birth outcomes
- *Who*—Pregnant women admitted in the hospital for delivery?
- *How much*—By 75 percent from baseline
- *By when*—Within 1 year of the start of the intervention

RESEARCH QUESTION	*AIM*	*OBJECTIVE*
Should follow FINER criteria	The objective of a study highlights the targets within the research's scope	Each target is addressed separately. Objective of a study should be **SMART**
Example:		
What is the impact of Janani suraksha yojna (JSY) on maternal mortality?	*Evaluating the impact of JSY on maternal mortality*	• *To explore the underlying factors of maternal mortality* • *To explore the trends of maternal mortality over the years* • *To assess the change in maternal mortality accounting for the JSY*

4.5 Understanding Reliability and Validity: An Essential Aspect in Research

Choosing a study design aims at maximizing the validity and dependability of the data while minimizing any potential errors and bias, which can be done by understanding what reliability and validity implies.

1. **Reliability (Syn: reproducibility or repeatability)** [6]: This refers to the "stability or consistency of information, i.e., the extent to which similar information is obtained when a measurement is performed more than once."
   - The consistency, precision or accuracy of the data is referred to as ***reliability***. Every time a variable is measured, an investigator tries to be certain that results are reliable and consistent. A study measurement is considered dependable when it produces the same outcomes when repeated two times. The measurement is not accurate if the outcomes differ.
   - When respondents are asked questions in surveys that they do not understand, cannot clearly recall, or are not very relevant to them, reliability issues can arise.

   Sources of Variation:

   (a) **Within-subject variation**: This refers and arises due to modifications in the characteristics being measured.

   (b) **Measuring instrument variation**: This refers to the variation between the reading by the same instrument or between instruments. This measuring instrument could be any tool like a questionnaire or any instrument also.

   (c) **Observer variation**: This implies the variations due to different people collecting the same information. This could be within-observer/intra-observer variation OR between-observer/inter-observer variation. *For example*: Women at the time of delivery may not be able to recall the ANC history or history of contraception usage prior to conception.

2. **Validity** [6] implies to the information that is not only reliable but also true. In other words, a measurement's validity refers to how well it achieves its goals.
   - The extent to which a measurement accurately reflects the genuine value of the attribute being measured. A measurement is considered reliable when it is valid. But even if it is reliable, it might or might not be true. Validity could be classified as *Internal and External validity*.
   - A study may not have high external validity even when it has high internal validity.
   - The degree to which the findings of a study can be applied to different contexts or people is known as external validity.
   - Internal validity refers how close are the results to the truth: When the outcomes are genuine and precise, one can confidently affirm whether a particular intervention did or did not have an impact in a specific geographical context, with a specific population group, at a specific moment in time.
   - Validity revolves around the question "Am I measuring what I intend to measure?". In research and testing, there are several types of validity, each addressing different aspects of a measurement's accuracy and relevance such as content validity, face validity, empirical, predictive, construct validity.

4.5.1 Types of Error

The null hypothesis can be accepted or rejected, and this determination may be accurate or inaccurate. Occasionally, due to chance alone, a sample may not accurately reflect the population, leading to findings that do not truly represent the reality of the population, with random error contributing to an incorrect conclusion. There are two types of errors in hypothesis testing named as Type I and Type II errors as shown in Fig. 4.2 [10, 11].

- **Type I error**: This happens in a case where null hypothesis is true in the population, but the investigator rejects it in its research. This error is often called a false positive error. The probability of this type of error is named level of significance and is denoted by Alpha (α).
- **Type II error**: This occurs in a case where null hypothesis is false in the population, but the investigator does not reject it in its research. This error is also termed as false negative error. This is denoted as Beta (β).

Statistical Power = ($1-\beta$) is the ability of research to detect the difference if at all there exists a difference (Table 4.3).

4.5.2 Types of Bias

"Any inclination that inhibits an issue from being considered objectively is known as bias" [12]. Research encounters bias when a specific outcome or response is favored or promoted over others in the course of testing or sampling. Bias can manifest at various stages of the research process, as illustrated in Table 4.4, encompassing study design, data collection, data analysis, and publication.

Some of the unique biases are:

- ***Attention/ Hawthorne bias***: Subjects alter behavior in a fear of being observed. Often seen in cohort study.

Fig. 4.2 Hypothesis testing outcomes

		Reality	
Research		The Null Hypothesis is True	The Alternate Hypothesis is True
	The Null Hypothesis is True	Accurate (1-α)	Type II Error (β)
	The Alternate Hypothesis is True	Type I Error (α)	Accurate (1-β)

Table 4.3 Difference between Random and Systematic error/bias

	Random error	Systematic error/ Bias
Reason	Biological variation	Will-full error
Results in	Lack of reliability	Decreased validity (internal)
Influence of sample size	Larger sample size reduces	Not affected
Preventable largely by	Can't be prevented	Robust methodology can remove it
Dangerous	Less	More

Table 4.4 Types of bias and measures to avoid such bias

Type of bias	Measures to be taken to avoid such bias
Bias encountered before study:	
Faulty study design	Defining risks and mitigation strategies.
Selection bias	Rigorous methodology for patient/participants selection. Defining and following patient selection criteria.
Channeling bias	Use strict criteria to divide patients into study groups.
Bias encountered during study:	
Interviewer bias	Standardizing how interviewer will interact with the respondent. Keeping interviewer unaware of exposure status.
Chronology bias	Chronological bias can be eliminated with prospective studies. Do not use historical controls.
Recall bias	Corroborate subjective data sources with medical records. Undertake prospective research because the results are unknown at time of patient recruitment.
Transfer bias	Designing ways to manage lost-to-follow-up of patients before start of study.
Exposure Misclassification	Define exposure prior to study.
Outcome Misclassification	Using diagnostic studies or validated measures as primary outcome.
Performance bias	Cluster stratification.
Bias encountered after study:	
Citation bias	Trial registration in recognized trial registries or publishing protocols.
Confounding	Known confounders can be addressed through data analysis or research design such as case control study or randomization process, or regression while analyzing. Randomization can control unidentified confounders.

- ***Neymann/prevalence***: Incidence bias: bias due to missing of fatal cases, mild/ sub clinical case or cases of shorter duration gets included.
- ***Golem effect***: Negative effect; researcher induced (Lazy person takes BP only once in 2 months).
- ***Pygmalion effect***: Positive effect; aggressive effect; If BP is taken day and night so patient tends to stop smoking; hence BP will automatically decrease; hence it will show positive effect always whether drug/ placebo is given.

Q.4.2 In reference to Ekjut trial, list down the probable confounders. How were those addressed?

Q.4.3 In reference to case study on Sex Selection Drugs, identify the potential biases during the conduct of the study to establish an association between Sex selection drugs (SSDs) and birth defects.

References

1. Kishore J, Vasundhra S, Anand T. Formulation of a research question. Indian J Med Spec. 2(2):184–8. [Internet]. [cited 2022 Aug 1]. Available from: https://web.s.ebscohost.com/abstract?site=ehost&scope=site&jrnl=09762884&AN=67675970&h=JXhd7NVA%2fI6LcIVEoiau%2fcg5Naw2mf6H8xcwZoYBgwWc19OaWlxPt8YdSLlP7YrRhKPcjtz5kGDPexOV%2-

bK%2fLDA%3d%3d&crl=c&resultLocal=ErrCrlNoResults&resultNs=Ehost&crlhashurl=login.aspx%3fdirect%3dtrue%26profile%3dehost%26scope%3dsite%26authtype%3dcrawler%26jrnl%3d09762884%26AN%3d67675970.
2. Alvesson M, Sandberg J. Generating research questions through problematization. AMR. 2011;36(2):247–71.
3. Bryman A. The research question in social research: what is its role? Int J Soc Res Methodol. 2007;10(1):5–20. Available from: https://www.tandfonline.com/doi/abs/10.1080/13645570600655282.
4. Ratan SK, Anand T, Ratan J. Formulation of research question—stepwise approach. J Indian Assoc Pediatr Surg. 2019;24(1):15–20.
5. Does exposure to mifepristone alone in pregnancy result in greater number of adverse outcomes for the woman compared with women who have not been exposed to mifepristone? [Internet]. 2022 [cited 2022 Aug 1]. Available from: https://www.crd.york.ac.uk/prospero/display_record.php?RecordID=324049.
6. Abramson JH, Abramson ZH. Research methods in community medicine: surveys, epidemiological research, programme evaluation, clinical trials. 6th ed. Wiley; 2008. Available from: https://www.wiley.com/en-gb/Research+Methods+in+Community+Medicine%3A+Surveys%2C+Epidemiological+Research%2C+Programme+Evaluation%2C+Clinical+Trials%2C+6th+Edition-p-9780470986615.
7. Farrugia P, Petrisor BA, Farrokhyar F, Bhandari M. Research questions, hypotheses and objectives. Can J Surg. 2010;53(4):278–81.
8. Hulley SB, Cummings SR, Browner WS, Grady DG, Newman TB. Designing clinical research. Philadelphia: Lippincott Williams & Wilkins, a Wolters Kluwer; 2022. Available from: https://books.google.co.in/books?hl=en&lr=&id=_7UWxJ5erSsC&oi=fnd&pg=PR13&ots=YPSzfQq1qL&sig=c-0kz9tDKEyGe-UahcDgMFF2iiU&redir_esc=y#v=onepage&q&f=false.
9. Riva J, Malik K, Burnie S, Endicott A, Busse J. What is your research question? An introduction to the PICOT format for clinicians. J Can Chiropr Assoc. 2012;56:167–71.
10. Banerjee A, Chitnis UB, Jadhav SL, Bhawalkar JS, Chaudhury S. Hypothesis testing, type I and type II errors. Ind Psychiatry J. 2009;18(2):127–31.
11. Friedman LM, Furberg CD, DeMets DL. Fundamentals of clinical trials [Internet]. Cham: Springer; 2010. Available from: https://link.springer.com/book/10.1007/978-1-4419-1586-3.
12. Pannucci CJ, Wilkins EG. Identifying and avoiding bias in research. Plast Reconstr Surg. 2010;126(2):619–25.

5 Context Setting Through Formative Research

Vinay Tripathi

Learning Objectives
After going through this section, participants will be able to:

- Describe the role and importance of formative research in public health interventions.
- Explain key stages in designing and planning formative research.
- Outline basic features of complex interventions.
- Describe the development of complex interventions using a specific framework.

5.1 Formative Research: An Overview

Formative research plays an important role and is essential in designing, implementation, and post-implementation stage of any public health intervention, be it simple or complex one. According to the Centers for Disease Control and Prevention (CDC), the formative research is a "*process by which researchers or public health practitioners define a community of interest, determine how to access that community, and describe the attributes of the community that are relevant to a specific public health issue*" [1].

In the literature, formative research is also referred to as "situation analysis" or "needs assessment" though the possibilities of conceptual differences between them cannot be ruled out. Formative research facilitates obtaining detailed information not only of targeted population but also around various contextual factors that can have a bearing on the success of any public health interventions. However, it is also important to understand that formative *research can be undertaken at any stage of an intervention. Therefore, the rationale for undertaking formative research is dependent on the needs and requirements of a given intervention.*

For instance, the requirement could vary from understanding and capturing the specific needs of the population which are being targeted under the intervention or to explore the factors which are inhibiting the uptake of some of the activities which are implemented in the interventions or for developing locale specific study tools or examining factors behind successful/unsuccessful interventions.

Nonetheless, one of the major reasons for undertaking formative research, particularly before designing the intervention, is to understand, examine and analyze contextual factors pertaining to the communities or population which are being targeted under the intervention. These factors could either be related to the social, cultural, economic or health-related aspects but can potentially influence the interventions (either

V. Tripathi (✉)
International Institute of Health Management Research, New Delhi, India
e-mail: vinay@iihmrdelhi.edu.in

S. Bandyopadhyay Neogi, A. K. Pandey (eds.), *Designing and Evaluating Public Health Interventions*, https://doi.org/10.1007/978-981-97-9574-1_5

positively or negatively) if due cognizance is not taken. Apart from this, formative research can also aid in understanding knowledge, attitudes, and behavior of population being targeted or covered under the project. Depending on the need for an intervention, formative research can also delve into specific health service provisions, policies, and programs, which are relevant to the issues being addressed under the intervention.

In order to elaborate on how formative research facilitates in designing a public health intervention, an abstract from a study [2] (which has used formative research) is presented below:

Evidences point out that health issues like under-five mortality and malnutrition can be addressed in developing countries if improved maternal and newborn care services as well as young child feeding practices are ensured in the population. In order to design interventions in these areas, researchers conducted formative research in the Lao PDR. The formative research found that the people were engaged in washing newborns immediately after delivery and were delaying breastfeeding to newborns, which was quite common there. Home deliveries without assistance from a trained provider were also common. Traditional beliefs with respect to diet during pregnancy were followed and pregnant women consumed those foods items which were believed to be affecting mother's health or breast milk. Traditional beliefs played an important role in determining how young children need to be fed.

Based on these findings of formative research, the researchers designed interventions which focused on low-cost technologies like keeping newborns warm. This was done by deferring washing for 24 hours and wiping, wrapping, and breastfeeding newborns immediately after delivery. Ensuring proper care during the umbilical cord and promoting 6-month exclusive breastfeeding to infants. The intervention also included promotion of food items to improve the quality and quantity of breast milk.

Considering the diversity in rationale for using formative research in public health interventions, it is important to *understand how formative research needs to be designed and carried out*. In the absence of definitive and sequential steps of the formative research which can be uniformly applied for different kinds of public health interventions, some of the broad and key steps are suggested below which could facilitate in designing and conducting formative research (these are adopted from the WHO work which focuses on using formative research for adopting global recommendations on HIV and infant feeding [3]:

1. Describe the scope of the formative research (more so when one knows that formative research can be undertaken in any phase of the intervention).
2. Outline a theoretical model (for better designing of the interventions as it aids in understanding the factors which are being addressed through interventions, apart from attributing the change).
3. Formulation of key questions (which needs to be answered via formative research).
4. Identification of study participants/informants and outlining of methods to obtain information or data from them (secondary review, primary data collection, secondary data collection, etc.)
5. Development of tools (relevant to the method which is being used).
6. Data collection and analysis.

While these steps are important, the iterative nature of formative research should not be overlooked. It is this iteration which makes formative research different from the other types of research, which can equally contribute to different phases of public health interventions. As mentioned earlier, the intervention could be simple or complex. But what makes an intervention simple or complex? What are those parameters which define an intervention as simple intervention or complex intervention?

According to the Medical Research Council (MRC) guidelines, the complex interventions are those interventions which "contain several interacting components" [4]. To elaborate it further, these guidelines highlight following aspects which make an intervention complex:

- Number of interacting components within the experimental and control interventions.
- Number and difficulty of behaviors required by those delivering or receiving the intervention.
- Number of groups or organizational levels targeted by the intervention.
- Number and variability of outcomes.
- Degree of flexibility or tailoring of the intervention permitted.

Against the complex interventions, the "simple" interventions in the health context are largely understood in terms of simple and linear pathways which primarily links or establishes the outcomes with their interventions (which mostly happens with the medical interventions). The complex intervention can be broken down into simple components relating it to the specified outcomes (mostly focusing on individual level). Though there could be differences in simple and complex interventions, few implementation researchers are of the view that it is the pragmatic perspective of a researcher which guides the implementation to be understood or stated as simple or complex [5].

An abstract and summarization of one such complex intervention, which has used MRC framework of designing and evaluating complex intervention, has been taken from a paper [6] and is presented as a case for further explanation. In the box, abstract of the paper is presented, which is followed by the summarized presentation of different components of interventions and its development across three different phases of MRC framework.

"Diabetes, which is a chronic illness, requires individuals to play an active role in taking their own care largely towards maintaining their glucose and blood pressure levels as close to normal as possible. Accordingly, individuals have been given instructions towards self-management. Traditionally, such instructions are part of the training programs which are delivered in didactic settings. However, there has been a focus to look for alternatives towards traditional delivery of diabetes care in recent time. For instance, 'peer support' concept does not emphasize much on professional domination rather it focuses on patient. This paper outlines the describe the development of a complex intervention of peer support in type 2 diabetes for a randomized control trial in a primary care setting.

To design the intervention, the MRC framework for developing and complex interventions for randomized control trials (RCT) was used. The preclinical phase of this framework, which focuses on understanding the existing literature, was used. Accordingly, a review of the literature relating to type 2 diabetes and peer support was undertaken. The phase 1 of the framework emphasize on defining the key components of the intervention. Accordingly, the qualitative data, which was collected from conducting focus group, in combination with the theoretical background facilitated in defining the main components of the intervention.

The four components of intervention which were identified from these two phases consisted of <u>*peer supporters*</u>; <u>*peer*</u>

<u>supporter training</u>; <u>retention and support for peer supporters</u>; and <u>peer support meetings</u>. The phase 2 focused on implementing the preliminary intervention. This was done via a pilot study which was conducted in 24 patients and 4 peer supporters. Additional qualitative data was collected by conducting focus groups and semi structured interviews to inform the development of the intervention. Findings from this phase allowed further modeling of the intervention, to produce the definitive intervention. The MRC framework was instrumental in the development of a robust intervention of peer support of type 2 diabetes in primary care."

There were four major intervention components, namely, peer support training, retention and support for peer supporters, and peer meetings. The "peer supporter" component of the intervention mainly included selection and identification of four peer supporters by the General Practitioners and Practicing Nurses. The criteria to include peer supporters were that they had type 2 diabetes for at least 1 year and are adhering to diabetes regime. Along with this, the peer supporters understand the confidentiality concept and can be in a position to liaise with practicing nurses or general practitioners, if required. Under the "peer support training" component, the identified peer supporters were given training, which was conducted by practicing nurses or general practitioners. The training was conducted locally and focused on contents like basics of diabetes, lifestyle and medication issues, communication skills. A peer supporter's handbook was also developed. Under the third component, which was "retention and support for peer supporter" the definitive intervention included putting a structure in place that could ensure peer supporters retention. This consisted of outlining the responsibilities of peer supporters, ensuring adequate training and resource pack, extensive support from project team, general practitioners and practicing nurse, constant telephonic interaction made by project manager after each session, reimbursement of travel and related expenses. Under the fourth component "peer meetings," nine peer-support meetings per group were held over the two-year duration of intervention in general practice. Each group had seven patients and each meeting started with a 10-minute structure component. The unanswered questions were told to research team at the end of each session and answers were discussed in next session [6].

It needs to be pointed out here that the above discussed complex intervention, which has been developed using MRC framework, involves Randomized Controlled Trial (RCT) to analyze the effectiveness of the interventions. However, it does not mean that every complex intervention needs to have RCT as part of analyzing the complex intervention (other designs could also be followed depending on the intervention). The complexity or simplicity of intervention should not determine the analysis, but rather the research question should guide the analysis that needs to be undertaken for assessing the complex interventions.

References

1. Formative research manual [Internet]. [cited 2022 Jul 19]. Available from: https://www.cdc.gov/hiv/pdf/statistics/systems/nhbs/nhbs-msm4-formativeresearchmanual.pdf.
2. (PDF) Using formative research to improve maternal and newborn care and infant and young child feeding in the Lao people's democratic republic [Internet]. [cited 2022 Jul 19]. Available from: https://www.researchgate.net/publication/242546220_Using_Formative_Research_to_Improve_Maternal_and_Newborn_Care_and_Infant_and_Young_Child_Feeding_in_the_Lao_People's_Democratic_Republic.
3. World Health Organization. What are the options? Using formative research to adapt global recommendations on HIV and infant feeding to the local context [Internet]. Geneva: World Health Organization. [cited 2022 Jul 19]. Available from: https://www.who.int/publications-detail-redirect/9241591366.
4. Craig P, Dieppe P, Macintyre S, Michie S, Nazareth I, Petticrew M, Medical Research Council Guidance. Developing and evaluating complex interventions: the new Medical Research Council guidance. BMJ. 2008;337:a1655. https://doi.org/10.1136/bmj.a1655.

5. Petticrew M. When are complex interventions 'complex'? When are simple interventions 'simple'? Eur J Pub Health. 2011;21(4):397–8. https://doi.org/10.1093/eurpub/ckr084. [cited 2022 Jul 19]. Available from: https://academic.oup.com/eurpub/article/21/4/397/438290.
6. Paul G, Smith SM, Whitford D, O'Kelly F, O'Dowd T. Development of a complex intervention to test the effectiveness of peer support in type 2 diabetes. BMC Health Serv Res. 2007 Aug;31(7):136.

Qualitative Research and Pragmatic Studies

6

Vinay Tripathi

Learning Objectives
After going through this section, participants will be able to:

- Describe qualitative research, associated methods, and approaches.
- Explain and appreciate the role of qualitative research in health settings.
- Differentiate qualitative and pragmatic studies.
- Describe pragmatic studies and their relevance in implementation research.

6.1 Qualitative Research: An Overview

Qualitative research with its foundations in the disciplines, such as anthropology, sociology, linguistics, psychology, etc., has transcended beyond these disciplines and is being increasingly used in many other fields including health. The reasons are manifolds and appear to be obvious to many of those who are engaged in conducting qualitative research. One of the key reasons for this proliferation is that qualitative research facilitates understanding those aspects which are difficult to capture with the mainstream methodologies of those respective disciplines alone.

But what is qualitative research, and can it be defined? Elucidating qualitative research in a standard definition may neither suffice nor can be appropriately justified. Accordingly, some key aspects of qualitative research are being mentioned here to elaborate it. Qualitative research primarily ***aims to explain social phenomena (which is under the study) mostly in its natural setting and investigate questions concerning behaviors, attitude, experiences, perceptions, norms,* etc.*, both at individual and societal level*.** In public health settings, qualitative research facilitates understanding (or in refining existing understanding) of health, health services and health related behaviors, which in turn, helps in improving health and healthcare. Two brief case studies are presented being presented below to further elaborate the point:

V. Tripathi (✉)
International Institute of Health Management Research, New Delhi, India
e-mail: vinay@iihmrdelhi.edu.in

S. Bandyopadhyay Neogi, A. K. Pandey (eds.), *Designing and Evaluating Public Health Interventions*, https://doi.org/10.1007/978-981-97-9574-1_6

Case Study 1: "Qualitative Research During the Ebola Virus Disease Outbreaks in Parts of West Africa (2014)" [1]

'During the Ebola Virus outbreak between 2014 and 2016, parts of West Africa had seen a rapid spread. Qualitative research was used to understand burial practices and their cultural implications across different communities. These practices, which were quite common among communities, were also high-risk practices compromising the containment efforts placed during the outbreak. The better understanding of these practices, in turn, facilitated not only in designing but also in monitoring the interventions for safe burials.

There was a sudden decline noticed in the number of cases and deaths in Liberia during October 2014. This decline contrasted with the disease modeling which predicted a significant increase in both cases and mortality. There was resistance among the communities to visiting testing centers and therefore the possibilities that patients not visiting the health facilities and engaging in occult burial were high. The officials carried out in-depth interviews and focus group discussions with the community members in order to assess the situation. Officials found that community members were not engaged in occult burial. They also learnt that in comparison to the previous years, the overall burial count was less. Other key findings of qualitative research included the readiness of funeral directors towards the response efforts, need of training the home workers engaged in funeral, and resistance in following the recommended practices of cremation. These findings helped the officials and their response in terms of opening a burial ground for Ebola decedents, extending support to private sector for enhanced testing, and imparting training to the workers from private sector engaged in funeral towards following practices leading to safe burial' [2].

Case Study 2: "Transformation of Primary Health Centers to Family Health Centers (FHC) in Kerala"

Qualitative research was carried out to understand patients' and healthcare workers' perspective towards the factors that facilitate and act as barrier to utilize services from these FHC in Central Kerala. The research found that the factors which facilitate utilization of services includes staff's good behavior, provision of having evening OPD and special clinics, better infrastructural facilities, clean premise of FHC, subsidized laboratory services, funding, giving rewards, and involving local government functionaries. The research found barriers related to staff crunch, staff workload, low awareness about the services provided from the centers among the general population, and medicines shortage. Addressing these barriers would facilitate in delivering quality health care if the model is scaled up to the country level.' [3].

Qualitative research plays an equally important role in implementation research. For instance, qualitative research can help in designing an intervention, explaining what aspects of an intervention are working or not working and can explore the reasons for the same. Similarly, it can also contribute to program monitoring and evaluation. Qualitative research employs a set of methods for doing what has been mentioned till now. Different studies discuss various methods which are used in qualitative research. The three most commonly used methods are as follows [4].

- **Interviews**

  Interviews can broadly be grouped into three categories, namely, structured, semi-structured, and open-ended interviews. Structured interviews involve asking questions, which are prepared as part of the study, to the respondents in a similar way and order. While semi-structured interviews involve asking questions which have closed-ended answers as well as open-ended questions. The open-ended interviews emphasize the open-ended questions related to the study and encourage a conversation pattern. In such interviews, both interviewee and interviewer strike up a conversation on the topic of interest. Probes, prompts or cues are part of open-ended interviews. These facilitate interviewers to get detailed information either by probing or following up for an answer in relation to the topic [3].

- **Focus group discussion (or group interviews)**
  It is another form of interview but involves more than one interviewee. Unlike the structured or semi-structured or open-ended interviews, the focus group involves 6–8 people. Depending on the purpose, these people can be identified and form a group. Since it involves more than one person, conducting group interviews are not relatively easy to conduct. Generally, a checklist is used to conduct such focus group interviews. These require a facilitator who is responsible to moderate the discussion and a note-taker who takes the note during the discussion [3]. Focus group requires a facilitator who moderates the discussion and note-taker, who takes the note.
- **Observation**
  Observation is another method via which qualitative data is collected. It is usually used in those situations where the researcher feels that other means or methods are not sufficient enough or have limitation to generate required data. For instance, people may respond to a question about behaving in a certain situation but may not necessarily practice that behavior in reality. Observing them may facilitate generating or collecting actual data on their behavior. Observation can also produce data for verifying or nullifying information provided in face to face can be an important method to generate the data which can either conform or contradict the data or information which is collected via interviews [3].

Like other research, there are different types of qualitative research. But rather than referring to them as types of qualitative research, it would be more appropriate to mention that different approaches are followed in qualitative research. Different references highlight various kinds of approaches. The most used approaches (in health context) are as follows:

- **Grounded theory**
- **Phenomenology**
- **Ethnography**

Understanding of each of these approaches requires extensive reading and in-depth information of qualitative research per se. Nevertheless, a brief and simplistic explanation is being provided below for each of these approaches (*several books have been written on each of these approaches, which can be referred to by readers for further understanding*).

Grounded theory, which is being extensively used in health research as well as in other fields, was developed by two sociologists Glaser and Strauss way back in late 60s. The primary aim of this approach is to generate a theory which needs to be based on the data that has been collected under the research. This explanation may sound easy, but the process involved in it is a complex one. The process requires iteration and involves passing through various stages, such as coding of data, memo writing, theoretical saturation, and theoretical sampling. Each of these stages requires a substantial amount of time, particularly the initial stages, wherein concepts are created and established in order to generate a theory.

Phenomenology is another approach of qualitative research but is also considered as a perspective which is used in health research. The approach is to focus upon the subjective experiences and interpretations of people with the purpose of understanding the "lived" experience of people being studied. It involves providing a detailed description of people who are studied in an extensive manner over a very long period of time.

Ethnographic approach, with its foundation in anthropology, is another approach of qualitative research which is used to study a culture or an organization in its natural setting with time span cutting across months. It requires extensive fieldwork with the researcher involved primarily in participant observation (there are other methods also which can be adopted by researcher). Over the time, the limitation in terms of time and resources as posed by this traditional approach, have also led to the emergence of different ethnographic studies, including focused ethnographic studies, with each one of their own advantages and limitations.

6.1.1 Pragmatic Research

Apart from qualitative research, there are studies which constitute pragmatic research. In pragmatic research, pragmatism refers to "action" or "change" and thereby is related with interventions. It needs to be mentioned here that an epistemological debate, which is beyond the scope of this chapter, exists in terms of qualitative and quantitative as well as pragmatic studies. The National Institutes of Health (NIH) explains the pragmatic research (in context of clinical trials and practice) and states that the research which is conducted in "***real world***"; It has all the parts of research like hypothesis making and testing, collection of data, data analysis, generating findings and answers. However, the way it is conducted and the questions which it tries to address are different [5]. On the continuum of translational research from T0 to T4, the pragmatic research falls in T3 or T4 research and includes both effectiveness and implementation research. The T0 leg represents basic science research stage dealing with preclinical and animal studies. The T1 leg represents translation to human stage consisting of first phase of clinical trials. The T2 leg represents translation to patient stage consisting of second and third phase of clinical trials. The T3 leg represents translation to practice stage consisting of fourth phase of clinical trials and clinical outcomes research. The T4 leg represents translation to community stage consisting of population level outcomes research. The leg from T0 to T2 depicts basic science transiting to human studies, while T3 and T4 leg depicts translation of new data into the clinic and health decision making [4].

Pragmatic research is also known as *"dissemination and implementation research"* or *"**knowledge translation.**"* An example is presented below to further explain about the pragmatic research:

"It is useful to know that those clinical psychologists who are well trained and hired under a study to deliver lengthy and controlled behavior treatments to the patients who otherwise do not have any other medical or psychological conditions and consequently demonstrate improvement in the patient's depression level. Equally important is also to know that same clinical improvements can be attained by the behavioral health providers in actual clinics working with complex patients under time and resource constraints." [4].

Another Example of Pragmatic Study (My Own Health Report—MOHR) Is Presented below to Explain the Applications of Such Studies in Real Settings [5]

"MOHR is an example of practice-level, pragmatic implementation study, wherein seven research centers with 18 clinics had partnered. It was a multisite pragmatic intervention trial which was implemented within the span of 18 months. The study was designed with the purpose of developing evidence in patient care which is quick and action oriented. The intervention was an online tool focusing on patient assessment and feedback being captured on health behaviors and psychological issues ranging from mental health or substance abuse to quality of life along with important demographic indicators. This online tool helps the patients who seek general care or wellness or chronic care and their care providers to mutually set the goals in collaborative ways. The tool, which is called MOHR, was designed with the purpose of testing whether a low-cost intervention can address multiple health issues at primary care level like health behavior, psychosocial and substance abuse in real-world settings. The findings suggested that it is quite feasible to implement the intervention as part of pragmatic research in real-world settings.

The whole study was conducted in 18 months duration, a relatively shorter time in comparison to traditional multisite trials. There were two reasons behind this namely, the extensive use of research networks and less time to get the funds which in turn helped the research team to save the time. Apart from these two reasons other factors such as presence of management team, site selection keeping collaborative and multi-site research experience in mind, focus on partnership, and conducting the study in a real-world community based primary care setting further helped the team to implement the intervention comparatively faster. The adaptive nature and engagement process adopted by the team that facilitated the team to quickly identify and address the evolving issues played a critical role in implementation of the study in shorter timeframe.

Conducting pragmatic research in a timely and efficient manner is very much possible. The insights from this research indicate that the identification and utilization of existing research network, designing and implementing interventions that can address local needs, involvement of relevant stakeholder right from the beginning and throughout the study duration, considering pragmatic decisions are some of the ways by which pragmatic research can be executed."

It is important to note that pragmatic studies are largely meant to assess the effectiveness of interventions in real-world settings (there are other designs and studies which are meant to assess both effectiveness and implementation efficiencies). Given the fact there is an emphasis on evidence-based interventions in health settings, the pragmatic studies will certainly play an important role in determining their efficacies in practice as well as in generating findings which can inform about the improvements that can be incorporated in such interventions for real world like situations.

***Q.6.1** In reference to the Ekjut trial: Trial was considered success to mobilize the community to reduce the neonatal mortality rate. How did the authors explore the mechanism of success of the intervention?*

References

1. Adongo PB, Tabong PTN, Asampong E, Ansong J, Robalo M, Adanu RM. Preparing towards preventing and containing an Ebola virus disease outbreak: what socio-cultural practices may affect containment efforts in Ghana? PLoS Negl Trop Dis. 2016;10(7):e0004852. https://journals.plos.org/plosntds/article?id=10.1371/journal.pntd.0004852
2. Family Health International, Mack N, Woodsong C, United States, Agency for International Development. Qualitative research methods: a data collector's field guide. North Carolina: FLI USAID; 2005.
3. Vijayan SM, Puliyakkadi S, Chalil S. Facilitators and barriers of service utilization: perspectives of stakeholders in a family health center of Central Kerala—a qualitative study. Indian J Public Health. 2021;65(2):136–41. https://doi.org/10.4103/ijph.IJPH_995_20. [cited 2022 Jul 19]. Available from: https://pubmed.ncbi.nlm.nih.gov/34135181/
4. Hancock B, Ockleford E, Windridge K. An introduction to qualitative research. National Institute for Health Research; 2009: 1–39. http://www.rds-yh.nihr.ac.uk/wp-content/uploads/2013/05/5_Introduction to qualitative-research-2009.pdf.
5. Glasgow RE, Kessler RS, Ory MG, Roby D, Gorin SS, Krist A. Conducting rapid, relevant research: lessons learned from the my own health report project. Am J Prev Med. 2014;47(2):212–9.

Observational Studies

7

Anuj Kumar Pandey and Sidharth Sekhar Mishra

Learning Objectives

After going through this section, participants will be able to:

- Describe different observational study designs that can be used in a program scenario.
- Explain and select an appropriate design for particular research question.
- Describe applicability of such study design in program implementation as well as for effectiveness assessment.

7.1 Study Designs: An Overview

There are different kinds of research study designs, and each having its own merits and demerits. These study designs are used to address a specific research question and it depends on the nature of the inquiry and the resources available. Broadly research methods fall into two major categories, namely the **Quantitative methods and Qualitative methods**. The qualitative method deals with "non-quantitative" elements, whereas quantitative methods deal with the "quantity" or numbers, or "measurement," which uses statistical methods. Identifying research design types, their advantages, and disadvantages, is crucial as they might influence study's validity.

A. K. Pandey (✉) · S. S. Mishra
Department of Health Systems and Implementation Research, International Institute of Health Management Research (IIHMR), New Delhi, India
e-mail: anuj@iihmrdelhi.edu.in

There are some terminologies that are used while categorizing study designs [1]:

- **Outcome v/s Exposure variables**
  A variable is a measurable characteristic that varies among the units of study. Age, sex, height, weight, health status (alive/dead, diseased/healthy), annual income, smoking status (yes/no), treated/untreated are some of the examples of variables. Researchers examine if one variable is related to or modifies values of other variables or not. The risk factor under examination, whose impact is being studied, is termed the exposure (or intervention). It is also known as the predictor variable or independent variable. The exposure is responsible for causing a change in the outcome (or predicted or dependent) variable.
- ***Interventional (or experimental) studies v/s Observational studies***
  As the name suggests experimental or interventional studies are research studies where researchers actively perform an intervention. For example, administration of a drug to set of study participants and providing usual care to other set of study participants to see drug efficacy.
  In contrary to this in observational studies, researchers document the natural occurring

S. Bandyopadhyay Neogi, A. K. Pandey (eds.), *Designing and Evaluating Public Health Interventions*, https://doi.org/10.1007/978-981-97-9574-1_7

relationship between the exposure and the outcome. No active intervention is being undertaken. Example—comparing the incidence of lung cancer amongst smokers and non-smokers. Observational studies could either be descriptive, i.e., describing the study subjects in context to person place and time or could be analytical, i.e., inferential that is proving the hypothesis.

- ***Analytical v/s Descriptive studies***
  Describing the study participants on one or more characteristics of a group of individuals is descriptive studies. Under descriptive studies we do not establish any relationship between the collected variables. Under analytical study section we attempt to test the hypothesis and establish causal relationship between the variables. Researchers assess the effect of an exposure on the outcome under study domain.
- ***Directionality—Retrospective v/vs. Prospective study designs***
  Study designs can be classified as **forward direction** or **backward direction**, based on direction of the investigation. In forward-direction studies, the researcher initially determines exposure to a risk factor and subsequently assesses whether the outcome occurs at a later time: such study design as cohort studies. In backward-direction studies, the researcher first identifies the presence of the outcome (cases vs. no cases, also known as controls) before investigating past exposure to a risk factor, and these are referred to as case-control studies.

7.2 Classification of Study Designs

An essential three-point methodology developed by the Centre for Evidence-based Medicine can be used to determine a research study's design from its methods section as shown in Fig. 7.1. All these study designs can be classified as either observational or experimental designs. In observational studies, the researcher observes but does not intervene. Observational studies can be categorized as descriptive or analytical.

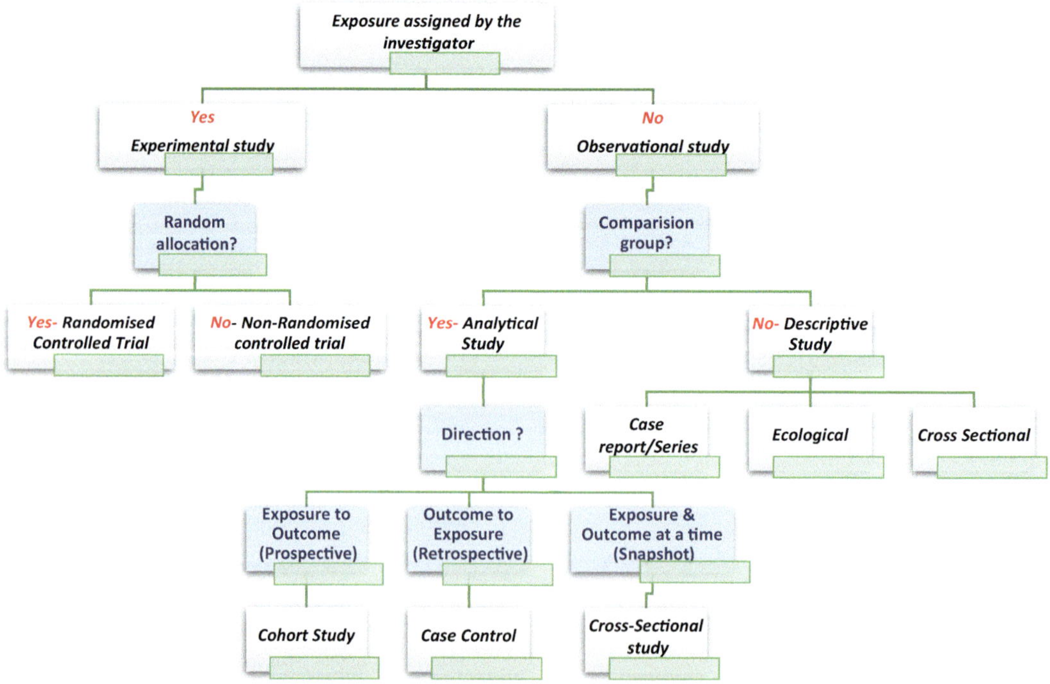

Fig. 7.1 Research study designs classification. *(Authors developed)*

Table 7.1 Advantages and Disadvantages of case reports, case series, and case study

Advantages	Disadvantages
One case to start (case report)	No control (uncontrolled)
Offer stronger evidence with multiple cases. (cases series)	Difficult to compare
Observational	Can't be generalizable
Educational	Selection bias
Easy to do (fast and no financial support needed)	Unknown future outcome/follow-up
Identify rare manifestations of a disease or drug	

- In **descriptive study** researchers undertake a description of the health-related status of a population and usually are the initial stage in any epidemiological investigation.
- An **analytical study** is further enhanced by examining relationships between health status and other variables.

This chapter will discuss the different types of quantitative study designs.

Almost all epidemiological studies are analytical in nature, with the exception of the most descriptive research. Purely descriptive studies are uncommon, although descriptive data from health statistics reports can be a good start for all epidemiological investigations when developing hypotheses. A more in-depth epidemiological study is frequently sparked by a lack of sufficient descriptive data, such as that found in case series when a number of patients with a particular condition are reported but not compared to a reference population. Every study design has its own merits and demerits depending upon the research question under consideration.

7.2.1 Case Reports/Case Series

Descriptive studies are used in case reports, case series, and case study research [2] to show patients in their natural clinical settings. Case reports, which often have three or less than three patients, highlights aspects of medical practice and perhaps spark new research questions that could advance our understanding of the literature. Case studies are qualitative research methods that incorporate in-depth assessments or experience inquiries of an individual or group in their actual environment and involve a number of patients. The context examination of many events or conditions and their relationships is the main focus of case study research. Some of the major advantages and disadvantages of such type of study designs are mentioned in Table 7.1.

> ***Q.7.1** Ref to the case study on Sex Selection Drugs (SSD) and discuss how the authors built upon the case series.*

7.2.2 Ecological Studies

Ecological research is an epidemiological study design in which an entire community serves as the unit of analysis instead of an individual. Ecological research, for instance, can examine the relationship between per capita income and infant mortality in Indian states. Ecological studies are valuable despite their flaws because they can be conducted quickly, simply, and inexpensively using data that is typically already available (Fig. 7.2). The outcomes of ecological research can offer the chance for more comprehensive investigations to expand on the preliminary findings.

> ***Q.7.2** Ref to the case study on JSY, which evidence triggered India to promote institutional deliveries? (Hint: Ref to evidence generated using an ecological study design)*

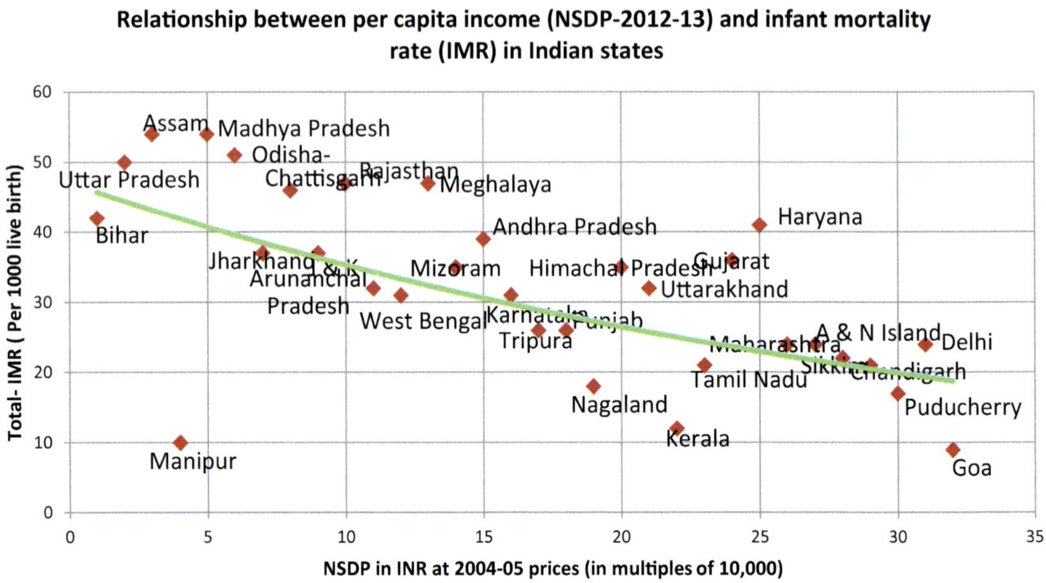

Fig. 7.2 Infant mortality rate and Per capita income (2012–13)
*Note: Developed by Author using NSDP (**Net state domestic product**) data of year 2012–13 and IMR data of 2013 available in public domain*

7.2.3 Cross-Section Studies

Cross-sectional studies [3, 4], also known as prevalence studies, assess the prevalence of a disease or a health condition (old and new cases in a community during a specific period of time). Cross-sectional studies are often named as a snapshot study as it provides the snapshot of the community at a given point of time. Such studies are being conducted for population-based surveys and also to evaluate the prevalence of any disease in clinic-based samples. Investigators in a cross-sectional study measure the outcome and the exposures at the same time as other directional investigations.

Measurements of exposure and effect (outcome or disease) are also made concurrently in a cross-sectional study. The most practical initial step in determining the reason can be a cross-sectional study to measure many exposures. The demands of populations in terms of healthcare can be determined with the use of cross-sectional study data. Trends can be identified utilizing data from repeated cross-sectional surveys using independent random samples and established definitions.

There are certain steps that need to be followed while undertaking any cross-sectional surveys-

- Defining the population and disease to be studied
- Measurement of disease
- Describing the health condition / disease by
  - Frequency
  - Distribution (Time, Place, and Person) and
  - Determinants (factors, if present, which increase the chance of getting the disease)
- Comparing with known indices (with other Districts, States, and National figures)
- Formulation of hypothesis

To examine the personal, demographic traits and other health/disease related information, various countries undertake cross-sectional surveys of a representative samples. National level cross-sectional surveys in India include National Family Health Surveys (NFHS), District Level Health Surveys and surveys conducted by National Sample Survey Organization (NSSO). Some of the strengths and limitations of cross-sectional studies as given in Table 7.2.

Table 7.2 Strengths and limitations of a cross-section studies

Strengths	*Limitations*
• Can usually be performed relatively fast and are inexpensive, particularly when compared to other study designs such as cohort, case-control.	• Since exposure and result are measured once, it is difficult to discern causal links from cross-sectional research.
• Such studies are being done either at a planning step for cohort studies or as a baseline for those investigations. These types of designs will provide data on the frequency of outcomes or exposures, and this data will be helpful in constructing the cohort study. • Planning, observing, and evaluating public health may benefit from these study designs.	• Certain biases are also possible in these investigations. • The prevalence of an outcome is influenced by both the disease's prevalence and the duration of survivorship after the outcome.

Q.7.3 Ref to the case study on Mental Health. Discuss the reason for a difference in the burden estimated from cross-section studies and meta-analysis.

7.2.4 Cohort Study Design

Cohort study design [5]- Synonyms: Incidence,, forward-looking, follow-up, concurrent, longitudinal, and prospective study designs.

This study design can be characterized as a collection of individuals who share a common characteristic or experience within a specified time frame. These studies commence with a group of initially disease-free individuals, who are later categorized into two subgroups based on their exposure to a potential cause of disease or outcome. Specific variables of interest are identified and measured, and the entire cohort is then monitored to observe the subsequent development of new cases of the disease (or other outcomes) and assess the differences between the groups with and without exposure. Cohort studies are longitudinal in nature, as the data on exposure and disease acquisition are collected at different points in time.

Cohort studies are also referred to as prospective studies, but this terminology can be misleading and should be steered clear of. The term 'prospective' pertains to the timing of data collection and not to the connection between exposure and effect, as illustrated in Fig. 7.3. Therefore, it's important to note that cohort studies can encompass both prospective and retrospective designs.

- **Prospective Cohort** (*Concurrent Cohort)*: Population under this cohort is followed up over a period of time to assess the outcome to a pre-determined exposure.
- **Retrospective Cohort** (*Historical Cohort)*: Historical exposure information is collected from the identified cohort.

Stages in Conducting a Cohort Study

- **Formulation of the objective:** It is essential to identify what we want to investigate.
- **Selection of study subjects:** The investigator decides on subjects, determines their extent of exposure and checks for the development of the disease over a period of time. The cohort can be selected from the general population or some specific group of people. Example: Smokers are followed up for a period of 10 years to check for development of lung cancer.
- **Obtaining data on exposure:** The feasibility of conducting cohort studies is significantly influenced by the challenges associated with measuring or obtaining pre-existing data on individual exposures. Additionally, if the disease is uncommon in both the exposed and unexposed groups, there may be difficulties in assembling a sufficiently large study cohort.
- **Follow-up:** The follow-up should continue till the occurrence of the defined outcome of interest in both the groups.
- **Analysis:** The risk ratio commonly referred to as relative risk is calculated as per the formula given below-

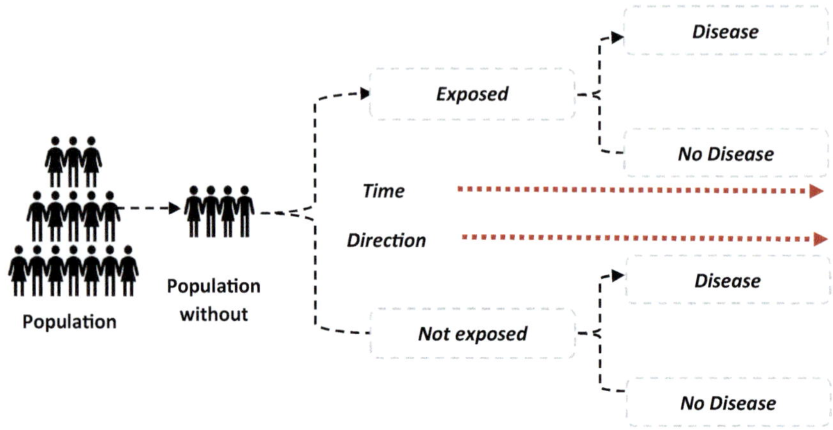

Fig. 7.3 Cohort Study design

Sample	Diseased	Non-diseased	Total
Exposed	a	b	$a + b$
Unexposed	c	d	$c + d$
Total	$a + c$	$b + c$	$a + b + c + d$

$$\text{Relative risk (risk ratio)} = \frac{\text{Incidence of disease in the exposed group}}{\text{Incidence of disease in the unexposed group}}$$

$$\textbf{Relative risk (risk ratio)} = \frac{[a/a+b]}{[c/c+d]}$$

- **Interpretation:** The risk ratio is used to quantify the etiological strength, or the degree to which a risk factor is associated with an outcome. If the incidence of the disease is the same in the exposed and unexposed groups, a value of 1.0 will be achieved, and this means that there is no evidence of an association between the exposure and the condition. A value higher than 1.0 denotes a strong correlation or an elevated risk for individuals who are exposed to the factor. Those exposed have a decreased risk or there is an inverse association, or the exposure is protective, if the value is less than 1.0.

7.2.5 Case-Control Study Design

Case-control studies [3, 6] provide more simpler way to check for association or relationship between two factors. They consist of individuals with the disease (or result variable) and a suitable control (comparison or reference) group of individuals who are unaffected by the expected disease or outcome variable. In such studies, the likelihood of the potential factors is compared between cases and controls. Data on illness occurrence at one point in time and exposures at a prior point in time are collected and studied. In contrast to cross-sectional studies, which are like a snapshot, case-control studies entail a longer time of investigation as shown in Fig. 7.4.

Stages in Conducting a Case-control Study

- **Formulation of the objective:** The definition of the disease or result of interest should be considered before designing a case-control study. What we want to investigate must be quite apparent to us.
- **Selection of case:** One of the first responsibilities is to create a strict case definition for the disease in order to ensure that the cases chosen for investigation represent a homogenous entity. The people with this ailment can be chosen from several sources once the criteria and definition of the sickness have been properly stated. The decision of whether to include incidence (new) or prevalence (new and old) cases is another crucial factor.
- **Selection of controls:** The most challenging and important aspect of designing a

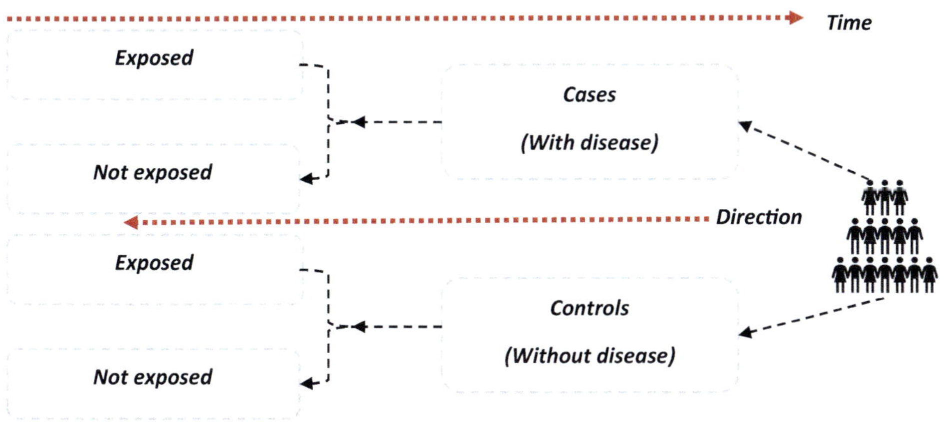

Fig. 7.4 Case-control Study design

case-control study is choosing an acceptable comparison group. Controls must be free of the disease being investigated. Except for the absence of the disease being studied, they must be as identical to the cases as possible. The source of selection of controls relies on the features and source from which the research group is selected.

- **Obtaining data on exposure:** For both cases and controls, the exposure information should be collected precisely the same way. This can be collected by interviews, questionnaires, records reviews, etc.
- **Analysis and interpretation:** The analysis of a case-control study is essentially a comparison of the exposure to a factor whose potential etiologic function is being assessed between cases and controls. Discovering the prevalence of exposure to the alleged illness-causing factor among cases and controls and estimating the risk of disease due to exposure are the last steps in the analysis (Odds ratio).

Sample	Cases	Controls	Total
Exposed	a	b	$a + b$
Unexposed	c	d	$c + d$
Total	$a + c$	$b + c$	$a + b + c + d$

$$\text{Odds ratio} = \frac{\text{Odds of exposure amongst cases}\left(a/c\right)}{\text{Odds of exposure amongst controls}\left(b/d\right)}$$

$$\textbf{Odds ratio} = \frac{\textbf{ad}}{\textbf{bc}}$$

OR of 1 means no association of disease with exposure. OR > 1 shows high risk for disease in presence of exposure, whereas OR < 1 means lower disease risk with exposure.

> *Q.7.4 Ref to the case study on Sex Selection Drug (SSD).*
>
> - *Identify the ideal study design for establishing the association b/w SSD and birth defect?*
> - *Can there be any other implication?*

References

1. Ranganathan P, Aggarwal R. Study designs: part 1—an overview and classification. Perspect Clin Res. 2018;9(4):184–6.
2. Sayre JW, Toklu HZ, Ye F, Mazza J, Yale S. Case reports, case series—from clinical practice to evidence-based medicine in graduate medical education. Cureus. 2017;9(8):e1546. https://doi.org/10.7759/cureus.1546.
3. The BMJ | The BMJ: leading general medical journal. *Research*. Education. Comment [Internet]. 2020 [cited 2022 Jul 28]. Chapter 8. Case-control and cross sectional studies | The BMJ. Available from: https://www.bmj.com/about-bmj/resources-readers/publications/epidemiology-uninitiated/8-case-control-and-cross-sectional.
4. Setia MS. Methodology series module 3: cross-sectional studies. Indian J Dermatol. 2016;61(3):261–4.

5. Berman NG, Parker RA. Cohort studies. In: Planning clinical research [Internet]. Cambridge: Cambridge University Press; 2016. p. 82–94. [cited 2022 Jul 28]. Available from: https://www.cambridge.org/core/books/planning-clinical-research/cohort-studies/4C8300CC5C479C214CCE9F6D8BB105EF.
6. Setia MS. Methodology series module 2: case-control studies. Indian J Dermatol. 2016;61(2):146–51.

Intervention/Experimental Study Design

8

Anuj Kumar Pandey and Sidharth Sekhar Mishra

Learning Objectives

After going through this section, participants will be able to:

- Describe different interventional study designs that can be used in a programme scenario.
- Describe the important elements and epidemiologic issues of randomized trials.

8.1 Experimental Study Designs: An Overview

The recommended approach to evaluate the effectiveness of any health or medical intervention is through an experimental research design [1]. In this type of study, a set of participants undergo an intervention and are compared to either a control group or another group that received a different intervention or no intervention. While there are situations where an experimental study design may be impractical or ethically challenging, but when feasible, well-designed controlled experiments provide robust information on the effectiveness of interventions, informing the development of a health policy/ programme.

A. K. Pandey (✉) · S. S. Mishra
Department of Health Systems and Implementation Research, International Institute of Health Management Research (IIHMR), New Delhi, India
e-mail: anuj@iihmrdelhi.edu.in

> ***"A well-planned and well-executed randomized controlled trial (RCT) is a highly reliable and effective method for evaluating the impact of any health program"*** [1]

As the name implies this study design is a technique of undertaking research in a controlled, objective manner. In most cases, the aim is to determine the effect of an intervention also called as an exposure on the outcome. Broadly experimental study designs may be classified as shown in Fig. 8.1:

The effects in experimental studies are being assessed by comparing the outcome in experimental arm with that of in the control arm.

(a) **Randomized controlled trials:** This type of study design aims to assess effect of an intervention (treatment/drug) hence often labelled as clinical trials. Subjects are randomly assigned to either intervention or control arm to avoid selection bias. This takes care of the confounders that can influence the study outcomes, positively or negatively.

(b) **Field trials:** Unlike clinical trials, participants under field trials are healthy and are assumed to be at risk. Data collection happens at the field. Such trials are often complex due to its methodology and are thus relatively expensive. ***Example*** *of such trials are "study to assess COVID vaccination efficacy and effectiveness at diverse settings". Such trials involve large field sites to examine a range of health outcomes.*

S. Bandyopadhyay Neogi, A. K. Pandey (eds.), *Designing and Evaluating Public Health Interventions*, https://doi.org/10.1007/978-981-97-9574-1_8

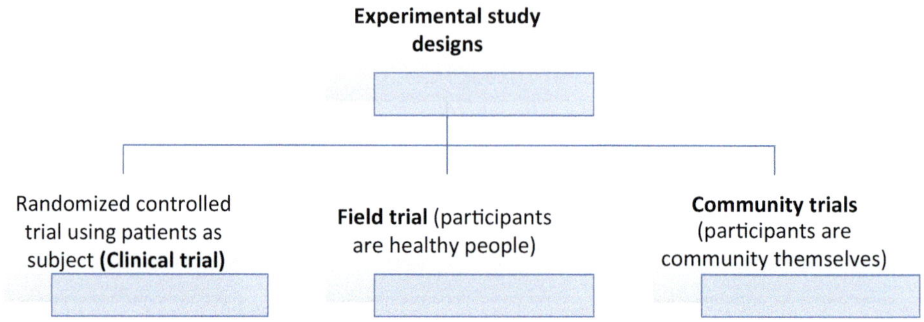

Fig. 8.1 Major experimental study designs

(c) **Community trials:** Under such trials, the treatment groups consist of communities rather than individual participants. Such trials are being undertaken when the disease conditions are guided by social conditions and under this prevention efforts are targeted by group behaviours.

Q.8.1 Ref to the case studies, classify them into RCT, field trial, and community trial

There are some terminologies that need to be understood before going into the details of the experimental study designs.

- **Intervention:** An intervention could be anything from a drug in a clinical trial setting to a behavioural change activity. These could be directed at individuals or communities.
- **Experimental group v/s Control group:** Experimental groups, often referred to as intervention groups, receive the planned intervention. In case a researcher wants to explore effectiveness of supplement X on micronutrient deficiencies amongst diabetics, the control group would be a group of diabetics not exposed to supplements, while the experimental group would receive the supplement. Usually control subset do not receive any treatment but in studies with objectives to compare new intervention to old/existing intervention, control group is assigned in the existing intervention arm.
- **Blinding (Masking):** This represents an essential part of randomized controlled trials [2]. Blinding in an epidemiological study imply that the trial participants, investigators, or the researchers remains uninformed of the assigned intervention to avoid a set of a biases at multiple stages of a study. Blinding or masking ensures privacy. Some of the potential benefits of blinding is shown in Fig. 8.2.

Type of Blinding/Masking [2]

- ***Non-blinded (open or open label)***: This means that everyone involved in the trial (participants, researcher, and investigators) knows details of participants in both intervention and under control arm.
- ***Single-blinded trial***: This means that amongst participants, researcher, or investigators, one group remains unaware of the intervention assignment throughout the trial. More often participants remain unaware of intervention rather than the investigators.
- ***Double-blinded trial***: Investigators and assessors usually stay unaware of the intervention allocation.
- ***Triple blinded trial***: All, participants, researcher, and investigators remain blinded of the intervention.

- **Contamination:** This refers to the issues arising when units in proximity are assigned different types of interventions. It also applies when one set of participants from the same organization or community receives the intervention and other set behaves as the control

Fig. 8.2 Potential benefit of Masking/Blinding [2]

Individua blinding	Benefits
Study participants	• Lowered bias towards psychological/physical appearance. • Lower chances to leave the trials in between i.e., loss to follow-up. • Participants comply well with trial regimens.
Investigators	• Investigators do not transfer their own inclination/attitudes to the study participants. Reduced chances to adjust the dose or withdraw a participants based on their own biases/perceptions.
Assessors	• Reduced chances to affect the outcome assessment.

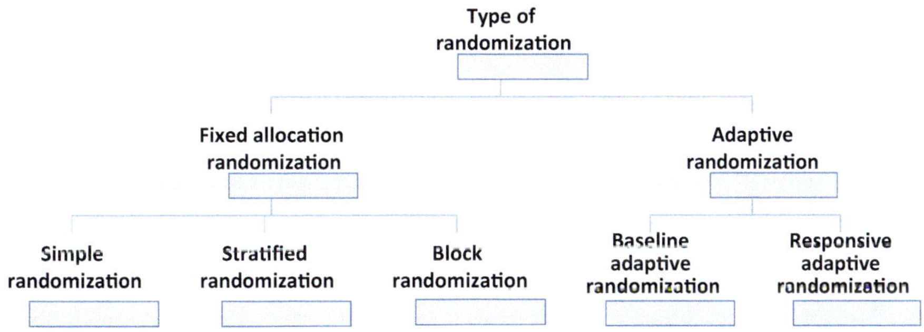

Fig. 8.3 Classification of types of randomizations

arm. For example, if half the nursing staffs of X hospital in the intervention arm are asked to use a new toolkit. Although just half of the nursing staffs are asked to use, they might share the toolkit with their colleagues, thus contaminating the effects of the intervention.

- **Randomization** [3, 4]. A well-designed and executed trial reduces the variability and offers an objective evaluation of the intervention by averting known or unknown confounding factors. Randomization ensures that each study participant is given an equal chance to receive intervention being studied; randomization makes comparable intervention groups that are similar in all ways. Randomization -
  - Reduces selection bias.
  - Increasingly comparability of groups (to the extent possible).
  - Stabilizes the two arms, i.e., the intervention arm and the control arm with respect to many known/unknown confounding variables.
  - Provides basis for an assumption of free statistical tests of equality of treatment.

Types of Randomizations There are several techniques for the random allocation of study participants to intervention or no intervention arm in any experimental study. Figure 8.3 provides an in-depth understanding of the same.

I. **Fixed Allocation randomization:** Under this mode of randomization, intervention to the participants is provided with a prespecified probability, more often this allocation is equal. This allocation is never altered during the entire study period. Some authors recommend unequal allocation with 2:1 ratio of intervention to control [5] but equal allocation is more commonly utilized with a ratio of 1:1 of intervention to control.

   (i) **Simple/complete randomization:** Most used type of randomization. Some of the commonly utilized methods include unbiased coin toss or rolling of dice or random number table or random number producing algorithm. For example, based on the results of a coin toss, participants are either assigned to group A or B. Not commonly used in large studies.

   (ii) **Stratified randomization:** To achieve between group comparability, this method is often utilized. Thus, within this method researchers first stratify (stratum = layer) the study population by each variable that is considered important and then participants are randomized within each stratum. Within each strata blocked randomization is used; usually simple random sampling can also be used. This concept is often used for larger studies or for many small studies when averaged.

(iii) **Block randomization:** This is sometimes referred to as Permuted block randomization. It is employed to prevent significant imbalance among participants assigned to each group. This technique guarantees that there will be no significant imbalance at any point during randomization, and at specific intervals, the number of participants in each group will be equal. This ensures comparable groups and maintains balance in groups even if the trial is terminated before completing the prespecified enrolment.

II. **Adaptive randomization:** This ensures a change in the allocation probabilities as study progresses which make the method a dynamic and real-time event; but for this to be done, the population recruited should remain stable over time and ultimately the method leads to a complicated data analysis.

(i) **Baseline adaptive randomization:** The Biased Coin Randomization procedure aims to equalize the number of participants in each treatment group based on prior assignments, without considering participant responses. This method randomizes participant allocation to groups A and B with equal probability when the number of participants in each group is equal or nearly equal. If there is an imbalance, the allocation probability (p) is adjusted to achieve balance in the number of participants in each group.

(ii) **Response adaptive randomization:** This approach incorporates participant response to the intervention throughout the trial to determine the allocation of the next participant.

8.2 Types of Intervention Study Designs

Intervention study designs can broadly be classified as shown in Fig. 8.4 [3, 6–8].

I. **True Experimental design:** Such study designs are the Gold Standard for explaining if the intervention is bringing out the desired change in the outcome or not. Such study designs explain the causality which is of a vital interest to an intervention manager. Based on the causality, decision on scalability or even continuing the intervention may be made. The subtypes are:

(i) **Pretest–Posttest control group designs:** RCTs often use this type of study designs. Participants in both the arms are randomly assigned. As shown in the figure, in this design type, participants from both the arm receive an initial measurement observation, i.e., O1 & O2—Pretest. Post-initial assessment participants get the intervention (X) and later a second set of measurements, i.e., observation is being made.

Since participants in both the arms were randomly assigned and intervention is only given in the intervention arm, researchers would be able to assess the difference due to the intervention and attribute differences between both the arms.

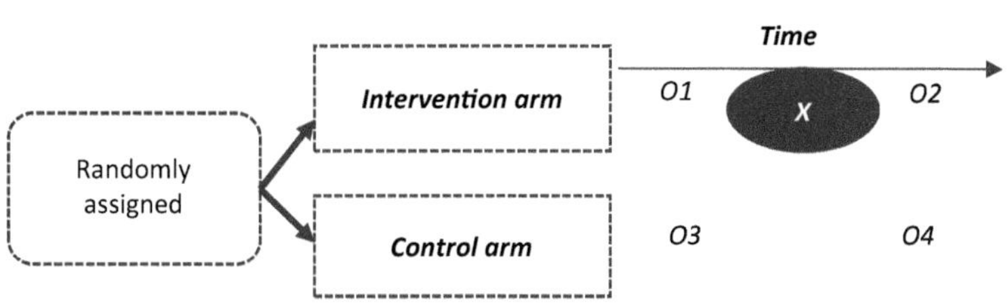

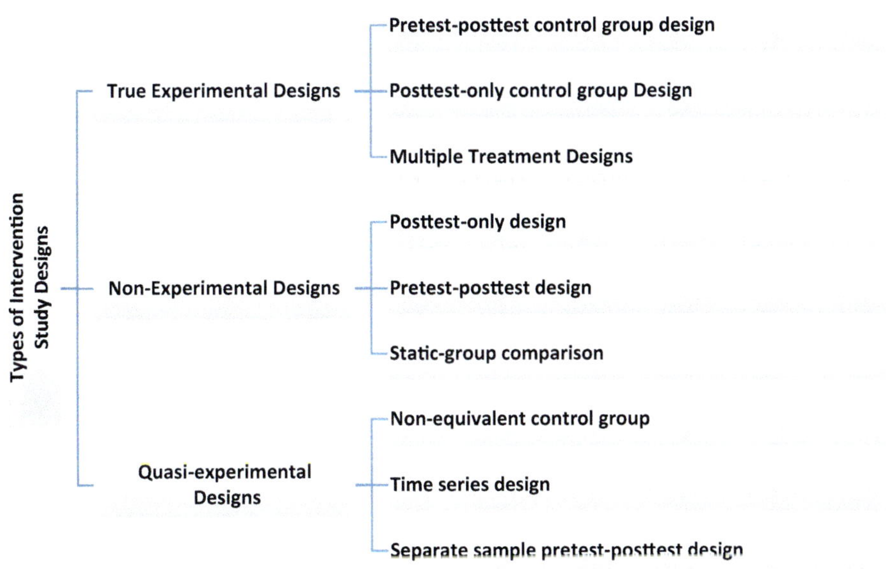

Fig. 8.4 Type of intervention study designs

(ii) **Posttest-only control group Design:** It has no pretest. Since participants are randomly assigned to both arms, it is presumed that these groups will be comparable prior to the intervention. This design enables the researcher to assess the impact of an intervention in the experiment arm. This design may be preferable in when investigator faces severe time or financial constraints, when pretest data are unavailable, when there are doubts about the testing effect, or when a sizable sample can be divided between the treatment and control groups. This design comes with certain limitations. Firstly, the lack of a baseline pretest assessment in the post-test-only control group design hinders the investigator from assessing the extent of change within the experimental group. Secondly, the absence of a pretest assessment makes it impossible for the researcher to make comparisons between patients before randomly assigning them to the experimental and control groups.

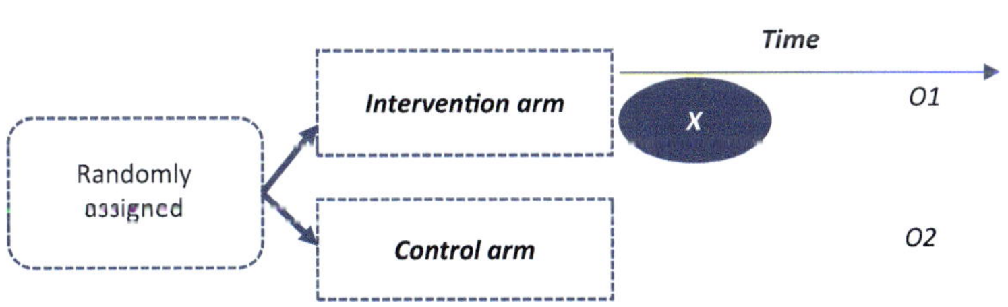

(iii) **Multiple Treatment Designs:** Researchers will be able to assess the relative efficacy of various therapies (X and Y) using this design as shown in the figure. This design enables researchers to compare the absolute effectiveness of each intervention with the randomly assigned controls. Without the control group, it would be impossible to determine whether X or Y was superior or more effective.

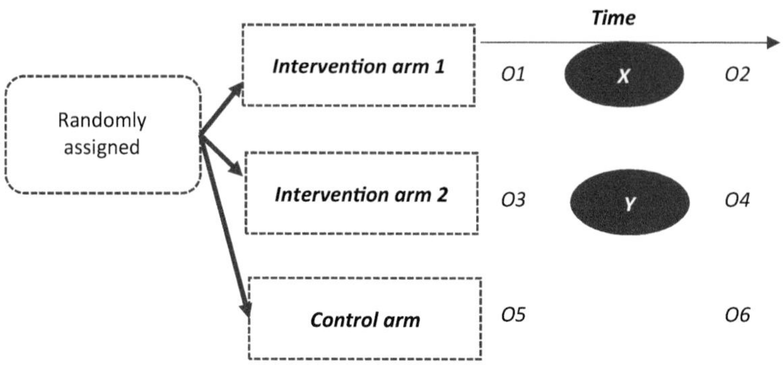

II. **Non-experimental design:** Such study designs are often used for descriptive study or for small case studies. Never being done for any evaluation studies.

(i) **Post-test-only design:** In this design as shown in the figure, the intervention (X) has been implemented, and a measurement observation (O1) is made some time after that. There is no way to compare the O1 measurement to any other measurement because there is no control group. The O1 measurement is only capable of providing ḥdescriptive data. Before picking this design, one should consider the risks to the validity of history, maturation, selection, and mortality since these risks cannot be controlled.

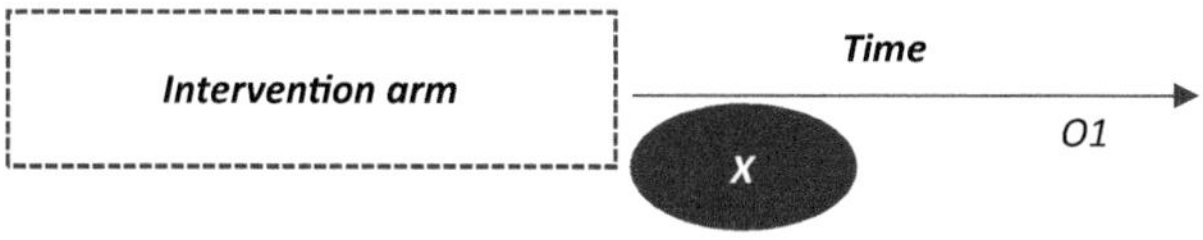

(ii) **Pretest-posttest design:** Although there is no control group in this design as shown in the figure, there is at least a measured observation(O1) before the intervention (X) that enables the researcher to look at changes over time. This design is vulnerable to various risks to validity.

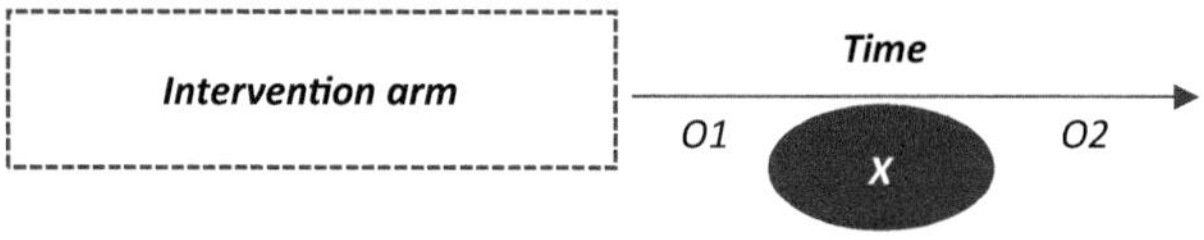

(iii) **Static-group comparison:** The third design, in contrast to the first two, includes a comparison group as shown in the figure. The intervention group then undergoes an observation (O1) after receiving programme intervention (X). The second observation (O2) without any intervention is then contrasted with this observation. It resembles the post-test-only comparison group concept that was previously addressed. It is important to note that a broken line (------) separates the two groups proves that a random procedure was not employed to divide the individuals into the two groups.

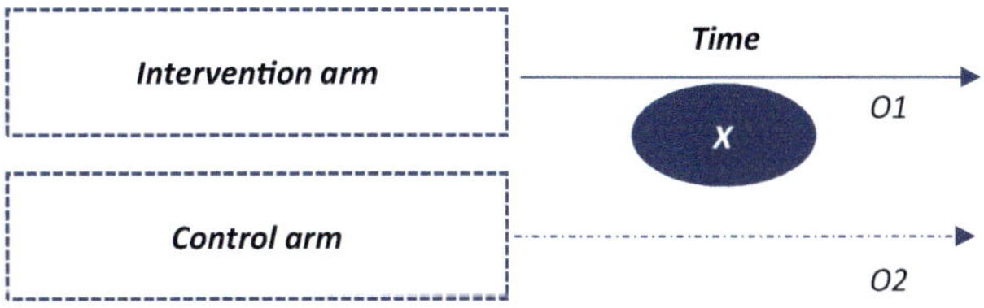

III. **Quasi-experimental design:** It is often difficult and expensive to achieve the random assignment requirements of an actual experimental design and at the same time threats to validity are also associated with the non-experimental study designs. A quasi-experimental design is frequently an acceptable compromise between the experimental and non-experimental study designs.
   (i) **Non-equivalent control group:** This design as shown in the figure is described by the use of a small number of collective units, like healthcare facilities, regions, or schools, each of which comprises a variety of people. The individuals within the collective units are not randomly allocated to experimental and control groups, and neither are the units themselves subject to random assignment (*Line between the treatment and comparison groups indicates lack of random assignment*)

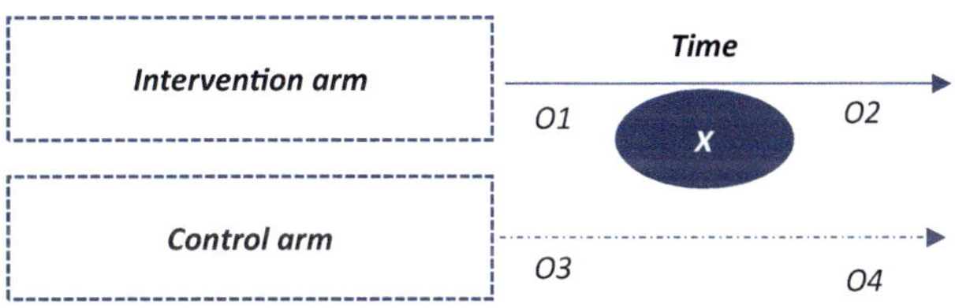

Example: A short training session on how to use personal protective equipment (PPE) (X) might be offered to the healthcare professionals in one hospital before the posttest (O1) (O2). A comparable group of healthcare professionals from a different hospital could take the same pretest at the same time (O3) and receive the same posttest for comparison's purpose (O4). The two pretests (O1 and O3) may be used in this case to determine how comparable the two groups of providers were. The two posttests would then be compared (O2 and O4).

   (ii) **Time series design:** The non-experimental pretest–posttest design is comparable to the time series design as shown in the figure. It has the advantage of repeated measurement observations both before and after the programme intervention X.

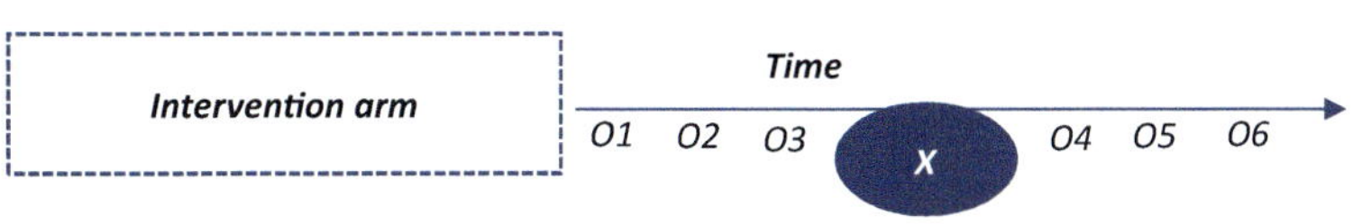

(iii) **Separate sample pretest-posttest design:** This study design does not account for history, maturation, mortality, or instrumentation effects, like the pretest–posttest approach. A baseline pretest (O1) is administered as part of the design to a sample that was randomly chosen from the study population. Following the introduction of the programme intervention (X) as shown in figure, a posttest measurement (O2) is conducted using a second randomly chosen sample from the same study group.

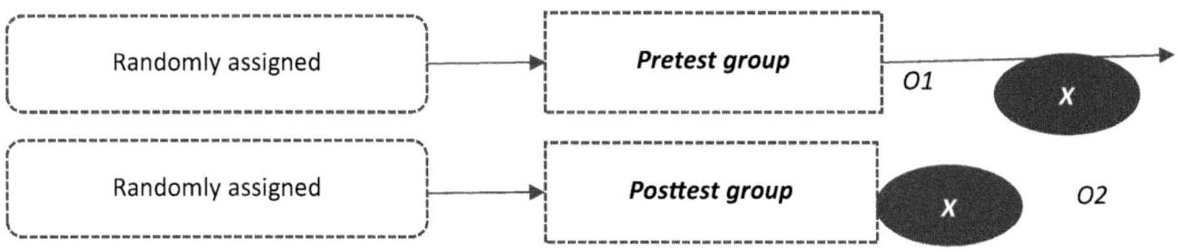

> *Q.8.2 Ref to the case study on HBNC. What was the study design used for evaluating the trial. Justify your answer.*

> *Q.8.3 Ref to the case study on IV Iron sucrose. Which analytical approach was used for the assessing the effectiveness.*

8.3 Data Analysis

The question of which patients to include in the data analysis frequently comes up [3]. After a trial has ended, some researchers might wish to exclude from the analysis subjects who did not meet the requirements for eligibility or who did not adhere to the protocol exactly. Others, on the other hand, think that once a person is randomized, they should always be monitored and considered in the study.

- ***The intention-to-treat principle (ITT)***: All randomized participants (as per the protocol) should be accounted for in the initial analysis.
- Other ways are "***modified intention-to-treat" analyses, or "per protocol" or "on treatment" analyses***, which states that only participants who have received at least some of the intervention should be included in the analysis.
- Some of the differences between these two types of analysis are explained in Table 8.1.

Table 8.1 Difference between Intention to Treat Analysis and Per Protocol Analysis

Intention to Treat Analysis	Per Protocol Analysis
Does not consider protocol violation	Analyse those who fully complied to protocol
Compare outcome according to randomized group (gold standard)	Includes cross over in final analysis
Also called as randomized or method effectiveness analysis; provide good idea on efficacy	Does not provide fair idea of efficacy for treatment
Randomization is not affected	May be biased (randomization compromised)

8.4 Interpretation of Results

Interpreting and summarizing the findings is the last step in any experiment, however the kind of analysis is decided at the beginning of the intervention. The results of an intervention can be summed up as:

- **Superiority:** *Intervention* ≥ *Control*, i.e., researcher identified that the intervention is proved to be more effective than the control.
- **Equivalence:** Intervention = Control, i.e., new drug/intervention is not "unacceptably different" as compared to the standard.
- **Non-inferiority**: Intervention is not "unacceptably WORSE" than control, i.e., the new intervention may be meaningfully less efficacious compared to the standard, but that lost efficacy is acceptable to us.

References

1. Britton A. Evaluating interventions: experimental study designs in health promotion. In: Thorogood M, Coombes Y, editors. Evaluating health promotion: practice and methods. 3rd ed. Oxford: Oxford Academic; 2010. [cited 2022 Jul 29]; Available from: https://academic.oup.com/book/12443/chapter/162055773.
2. Schulz KF, Grimes DA. Blinding in randomised trials: hiding who got what. Lancet. 2002;359(9307):696–700.
3. Fundamentals of Clinical Trials [Internet]; [cited 2022 Jul 31]. Available from: https://link.springer.com/book/10.1007/978-1-4419-1586-3.
4. Fisher A, Foreit J, Laing J, Stoeckel J, Townsend J. Designing HIV/AIDS intervention studies: an operations research handbook. HIV and AIDS [Internet]; 2002. Available from: https://knowledgecommons.popcouncil.org/departments_sbsr-hiv/721.
5. The James Lind Library [Internet]; 2015 [cited 2022 Jul 31]. M Peto R (1978). Available from: https://www.jameslindlibrary.org/peto-r-1978/.
6. Campbell DT, Stanley JC. The James Lind Library [Internet]; 2016 [cited 2022 Jul 31]. Available from: https://www.jameslindlibrary.org/campbell-dt-stanley-jc-1963/.
7. Designing HIV/AIDS intervention studies: an operations research handbook [Internet]. Population Council; 2002 [cited 2022 Jul 31]. Available from: https://knowledgecommons.popcouncil.org/departments_sbsr-hiv/721.
8. Gordis L. Epidemiology. 5th ed. Philadelphia: Elsevier; 2014. Available from: https://ak.sbmu.ac.ir/uploads/epidemiology_gordis_5_edi.pdf.

Project Implementation

9

Rupsa Banerjee

Learning Objectives

After going through this section, participants will be able to:

- Enumerate the steps in project implementation.
- Describe the steps of project implementation.
- List the stakeholders in healthcare research.
- Describe the roles and responsibilities of stakeholders in healthcare research.

9.1 Introduction to Project Implementation

A project is any complex task to be completed within a specified time with the help of defined organizational resources. A newly designed health intervention is initially implemented as a pilot project, which is then evaluated for effectiveness and efficiency before being scaled up or incorporated into a health program. A typical healthcare project goes through the stages of project formulation, objective, and target setting, planning of project activities, project implementation and termination of project. Projects in implementation research involve several stakeholders, each of whom has a distinct and defined role in implementation and evaluation of the project.

Project management is the discipline which deals with overseeing the stages of project implementation from initiation till completion to ensure that it is delivered as planned. In healthcare projects, technical planning and activities of the project are usually of high quality but the managerial aspects are often neglected. Project management is necessary to ensure that the project is completed within the planned timeline, while adhering to the allocated budget and maintaining the required quality and functionality.

This chapter has two sections. The first section discusses the stages of project implementation including basics of project management, while the second section focuses on the roles and responsibilities of different stakeholders involved in project implementation.

9.2 Stages of Project Implementation

The implementation of a healthcare project involves following stages as shown in Fig. 9.1 [1–3]:

1. Initiating the project.
2. Specifying and scheduling the work.
3. Clarifying authority, responsibility, and relationships.

R. Banerjee (✉)
Department of Health Systems and Implementation Research, International Institute of Health Management Research, New Delhi, India
e-mail: rupsa@iihmrdelhi.edu.in

S. Bandyopadhyay Neogi, A. K. Pandey (eds.), *Designing and Evaluating Public Health Interventions*, https://doi.org/10.1007/978-981-97-9574-1_9

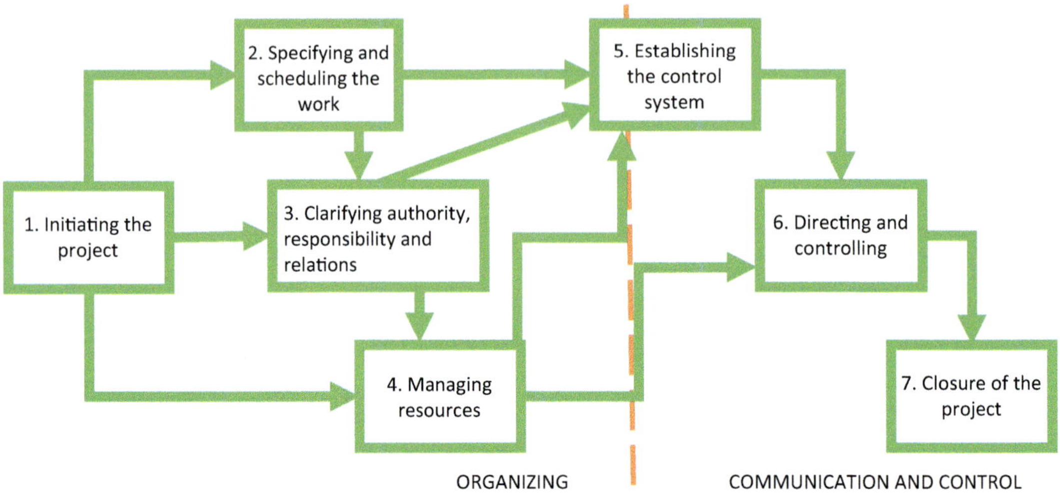

Fig. 9.1 Stages of project implementation (Adapted from Bainbridge and Sapirie [1])

4. Obtaining resources.
5. Establishing the control system.
6. Directing and controlling.
7. Terminating the project.

Each of these stages involves multiple activities which are discussed in detail below. Two documents are relevant for project implementation. A *project charter,* which is a document that outlines the project vision, scope, objectives, stakeholders, and their responsibilities. A *project implementation plan* which is a more detailed document which describes all activities to be undertaken to initiate and run the project in order to achieve the project objectives, the timeline within which each phase of the project and the associated activities need to be completed, the resources allocated to each activity, control system, and responsibilities assigned and feedback mechanism to monitor the progress of the project activities as planned.

9.2.1 Step 1: Initiating the Project

Project initiation largely involves the following groups of activities as shown in Fig. 9.2:

(i) Obtaining approval for conducting the project from relevant authorities (may include Ministry of Health, hospital authorities, etc.)
(ii) Obtaining approval of the relevant budgets from the respective funding agency (government and other sources).
(iii) Selecting and assigning a project manager who will be responsible for further implementation of the project.
(iv) Recruitment of full-time project staff.

The principal person/team who will take responsibility for each of the above activities is to be decided at the outset. Initiating the project may take a considerable amount of time, particularly the process of obtaining approvals. Planning for project approval process should be meticulously done (including mapping of approving authorities, preparing documents to be presented to the authorities, deciding who will brief each authorizing agency, preparing a timeline of these and related activities).

Once the project is approved in principle, the process of selection and recruitment of project manager is to be initiated. This includes defining the project manager's qualifications, functions and terms of reference, searching for acceptable candidates, interview process, recruitment of a suitable candidate, completion of administrative processes for assignment of candidate to the project and briefing of the candidate. The project manager, along with the chartering agency, then proceeds to recruit the full-time project staff.

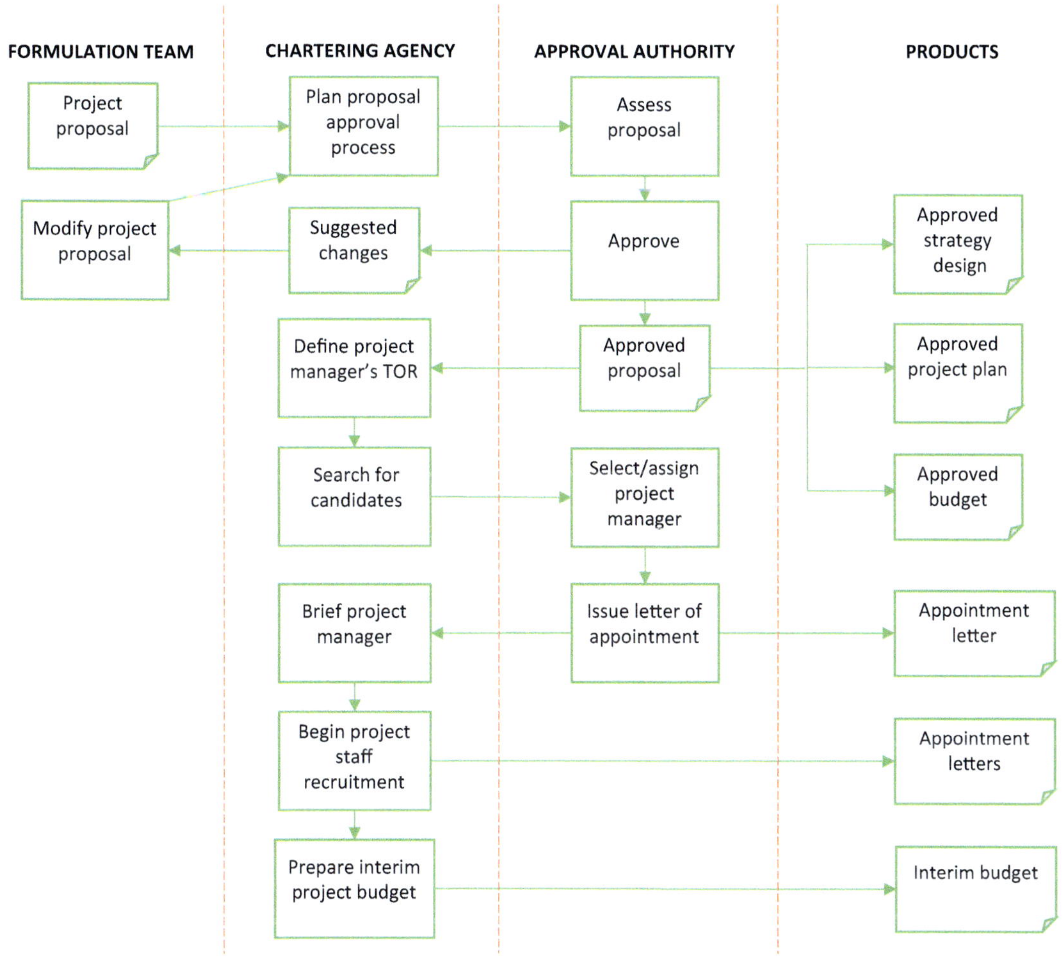

Fig. 9.2 Steps to be considered while initiating the project (Adapted from Bainbridge and Sapirie [1])

9.2.2 Step 2: Specifying and Scheduling Project Work

This step is necessary to detail each project activity (Fig. 9.3) and sub-activities which are to be done, when and how they will be done, who will do them and who will supervise at which level. The following are done at this stage:

(i) Assigning project activities to appropriate staff.
(ii) Involving the staff in detailing out sub-activities (with the project manager guiding the process).
(iii) Defining intermediate and end products/ outcomes in detail.
(iv) Reviewing and finalizing complete list of project activities and sub-activities.
(v) Determining interrelationships among activities.
(vi) Defining resource requirements and activity durations.
(vii) Grouping the activities of potential activity managers.
(viii) Preparing detailed budgets and activity schedule.
(ix) Review of the final schedule and budget by the project supervisor/chartering agency.

Details of the project activities need to be specified, if not sufficiently detailed out in the

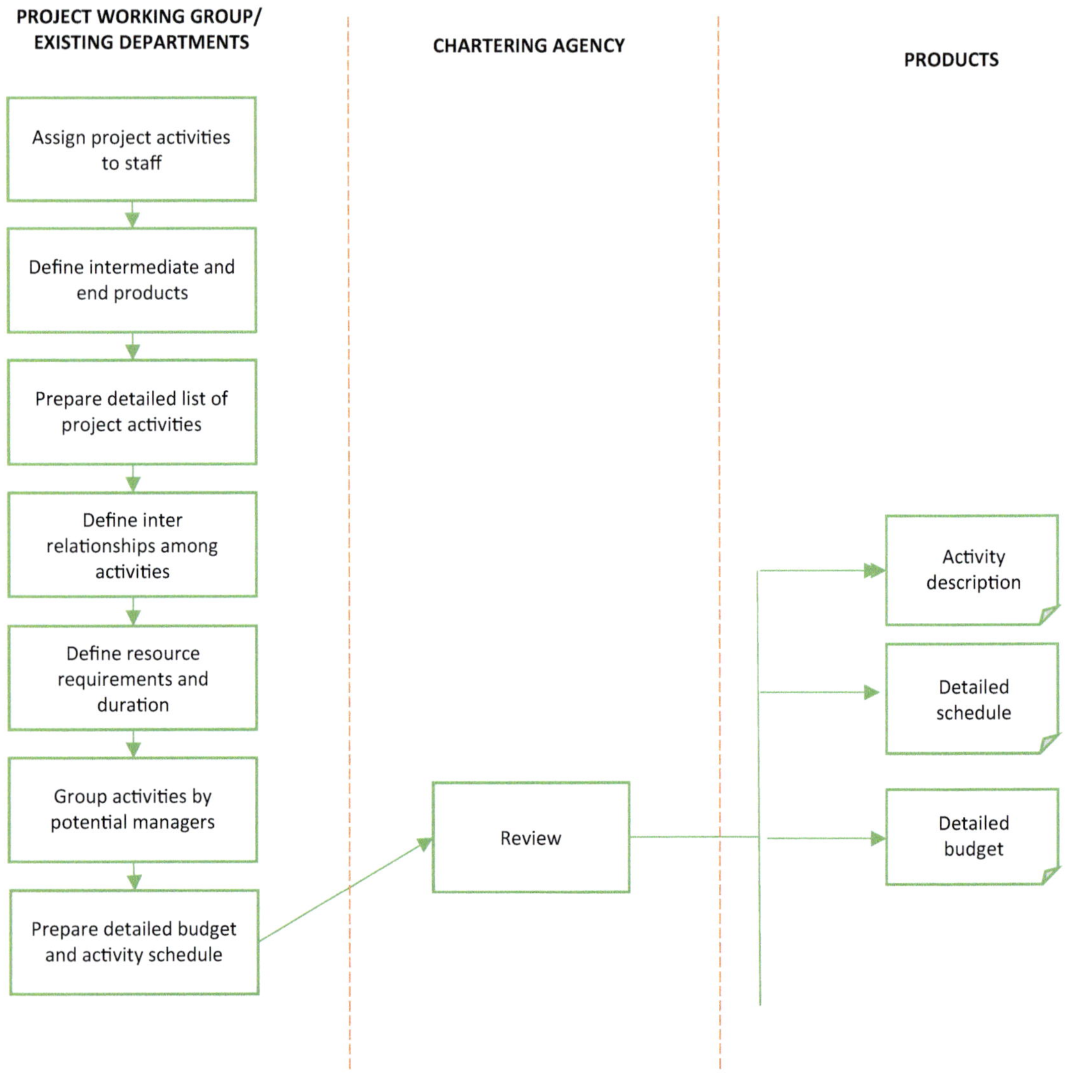

Fig. 9.3 Specifying and scheduling project work (Adapted from Bainbridge and Sapirie [1])

protocol. It is a good idea to prepare an activity schedule at this point and group them according to the teams which will be handling a specific cluster of activities. Schedule of project activities can be done by using a Gantt chart (Fig. 9.4) or by constructing a project network (which depicts the inter-relatedness of activities). If the full-time project staff have already been recruited by this point, they should be involved in scheduling project sub-activities as it will contribute to increasing their ownership and motivation.

While defining resource requirements, it is useful to specify the resources required for each activity in terms of the type of resource, preferred source, and time period when each resource will be used. The project implementation budget is prepared in detail under each major expense heading—non-recurrent cost/development budget and recurrent cost, and overhead costs are calculated on the total budget (Fig. 9.5). The budgetary estimate is usually prepared separately for annual or semi-annual periods, depending on the funder's requirement.

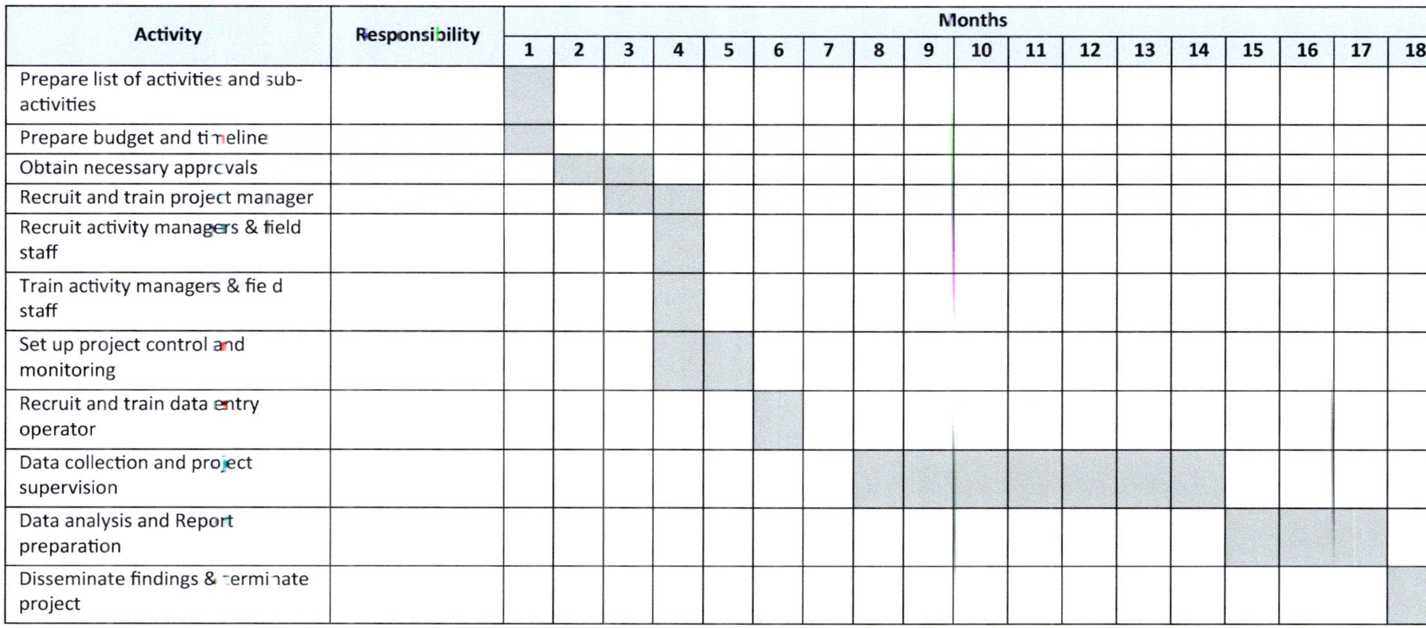

Fig. 9.4 Model Gantt chart

Budget head	Unit cost (X)	Total no. of units (Y)	Total cost (X*Y)	Justification
Human resource costs (A)				
Research officer	a (salary)	N*no of months		
Field investigator	b (salary)	N*no of months		
Data entry operator	c (salary)	N*no of months		
Contingency costs (recurring) (B)				
Communication cost	Cost per month	No of months		
Stationery	Cost per month	No of months		
Review meetings	Cost per meeting	No of meetings		
Contingency costs (non-recurring) (C)				
Laptop	Cost	-		
Tablets	Cost	-		
Training cost	Cost	-		
Field work cost (D)				
Travel cost for investigators	Cost of travel per head	N*no of visits		
Stay and subsistence costs for investigators	Cost per day	N*no of days		
Travel cost for field teams	Cost of travel per head	N*no of visits		
Stay and subsistence costs for field teams	Cost per day	N*no of days		
Sub total (A+B+C+D)				
Overhead cost (at the rate of 'x'%) **(E)**	Calculated on the subtotal			
GRAND TOTAL (A+B+C+D+E)				

Fig. 9.5 Model project budget

9.2.3 Step 3: Clarifying Authority, Responsibility, and Relationships

In any project, it is essential for all members of the project team members to have a clear understanding of their responsibilities. This increases the efficiency of project implementation by removing duplication of efforts and underutilization of resources [4, 5]. Following aspects can be taken into consideration (Fig. 9.6):

(i) Clarifying each project team member's responsibilities (what activities they are assigned) and reporting officer/activity manager, who will supervise them).
(ii) Obtaining manpower commitments (respective governmental departments and other relevant agencies).
(iii) Determining the organizational location of the project (as per existing hierarchy in the organization- Determining the location of the project with respect to organizational hierarchy is done to avoid any conflict in relationships between the existing organization and the project team.)
(iv) Establishing a project coordination committee/core group, with representatives from the chartering agency, funding agency and implementing agency.
(v) Defining the authority and responsibilities of project coordination committee, chartering agency officials, project manager, activity managers and other liaison persons.

There might be some outside agencies and organizations which are involved directly in project formulation and implementation and need to cooperate and/or provide support to the project. For example, in obtaining resources, implementing the intervention, obtaining feedback, etc. It is useful to have a written agreement of these commitments specifying the details of involvement including time dedicated to the project. The clarification of authority of each level of project supervisor and manager should be decided at the outset.

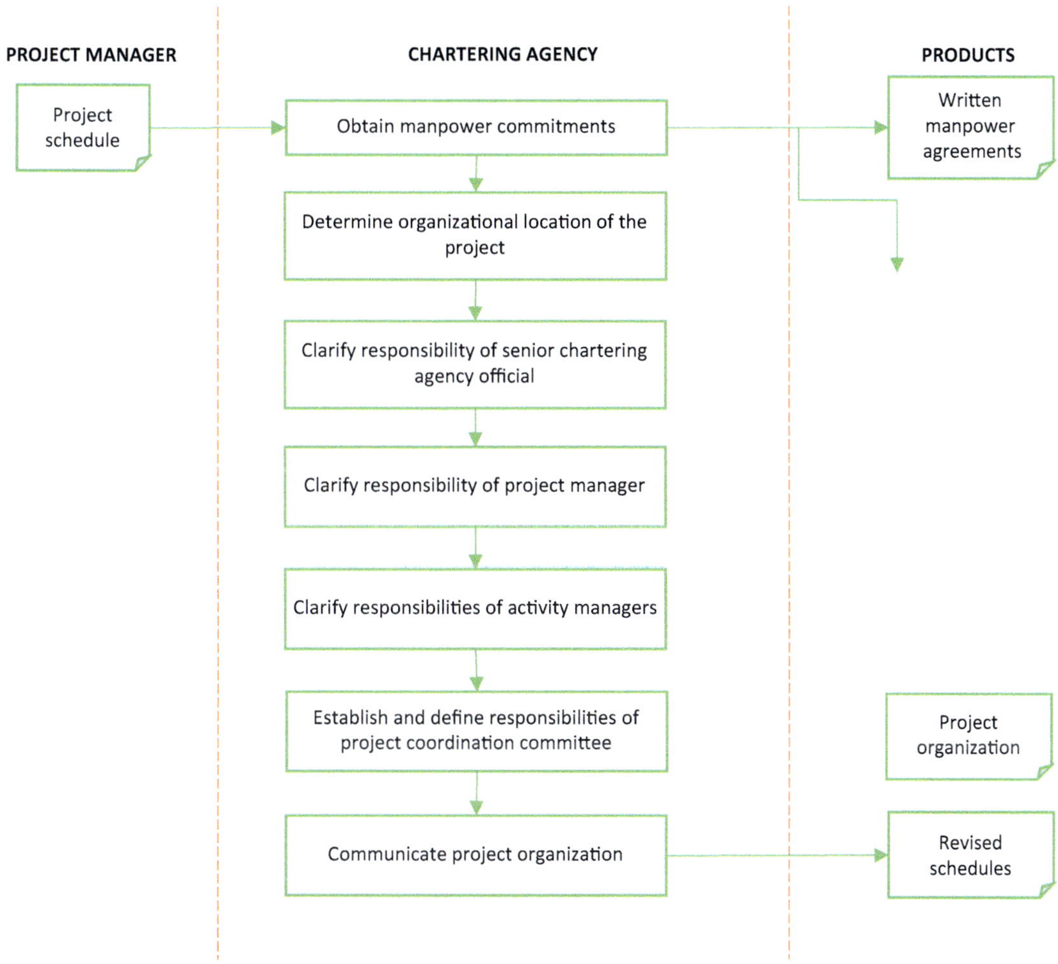

Fig. 9.6 Figure depicting authority, responsibility, and relationships (Adapted from Bainbridge and Sapirie [1])

9.2.4 Step 4: Obtaining Resources

This step is to ensure that all the resources that are budgeted for the project are available in a timely manner and include funds, infrastructure, manpower and supplies. The activities of this stage are often done parallel with the previous steps, especially obtaining human resources for the project (Fig. 9.7).

Several standard administrative procedures are required to obtain the necessary resources for a project. The project managers must familiarize themselves with these procedures by getting acquainted with the relevant officials. In order to ensure that resources are available for use in time, a schedule of administrative processes required (to obtain the resources) can be prepared. This timetable needs to be monitored to ensure that all permissions and procedures are undertaken as planned so that funds, supplies and other resources are available for utilization in the project in a timely manner. Contingency plans should also be kept in place in the event of any unforeseen circumstances, so that the project activities do not get stalled.

Project activity log can be maintained by the project team for monitoring by the activity managers and activity schedule updates can be provided by activity managers to the project manager. The project manager can keep track of resources and schedule of the project with the help of expenditure log and Gantt chart. A list of all logs,

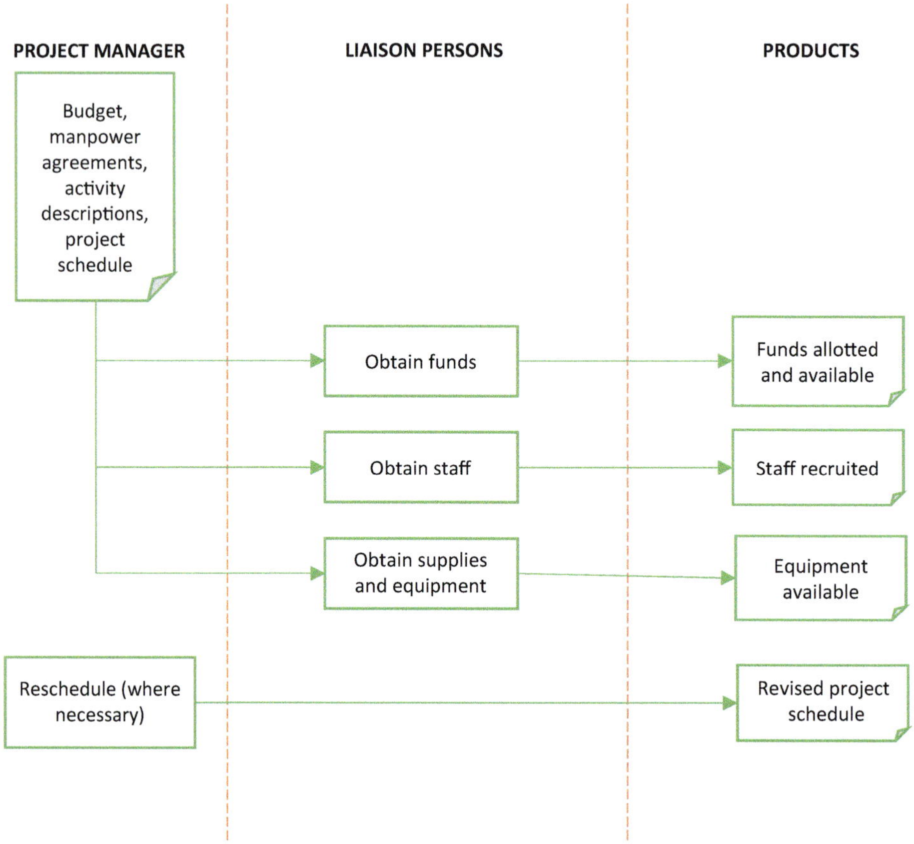

Fig. 9.7 The process of obtaining resources (Adapted from Bainbridge and Sapirie [1])

people responsible and frequency of recording and reporting is drawn up for testing and modification if required (Fig. 9.8).

9.2.5 Step 5: Establishing the Control System

Project control or monitoring system is the mechanism which ensures that all project activities are functioning as planned. It monitors the progress of activities to ensure that the project is running on schedule and resources are being utilized as planned. A feedback mechanism alerts if there is any deviation from the plan, in which case corrective actions are taken. Setting up a project control system involves the following:

(i) Selecting control (monitoring) indicators.
(ii) Identifying sources of information.
(iii) Designing the control system.
(iv) Testing and implementing the system.

The control system is designed at different levels of management, and each monitors the progress of the project at that particular level—activity manager level (to ensure a specific group of activities are running as planned), project manager level (to ensure the project as a whole is functioning as planned) and chartering agency official level (to ensure conformity to project goals and objectives).

The following components must be designed into the project control:

- An indicator which measures any aspect of the project's output.
- A set standard against which the indicator is measured.
- A threshold of tolerance for each measured indicator (compared to the expected output).

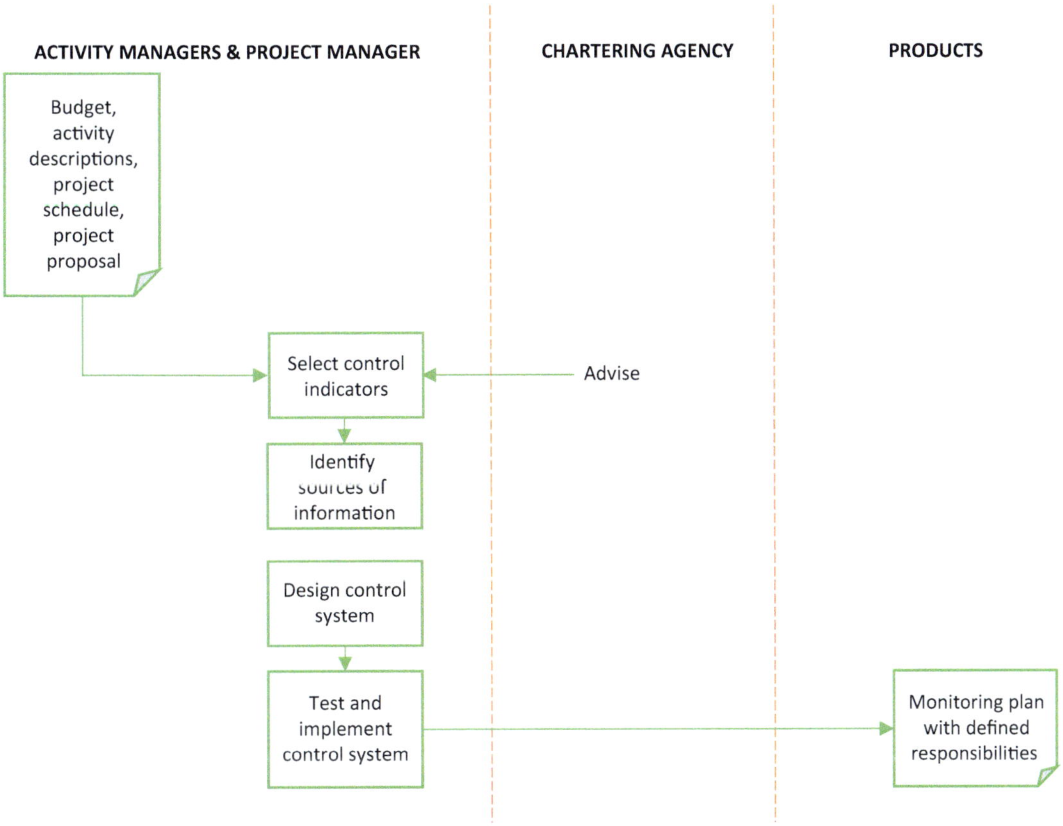

Fig. 9.8 Establishing the control system (Adapted from Bainbridge and Sapirie [1])

- A decision-making system on the corrective action to be taken.

Control indicators are selected on the basis of the project objectives, the project schedule, and the project activity descriptions. Both performance and output indicators may be devised, and all indictors can be built into the project as far as possible so that regular progress monitoring can be done. Indicators at the level of activity manager are prepared based on the activity descriptions. The project manager monitors whether the project is adhering to the time schedule, budget, and overall performance standards. For this purpose, they also have to identify crucial activities that can slow down the project/can easily exceed the budget/whose outputs can be used as effectiveness indicators and pay close attention to these.

For each control indicator, a source of information is identified. Some information may be obtained from an existing mechanism of reporting (for example, monthly reports prepared by healthcare workers). For obtaining information on other indicators, new mechanisms may need to be established.

Designing the control system involves establishing the frequency of obtaining monitoring reports, deciding who is responsible for generating the reports, establishing reporting mechanisms and structure, etc. For large projects, regular audits and process monitoring exercises are carried out to assess the progress of the project.

9.2.6 Step 6: Directing and Controlling

This step is about running the project once the planning and organization stages are complete. It

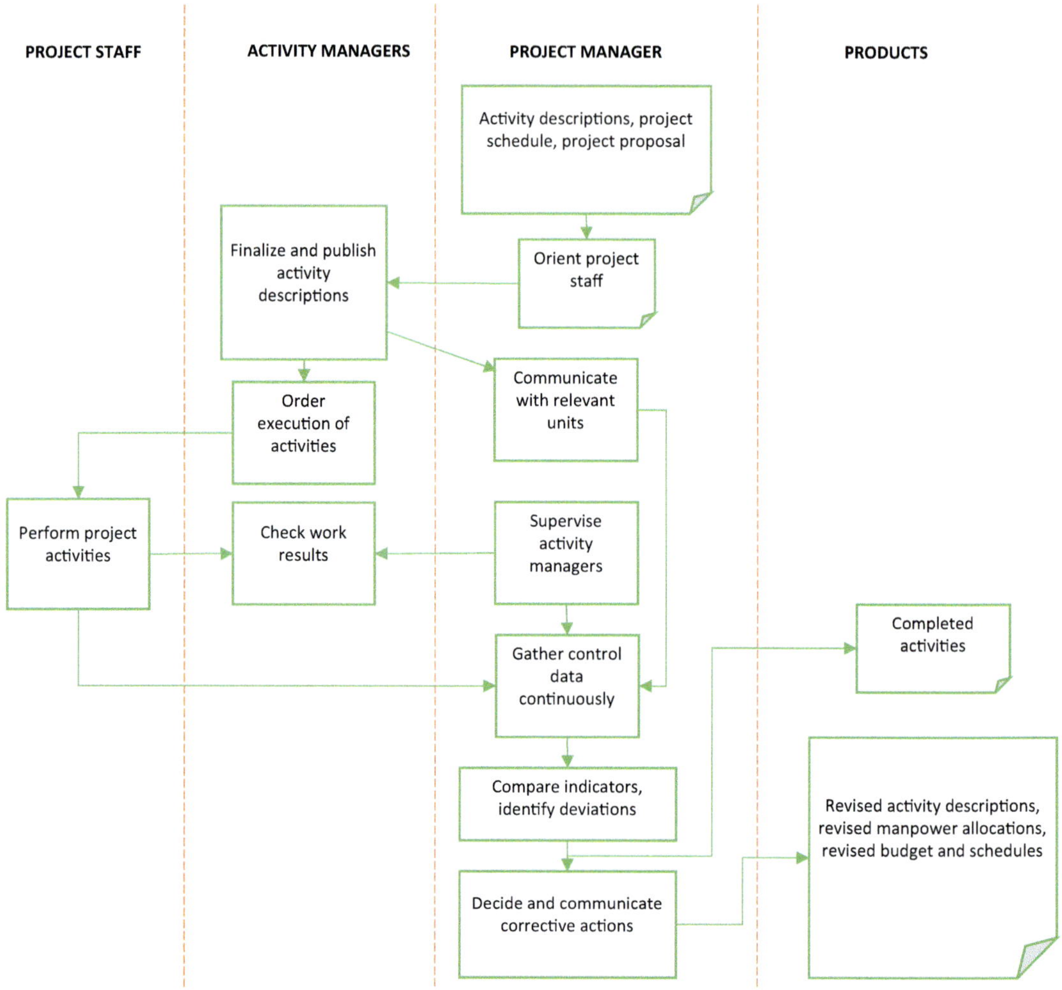

Fig. 9.9 Figure depicting directing and controlling as part of project management (Adapted from Bainbridge and Sapirie [1])

deals with ensuring that the project team carries out their responsibilities in executing the project activities and maintaining quality in project functioning (Fig. 9.9).

(i) Communicating with and motivating the project team to do their work.
(ii) Executing the project activities.
(iii) Managing the project staff through the project.

Orienting the project staff about their roles, so that each member has a clear understanding of their responsibilities under the project, helps in improving efficiency of the project. Motivating the project staff regularly is necessary for them to perform well. Factors like achievement, recognition, responsibility, and advancement (satisfiers) should be adopted to motivate the project team rather than giving them rewards or punishing them. Motivation becomes more important in cases where organizational staff are assigned project work rather than recruiting dedicated project staff. The project manager also communicates and liaises with other stakeholders involved in the project whenever necessary, on a regular basis, to inform them regarding project status, involve them in decision-making, review, auditing, etc.

Execution of the project deals with performing project activities, obtaining feedback regularly from the project staff, troubleshooting, running project controls, identifying any deviations from project protocol, decision-making and communicating corrective actions to be taken and monitoring their adoption. The managers at all levels carry out these activities and also supervise the project staff and manage any conflict arising within the project team to ensure smooth execution of project activities according to plan.

An important component of project management is ensuring quality in the project activities and products. A quality management and assurance plan is usually included as part of a project protocol. Quality management refers to processes to oversee that all project activities are performed according to set standards.

9.2.7 Step 7: Closing the Project

A project is usually closed after it has accomplished its objectives and/or achieved the deliverables either on time and within resources or later than the due date (due to operational or other reasons). Projects may also be terminated early under unforeseen circumstances or situations, for example, scarcity of resources or competing priorities. In some cases, the project is not terminated or closed but the activities continue and are adopted in the operations of the implementing agency or are adopted into an existing program. The steps involved in project closure are (Fig. 9.10):

(i) Dissemination of project findings to relevant audience (including specifying any future steps to be taken by others as a result of the project).
(ii) Post project review with the project team to assess performance against the project implementation plan in terms of objectives, timeline, and budget.
(iii) Rewarding and reassigning the project team to other tasks if applicable.
(iv) Preparing the final project report.

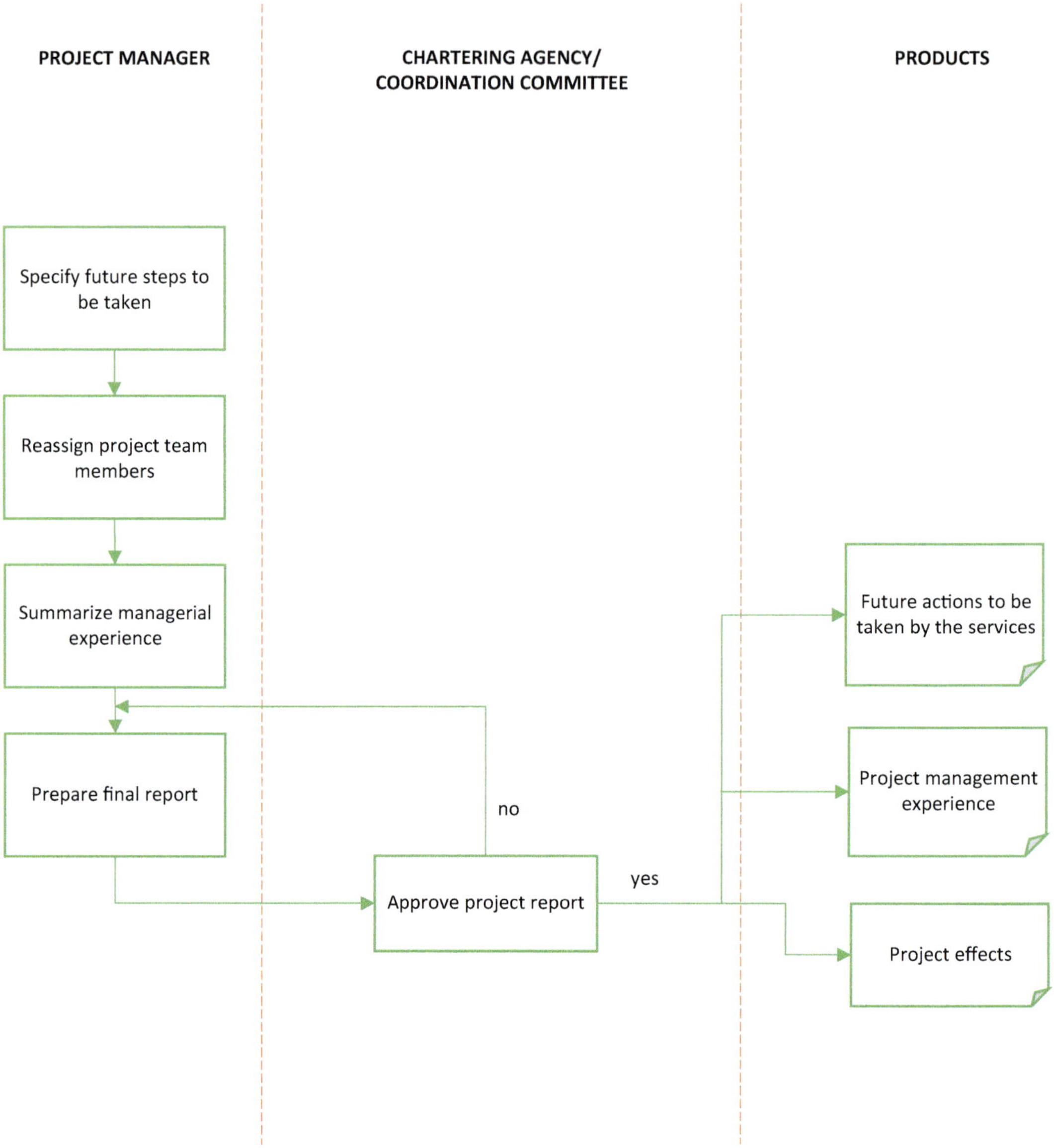

Fig. 9.10 Terminating the project (Adapted from Bainbridge and Sapirie [1])

9.3 Stakeholder Engagement in Project Implementation [6, 7]

9.3.1 Who Are Stakeholders in Health Research?

A stakeholder in health research is any individual or group of persons who are either responsible for planning and/or conducting the research, acting on the findings of the research or are affected by the healthcare decisions that are informed by research evidence. Often, a gap exists between the conduct of research and application of its findings in healthcare practice. Even though there has been a growth of collaborative research in the public health sector, patient-centered outcomes research is still lacking in practice (partnership between researchers, policymakers, managers, and the population whom the research findings are intended for).

Stakeholders in health research can be primarily categorized as follows (seven P's framework)

1. Patients and the public, i.e., the consumers of healthcare services or products which are the outcomes of research.
2. Providers, i.e., the individuals and organizations who practice evidence-based healthcare, are informed by research.
3. Purchasers, i.e., individuals and organizations responsible for underwriting the costs of healthcare (e.g., employers or self-insured individuals).
4. Payers, i.e., individuals and agencies responsible for reimbursement of costs incurred in obtaining healthcare (e.g., insurers).
5. Policymakers, i.e., governmental entities who make informed decisions based on research evidence.
6. Product manufacturers, i.e., industries engaged in production of drugs and devices.
7. Principal investigators, i.e., who are involved in planning, implementing, and funding the research project.

9.3.2 Why Is It Important to Engage Stakeholders in Health Research?

Involving communities, planners, policymakers, and healthcare providers in all stages of research ensures that the research process is more meaningful and need-driven and also enables dissemination of research findings to the appropriate audience (policymakers) and utilization of evidence generated by the research study in actual healthcare practice.

- *Improved quality of research*: Including the perspective of stakeholders leads to formulating research questions and objectives which are more relevant and responsive to the needs of the communities and other stakeholders. It also improves applicability of research findings especially to hard-to-reach, marginalized populations.
- *Empowering communities*: Community engagement in the research process can be valuable in conducting needs assessment and can also result in people playing an active role in decision-making and availing healthcare services.
- *Increased translation, dissemination, and uptake of results*: Involving all relevant stakeholders can accelerate the dissemination of research findings and improve the "actionability" of research results and their adoption into practice.
- *Democracy and accountability*: If communities or patients are involved in research planning, it improves the allocation of resources to serve public interest and increases transparency and accountability of the research.
- *Moral obligation*: End-users and communities have a fundamental right to be involved in the research process beyond their role as study subjects.

9.3.3 Roles and Responsibilities of Stakeholders in Research

There is a need to ensure that healthcare research is informed by public health and clinical health priorities and the evidence generated, in turn, informs public health and clinical practice with the overall aim of improving the health of the population. The roles and responsibilities of stakeholders in research are centered around this principle. It is important to include stakeholders in all stages of the research and translation process.

Healthcare policymakers and managers are engaged in identifying health priorities of the community. For this process, the patients/ citizens/community members are involved in conducting health needs assessments and identifying their health demands. Academicians/research investigators liaise with health program managers in translating health needs to researchable questions and objectives. Community members/ patients are included in the conduct of research, as study participants and evaluators. Healthcare providers should also be engaged to collaborate in the research to provide the clinical and on-ground perspective to study interventions. Political will is essential to facilitate translation of research evidence to policy and practice. The investigators are responsible for dissemination of findings from research studies to the suitable audience including clinicians, manufacturers of drugs and supplies, program managers, health-care organizations, insurance companies, and the public.

Q.9.1 *In reference to case study on Mental health and Solidarity trial, enumerate and explain the steps involved in project implementation.*

References

1. Bainbridge JK, Sapirie SA. Health project management: a manual of procedures for formulating and implementing health projects [Internet]. World Health Organization; 1974. [cited 2022 Jul 20]. Available from: https://apps.who.int/iris/handle/10665/37111.
2. Mantel SJ, editor. Project management in practice. 4th ed. Hoboken, NJ: Wiley; 2011. p. 312.
3. Billingham V. Project management. How to plan and deliver a successful project. New Delhi: Viva Books Private Limited; 2010. [Internet]. [cited 2022 Nov 5]. Available from: https://www.goodreads.com/book/show/21348808-project-management.
4. PCORI. The value of engagement [Internet]. [cited 2022 Nov 5]. Available from: https://www.pcori.org/engagement/value-engagement.
5. Boaz A, Hanney S, Borst R, O'Shea A, Kok M. How to engage stakeholders in research: design principles to support improvement. Health Res Policy Syst. 2018;16(1):60.
6. Concannon TW, Meissner P, Grunbaum JA, McElwee N, Guise JM, Santa J, Conway PH, Daudelin D, Morrato EH, Leslie LK. A new taxonomy for stakeholder engagement in patient-centered outcomes research. J Gen Intern Med. 2012;27(8):985–91. https://doi.org/10.1007/s11606-012-2037-1. [cited 2022 Nov 5]. Available from: https://pubmed.ncbi.nlm.nih.gov/22528615/
7. Esmail L, Moore E, Rein A. Evaluating patient and stakeholder engagement in research: moving from theory to practice. J Comp Eff Res. 2015;4(2):133–45.

10 Monitoring and Evaluation of Public Health Interventions

Anuj Kumar Pandey and Preetha G. S.

Learning Objectives
After going through this section, participants will be able to:

- Describe the concepts of monitoring and evaluation.
- Review the strategic planning, design, and efficiency of implementation of a public health intervention.
- Describe various evaluation designs and methods to assess the impact of an intervention.
- Describe various monitoring, and evaluation frameworks.
- Track the progress of program/project activities and indicators and goals.

As explained in Fig. 10.1, this chapter will begin with a broad overview of monitoring and evaluation, describing the goals for monitoring and evaluation (M&E), and later explaining independently the processes involved in monitoring and evaluation of an intervention.

A. K. Pandey
Department of Health Systems and Implementation Research, International Institute of Health Management Research (IIHMR), New Delhi, India
e-mail: anuj@iihmrdelhi.edu.in

Preetha G. S. (✉)
International Institute of Health Management Research, New Delhi, India
e-mail: preetha@iihmrdelhi.edu.in

S. Bandyopadhyay Neogi, A. K. Pandey (eds.), *Designing and Evaluating Public Health Interventions*, https://doi.org/10.1007/978-981-97-9574-1_10

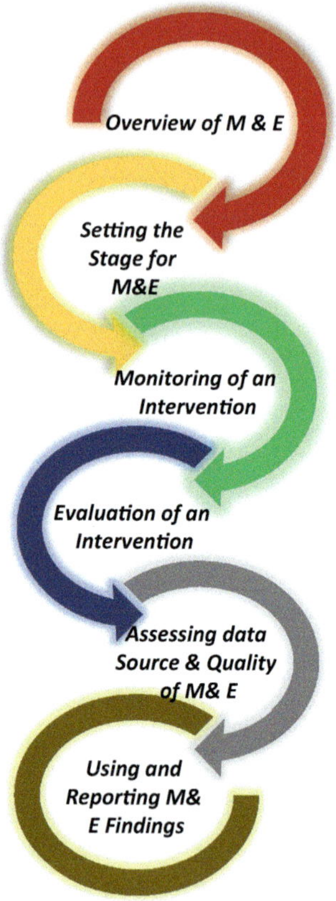

Fig. 10.1 Steps involved in the M&E of an intervention

10.1 Understanding the Basis of Monitoring and Evaluation (M&E)

At the planning and implementation phase of a program/project, it is essential to enquire about certain questions like:

- Is the planned intervention/program progressing as per plan?
- Are the planned activities proceeding as per schedule?
- Is the intervention covering and serving the targeted population?
- Are the program strategies and activities cost effective?
- What is the impact of intervention on health outcomes?
- Would the program outcome be different without the public health intervention?
- What is the effectiveness of the program activities?
- What is the scope of improvement?

These questions can be answered by robust M&E techniques; thus *M&E represents two essential aspects of a program-for continuous gathering of information and assessing the same (1) to determine whether the progress is being made toward the specified aims and objectives and (2) to emphasize if there are any unplanned effects from the project or its activities.* In broad terms, Monitoring and evaluation techniques will help improve performance and achieve results. The primary objective is to measure and evaluate performance to enhance the effective management of outcomes and outputs [1, 2].

Before moving forward and seeking how M&E provides answers to these questions it is essential to understand the program life cycle and M&E in the program life cycle. This cycle is a tool to understand the various tasks and functions that needs to be performed during the whole intervention phase or a program cycle [3].

As explained in Fig. 10.2, the project cycle is a tool for explaining various tasks that must be performed during the entire project duration which contains stages of design, implementation, monitoring, and evaluation.

> **Monitoring**
> *Tracks changes in program performance over time* [4]

Salient features of Monitoring:

- ***It is a continuous process*** in which inputs utilized and outputs achieved are measured at regular intervals.
- ***Counting the performance as*** what has been done as compared to previous measurement.
- This series of data recordings ***track the changes*** as per the desired plan over a particular period. This ensures optimum result as per the plan and that too during implementation phase.

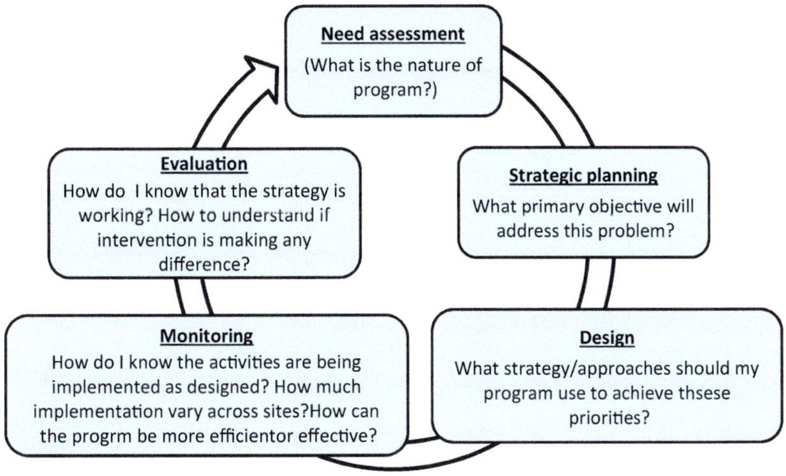

Fig. 10.2 Program Cycle explaining various strategic information that are needed at all stages of the program lifecycle [3].

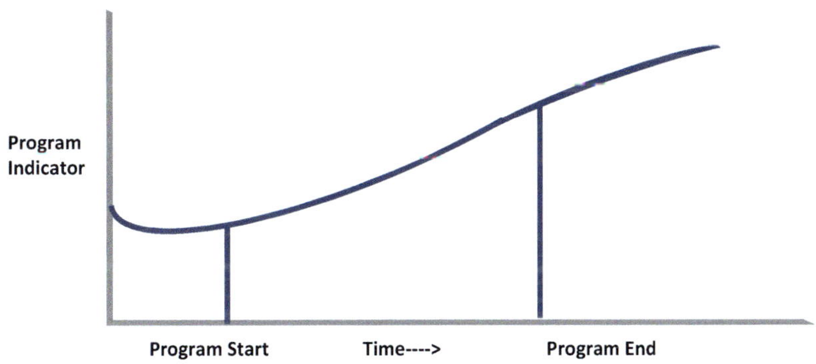

Fig. 10.3 Illustrates Monitoring of the program/intervention *(Developed by author)*

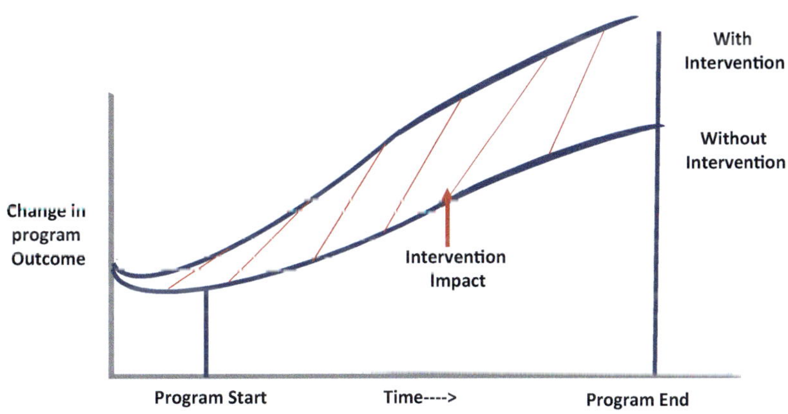

Fig. 10.4 Illustrates Evaluation of the program/intervention *(Developed by author)*

Figures 10.3 and 10.4 depict an intervention monitoring framework. In the graph, vertical axis is an intervention, whereas horizontal axis is the time indicating program duration. Bars indicate periodic measurement of the indicator (i.e., monitoring).

Thus, monitoring is performed after an intervention has started and continues throughout the intervention implementation phase. Monitoring requires (or generates) data which is in turn used to compute indicators for the outcomes of interest various time points.

> **Evaluation** [4]
> *Determines whether program activities led to changes in behaviors or some other outcome*

Evaluation focuses on anticipated and realized activities, analyzing the results chain—comprising inputs, activities, outputs, outcomes, and impacts—to comprehend accomplishments or shortcomings.

Evaluationalsoinvolvesthreeimportantaspects-

- Evaluations are carried out at the ***end of the project /program called end term evaluation*** or in the ***middle of the project called mid-term evaluation***.
- Evaluation measures the ***performance of the project against the desired goals and objectives*** of the program.

Evaluations are carried out in a systematic manner and based on scientific methods used to investigate the implementation of interventions and outcomes of a particular intervention.

Thus, as explained in Fig. 10.5, the primary reason for monitoring and evaluation is:

To use the data and evidence to inform decision-making at each stage of the program life cycle. To assist project/program implementation with accuracy and make it more evidence based.

To contribute to organizational learning by sharing experiences and lessons learned from what and how we do various activities. To assess if the work was undertaken as planned/ as per protocol or established standards. To disseminate the work by highlighting major accomplishments and achievements.

> ***Q.10.1*** *In reference to case study on Pulse polio, explain the steps involved in monitoring. How can monitoring be conducted effectively for PHIs (Stakeholders involvement)*

10.2 Setting Up the Stage for Monitoring and Evaluation

There are some steps that need to be performed before initiation of the monitoring and evaluation activities that includes:

1. **Conducting a situation analyses or a needs assessment** [6] -
   - A comprehensive review of the situation needs to be done to provide an understanding of various contextual factors regarding the basis of intervention.
   - Needs assessments to assess knowledge gap.
2. **Developing a monitoring and evaluation framework** [4]

   A well-defined framework is essential, delineating how the intervention is expected to operate. It should outline the various components of the intervention, their sequence, and the necessary steps to attain the desired outcome. Frameworks serve as the initial

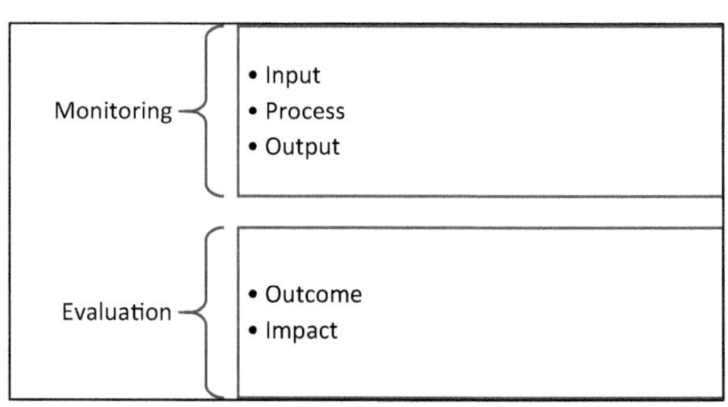

Fig. 10.5 Diagram indicating interaction in monitoring and evaluation activities [5]

stage in formulating the Monitoring and Evaluation plan.

The framework explains:

a. How will the intervention work?—the aim and the objective(s)
b. How to achieve goals and objectives?
c. How the program's progress toward achieving objectives and contributing to the goal will be assessed?
d. What are the connections between critical implementation factors and other elements that may influence the program's success?
e. How the program or intervention will be monitored, examined, or evaluated comprehensively.

10.3 Type of M & E Frameworks

1. The Conceptual Framework
2. The Logic Model; The Logical Framework (or log Frame Matrix)
3. Result Framework

All these frameworks serve to guide the overall intervention and facilitate the monitoring and evaluation of the implemented intervention. Table 10.1 presents a synopsis of all the Monitoring and Evaluation (M & E) frameworks. The conceptual framework contextualizes the health problem, and either a results or a logical framework is employed to comprehend the interconnections among factors pertinent to the program. Logic models assist in illustrating the logical relationships between the inputs, processes, and outputs of an activity, as well as its connection to the program's objectives (outcomes) and goals (impact).

10.3.1 Conceptual Framework

Conceptual framework [7] are "representations that identify and illustrate the relationships among various factors like systems, organizations, government or institutional policies, infrastructure, population characteristics, or other features of the operational landscape that influence program implementation and successful achievement of goals."

- They aid in identifying the factors that will impact the intervention and delineate how each of these factors may be connected to and influence the outcomes.
- They do not serve as the basis for monitoring and evaluation activities but contribute to explaining the results.

The conceptual framework shows a range of variables that might influence the capacity and performance of intervention and thus help at design stage to determine the scope and focus of an Intervention. This framework also elucidates

Table 10.1 Summary of all the M & E frameworks

Framework	Details		Basis for Monitoring & Evaluation
The Conceptual Framework	Establish causal pathway and interaction of intervention and environmental factors	Determine factors influencing the intervention	No, only aids in explaining the results.
The Logic Model	Logically linked intervention objectives	Presents logical link between intervention goal, objectives, and sub-objectives	Yes—at objective level
The Logical Framework (or log Frame Matrix)	Shows logical flow of the inputs, process, output, outcomes, and impacts	Helps in determining key program elements to be tracked	Yes—at all stages. (Inputs to process to output to outcomes)
Results Framework	Shows logical link between program activities, outputs, outcomes, and goal; specific risks/ assumptions	Lists risks and assumption that may affect program success	Yes–at the activities, output and outcome level

the assumptions regarding the causal connections among significant elements of the program context. Identifying such risks and planning mitigation strategies are must for a successful intervention.

Figure 10.6 is a classic example of a conceptual framework for a health program. The framework possesses characteristics that may impact the intended outcome, encompassing factors beyond the program's control, such as individual factors. Each parameter is interconnected with other elements that ultimately influence a health outcome. The arrows in the framework signify the relationships between these factors, encompassing individual, systemic, and program variables.

Proximate determinants: These determinants take the intermediate position between underlying determinants and biological determinants. Biological determinants further affect the outcome.

Researchers influence the proximate determinants because it is easier to achieve the outcome by improving the proximate determinants. An example [8] is can be seen regarding *a framework for analyzing the determinants of maternal mortality and morbidity.*

10.3.2 Logic Model or the Strategic Framework

10.3.2.1 Synonyms: Log Frames or Logical frameworks

This framework demonstrates the logical relationship between intervention goal, objectives, and sub-objectives. These models illustrate the linear relationships in different heads (Fig. 10.7).

This is a tool used for:

- Identifying and depicting the operational factors crucial for attaining a desired outcome or goal.
- It is the sole model capable of directly indicating indicators for process monitoring.
- One of its advantages is that it can pinpoint linkages and key processes, emphasizing the connection between resource allocation and the output generated, as well as identifying potential issues if goals are not met.
- They offer a streamlined perspective on the most pivotal processes directly contributing to program outputs and outcomes, elucidating the linear relationships between program decisions, activities, and outputs.

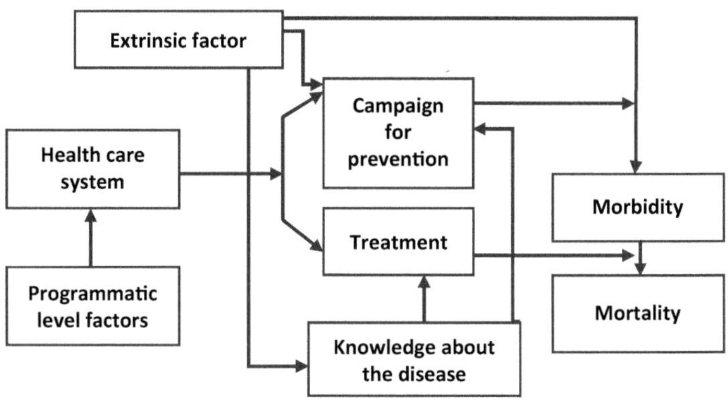

Fig. 10.6 An example of a conceptual framework (developed by author)

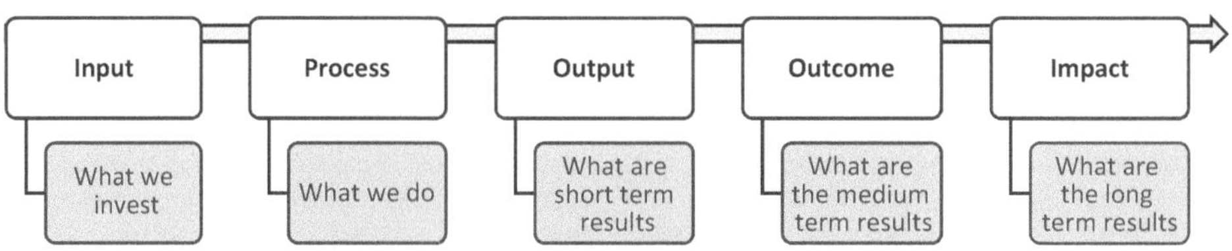

Fig. 10.7 *An example of the concepts of Logic Model* (developed by author)

Logic model tries to focus on the intervention's activities and their impacts. This provides an overview of the design of the intervention. Very often these models also include assumptions between inputs and processes, processes and outputs, outputs and outcomes, and outcomes and impact.

> *Q.10.2 In reference to case study on Ekjut, please go through the logic model. Develop a similar model for VAPE.*

10.3.3 Logical Framework Matrix (LFM)

This is a standard analytical analytic product of the Logical Framework Approach. As explained in Fig. 10.8, it comprises of four columns and four rows to summarize program activities.

- Activity description: What activity and what will be the outcome of the activity.
- Description of each activity.
- Assumptions related to the program.

The vertical logic explains causal relationships between objectives. **The horizontal logic** explains how the activity's achievement will be measured, monitored, and evaluated (Indicators and means of verification).

The **risk and assumptions** are considered as conditions affecting program's progress but not under direct control of project management. **An *assumption* is a *positive* statement** whereas a ***risk* is a *negative* statement**.

10.3.4 Results frameworks

10.3.4.1 Synonym: Strategic Frameworks [7, 9]

This framework depicts the direct connections from the intermediate outcomes of activities to the overarching objectives and goals. It delineates the causal link between program objectives, detailing how each intermediate result/output and outcome is connected to and supports the attainment of each objective. It also illustrates the relationships between objectives and their contribution to one another and the ultimate goal. It forms the basis for monitoring and evaluation activities. An example of Result Framework can be studied from elsewhere [9].

This framework presents the connection between the progressive outcomes of the key activities, extending to the overall objective or goal of an intervention. Developing a framework focused on program results clarifies the points at which results can be monitored and evaluated. This framework also depicts the causal relationships that the project design assumes will connect.

- Creating a results-oriented framework helps elucidate the stages where results can be monitored and evaluated.
- Additionally, this framework illustrates the assumed causal relationships that the project design expects to establish.

Developing a Results framework:

- We keep the overall goal on top of the diagram by adding the objective/s linkages with the

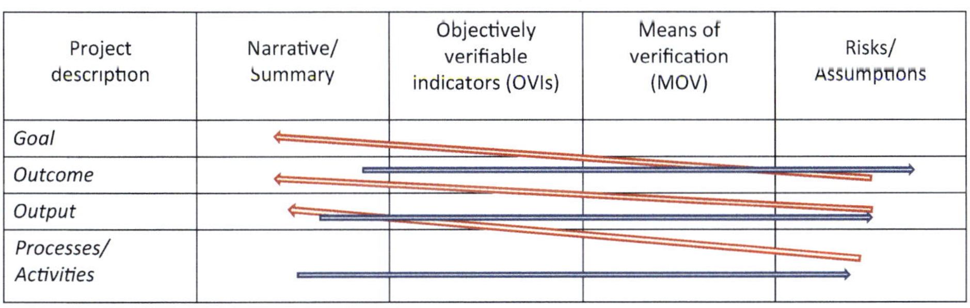

Fig. 10.8 An example of the Logical Framework Matrix (LFM) (developed by author)

goal. These objectives are called strategic objectives (SO).

- Each of these objectives is attained by reaching multiple intermediate results (IR); which we put below to the strategic objective/s in the diagram.
- An example of the result framework of *Tb control program* can be seen from "Handbook on Planning Monitoring and Evaluating for Development Result."

10.4 Monitoring and Evaluation of an Intervention

Figure 10.9 provides an insight on various components of the M&E [10].

As shown the components are explained as:

- **Functionality**: Represents a "characteristic which assesses the degree to which an intervention meets the stated and implied needs"
- **Stability:** The likelihood that the intervention will not fail under both normal and adverse events.
- **Fidelity:** This measure whether an intervention is delivered as planned.
- **Quality:** A measure of excellence.
- **Feasibility**: Assess if intervention works as proposed.
- **Usability**: Evaluate whether the intervention is used as intended.
- **Efficacy**: Assess whether the intervention achieves the expected results (controlled setting).
- **Effectiveness**: Measure if the intervention achieves the expected results (uncontrolled) setting.
- **Implementation research**: Assess the uptake, institutionalization, and sustainability of the planned interventions in a given context, including policies and practices.

10.5 Approaches to the Evaluation

To generate evidence of the effectiveness for an intervention, various study designs may be used as appropriate [10].

- **Implementation research**: This is a systematic study of processes involved in the application of research findings into policy and practice [11].
- **Formative evaluations v/s Summative evaluation:** The formative evaluation aims to inform the development of effective intervention strategies. In contrast to that the summative evaluations are conducted at the end of an intervention to determine the extent to which anticipated outcomes were produced. (Table 10.2)
- Other study designs are mentioned in Table 10.3. These are further explained in Chaps. 7 and 8 which further aims to inform decision-making on evidence generation and the scope of monitoring and evaluation (M&E) activities [12, 13].

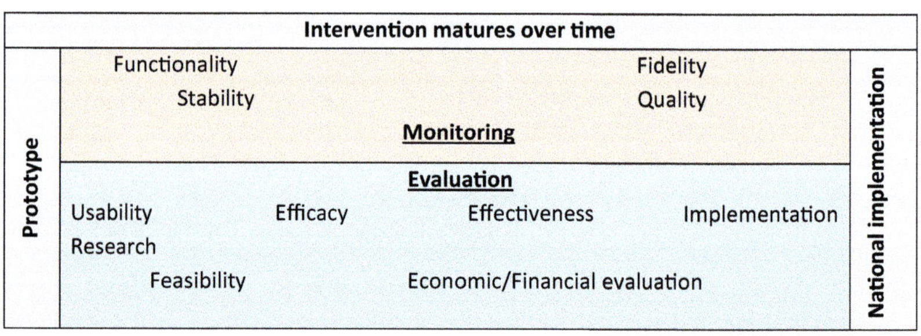

Fig. 10.9 Schematic diagram showing components of the Monitoring and Evaluation (developed by author)

Table 10.2 A detailed assessment of the formative and summative evaluations

Formative	
Need assessment	Determines the need and activities.
Process evaluation	Measures outputs arising due to the intervention activities or inputs.
Implementation evaluation	Monitors the reliability
Summative	
Performance or outcome evaluation	Evaluates the impact of intervention activities on immediate and intermediate changes in crucial outcomes, such as knowledge, service provision, utilization, and coverage.
Impact evaluation	Assesses the enduring net consequences or influence of the intervention on significant health outcomes, encompassing mortality, morbidity, and disease risk, at the community level or beyond.
Economic evaluation	To determine value for money.
Secondary analysis	To explore new research questions or methods.
Meta-analysis	Seeks to amalgamate evidence regarding the effects (impact) of various interventions on essential outcomes of interest.

Table 10.3 An overview of study designs

			Advantages	Limitations
Analytical	Experimental	Randomized controlled trials (RCTs) Individually randomized. Cluster randomized. Parallel Crossover Stepped wedge	Gold Standard study design	Ethical issues Randomization may be difficult as per the area of study Expensive May not be the right choice for many public health interventions.
		Quasi-experimental studies Without Control With Control but no pretest With Control and pretest Interrupted time-series design	Can be used with small sample size and if randomization is not possible. Easier than RCTs Minimizes threats to ecological validity. Generalizability May minimize the ethnical and other concerns	Lack of randomization
	Observational	Cohort	Conducted prospectively or retrospectively	Loss to follow-up Lack of randomization
		Cross-sectional	Less expensive than alternatives	Don't establish causality Recall bias Confounders may be unequally distributed
		Case Control	Relatively inexpensive and can be done in short span of time than alternatives	Results confounded by other factors Difficult to establish timeline of exposure
Descriptive	Surveillance		Provides ongoing, systematic information essential for planning, and service delivery	Resource intensive
	Cross-Sectional Survey		Less expensive than alternatives	Both exposure and outcome are determined at the same time
	Ecological correlational studies		Less expensive than alternatives	Cannot link exposure to outcome in individuals Can be difficult to control for confounding
	Case Report		Can be used to spur subsequent research	Least publishable unit in the medical literature
	Case Series report		Can be used to spur subsequent research	Difficult to publish in the medical literature

10.6 Evaluation Methods

The evaluation methods are grouped into four categories:

- Qualitative approaches- yields data in the form of text, image, or audio/video formats (views, behaviors etc.). Qualitative data is collected using focus group discussions (FGDs), in-depth interviews (IDIs), participatory action research (PAR). (Explained in detail in Chap. 6)
- Quantitative approaches (e.g., survey data collection) yield numeric data that can be analyzed using statistical methods.
- Mixed methods are the combination of both qualitative and quantitative approaches.
- Financial and economic evaluations assess financing and affordability, whereas economic evaluations aim to determine a probable value for money from an intervention. (Detailed explanation is given in Chap. 11)

10.7 Indicators

Once the frameworks are conceptualized and drafted, identifying the indicators is necessary. These are the signs of progress which are used to assess if the intervention is progressing as planned to achieve the defined objective and the goals.

- The indicators should be "Specific, observable and of measurable characteristic."
- It is essential to have at least one indicator for each outcome.

M&E plans need to be drafted after the planning phase and before the design phase of an intervention.

These plans should include.

- Underlying assumptions on which the success of the intervention depends.
- Anticipated relationship between activities, output, outcome using the frameworks.
- A defined conceptual framework
- Questions and tools
- Identified indicators for the assessment along with baseline assessment data.
- A timeline and a budget explaining the details of the resources required.

10.7.1 Evaluation Questions

- These inquiries convey the main issue to be explored by the assessment. These are detailed after finalizing the goal and objectives supported by the activities of the intervention.
- Sorting the evaluation questions into categories or groups that are relevant to the intervention and deciding which evaluation question to answer.

10.8 Data Quality Assessment

This assessment must be conducted to enhance the ability of researchers to support their intervention's claims with reliable data. Flowchart (Fig. 10.10) below explains different components of data quality assessment [10].

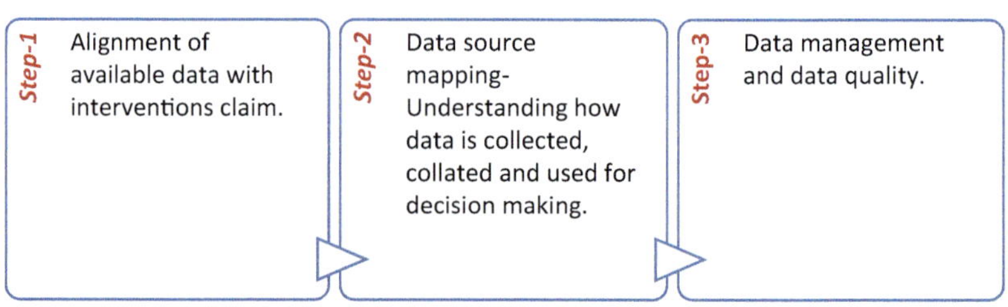

Fig. 10.10 Flowchart explaining components of data quality assessment (developed by author)

10.9 Using and Disseminating M&E Results

Why Use and Disseminate M&E Results [14, 15]?

- To improve program management and planning
- To identify weaknesses of program implementation, and to determine demand for service modification or expansion, to assess quality of care and to identify future research needs and to strengthen funding proposals. There are various reporting and disseminating formats which can be used and explained in detail in Chap. 14.

References

1. ME-Handbook.pdf [Internet]. [cited 2022 Feb 17]. Available from: http://web.undp.org/evaluation/documents/HandBook/ME-Handbook.pdf.
2. UNDG-UNDAF-Companion-Pieces-6-Monitoring-And-Evaluation.pdf [Internet]. [cited 2022 Feb 17]. Available from: https://unsdg.un.org/sites/default/files/UNDG-UNDAF-Companion-Pieces-6-Monitoring-And-Evaluation.pdf.
3. M&E in Project Cycle Management [Internet]. [cited 2022 Feb 17]. Available from: https://csnm.kku.ac.th/learning/course/module/lesson/116-me-project-cycle-management.
4. Monitoring and Evaluation Frameworks (3 parts) [Internet]. [cited 2022 Mar 28]. Available from: https://www.endvawnow.org/en/articles/335-monitoring-and-evaluation-frameworks-3-parts.html.
5. WHO.-Monitoring-and-Evaluating-Digital-Health--Interventions.pdf [Internet]. [cited 2022 Mar 28]. Available from: https://saluddigital.com/wp-content/uploads/2019/06/WHO.-Monitoring-and-Evaluating-Digital-Health-Interventions.pdf.
6. Situation analyses/Needs assessments (Formative research) [Internet]. [cited 2022 Mar 28]. Available from: https://www.endvawnow.org/en/articles/334-situation-analyses-needs-assessments-formative-research-.html?next=332.
7. Monitoring and Evaluation Frameworks (3 parts) [Internet]. [cited 2022 Mar 31]. Available from: https://www.endvawnow.org/en/articles/335-monitoring-and-evaluation-frameworks-3-parts.html.
8. McCarthy J, Maine D. A Framework for Analyzing the Determinants of Maternal Mortality. Studies in Family Planning. 1992;23(1):23–33.
9. Handbook on Planning Monitoring and Evaluating for Development Result. 232.
10. WHO.-Monitoring-and-Evaluating-Digital-Health--Interventions.pdf [Internet]. Available from: https://saluddigital.com/wp-content/uploads/2019/06/WHO.-Monitoring-and-Evaluating-Digital-Health-Interventions.pdf.
11. Meadows KA. So you want to do research? 3. An introduction to qualitative methods. Br J Community Nurs. 2003;8(10):464–9.
12. epidemiology_gordis_5_edi.pdf [Internet]. [cited 2022 Apr 1]. Available from: https://ak.sbmu.ac.ir/uploads/epidemiology_gordis_5_edi.pdf.
13. Classification of epidemiological study designs | International Journal of Epidemiology | Oxford Academic [Internet]. [cited 2022 Apr 1]. Available from: https://academic.oup.com/ije/article/41/2/393/697874.
14. Chapter9–1.pdf [Internet]. [cited 2022 Apr 1]. Available from: https://www.measureevaluation.org/resources/training/capacity-building-resources/basic-me-concepts-portuguese/Chapter9-1.pdf.
15. Reporting.pdf [Internet]. [cited 2022 Apr 1]. Available from: https://www.intrac.org/wpcms/wp-content/uploads/2017/01/Reporting.pdf.

Economic Evaluation of Interventions

11

Sidharth Sekhar Mishra and Samraj Sahay

Learning Objectives

After going through this section, participants will be able to:

- Explain the need for economic evaluation in an intervention study.
- Enumerate types of economic evaluation and elaborate the steps of evaluation.

11.1 Introduction: An Overview of Economic Evaluation

Unlike usual treatment and management strategies that have limited scope, public health interventions are targeted at the masses, and this is generally a costly affair. No matter how effective an intervention might be, the fact remains that its inclusion into the health programmes requires a great deal of introspection into the gains achieved for investment that the health systems would have to make. This requires the decision makers to be well informed with the return in terms of the value a programme provides for the costs incurred. So, for the intervention to be included in policies and programmes, economic evaluation of the interventions becomes essential.

The overarching goal of public health interventions is to maximize the health outcomes. More often, the resources available for public health are limited. This makes the cost of the interventions as one of the main factors in deciding on the implementation, continuation, and scaling up of the interventions. The effectiveness of the interventions and programme in achieving the intended goals of improvement in health outcomes are evaluated using different approaches. Economic evaluation offers an approach to analyse the effectiveness of the interventions both in terms of their cost as well as health effects; crucial for decision making. It serves to provide information on the most effective intervention based on the magnitude of the effect, optimal intervention mix, the overall benefits achieved through the intervention for the available or allocated level of resources, cost-effectiveness, and cost of scaling up. Economic evaluation is used for providing evidence to the decision makers, stakeholders, and funders. It provides a comparative analysis of the interventions which helps in the decision to scale up, identify the most effective intervention, and subsequent budgetary allocation. Figure 11.1 summarizes the major questions addressed and the uses of economic evaluation of public health intervention.

One of the main objectives of economic evaluation is to facilitate evidence-based decision

S. S. Mishra
Department of Health Systems and Implementation Research, International Institute of Health Management Research, New Delhi, India

S. Sahay (✉)
Independent Researcher, New Delhi, India

S. Bandyopadhyay Neogi, A. K. Pandey (eds.), *Designing and Evaluating Public Health Interventions*, https://doi.org/10.1007/978-981-97-9574-1_11

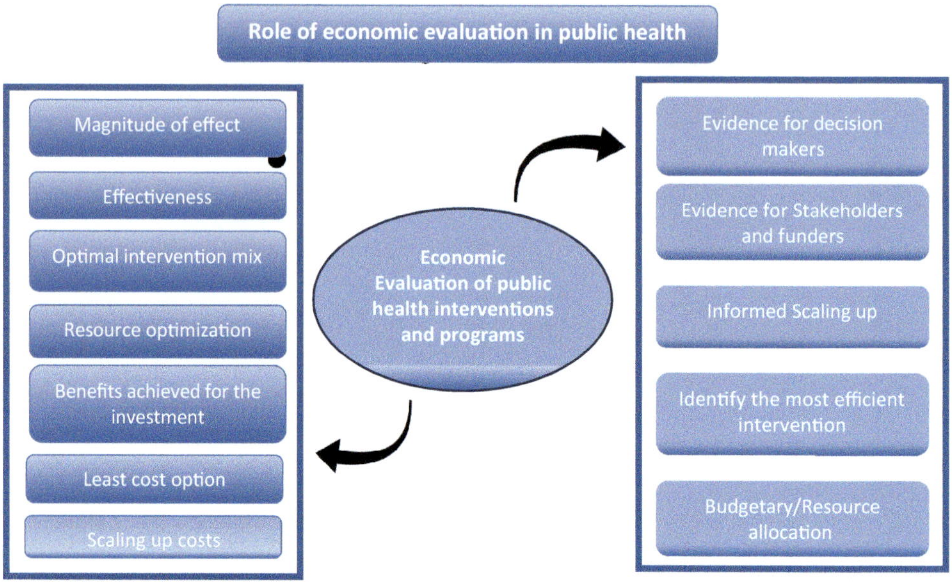

Fig. 11.1 Role of economic evaluation

Fig. 11.2 Scheme for conducting economic evaluation

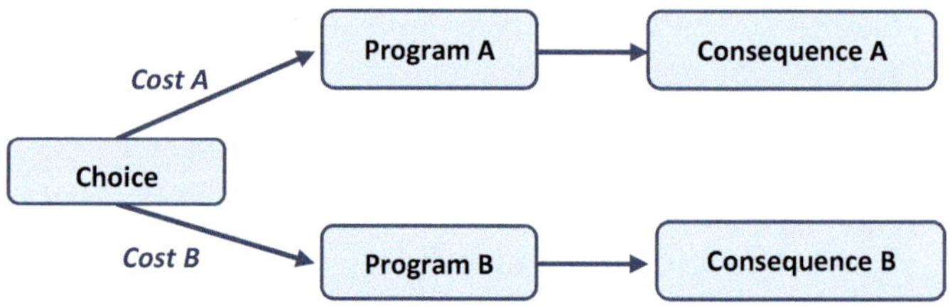

making in healthcare. This requires a comparative analysis of the interventions. Economic evaluation achieves this as it mainly deals with the costs and health outcomes and is concerned with the choice of alternative interventions. Economic evaluation, therefore, involves identifying, measuring, valuing, and comparing the cost and the health outcome of competing interventions and programmers. Figure 11.2 presents a schematic of any economic evaluation which involves comparative analysis of alternative programme A and B. The choice depends on the costs of the two programme and the subsequent consequences.

11.2 Economic Evaluation—Methodological Approaches

Economic evaluation of the interventions and programmes is achieved using different methods depending on the objective of the evaluation. The evaluation approaches have been classified into two broad categories—partial and complete economic evaluation (Table 11.1).

Partial economic evaluation—involves only the cost and does not include any evaluation of the effectiveness of the outcome or consequences. It provides vital information on the use of resources for a specific programme. It serves as a component of full economic evaluation as it is used in the estimation of full economic evaluation approaches along with the health outcome assessment. The approach includes the cost or costing analysis such as programme cost analysis which measures actual cost of implementing the programme and cost-of-illness analysis which measures the average cost incurred over a patient's lifetime.

Full economic evaluation—involves analysis of both the costs as well as the outcome of the programme. The economic effectiveness of the programme is evaluated based on the output from

Table 11.1 Types of Economic Evaluation

Partial	**Considers only cost**	
	Programme cost analysis	Cost description of the programme
	Cost-of-illness analysis	Cost incurred on illness
Full	**Consider both cost and outcome**	
	Cost-effectiveness analysis	Cost and desired health effects
	Cost-utility analysis	Cost and health outcome as utility (DALY/QALY) *
	Cost-benefit analysis	Cost and health outcome (benefit) in monetary terms

Note: * DALY: Disability-adjusted life year; QALY: Quality-adjusted life years

the costing analysis and the health outcome measured as natural health units, utility, and monetary terms. The approaches include the cost-effective analysis, cost-utility analysis, and cost-benefit analysis.

11.2.1 Costing Analysis

Cost analysis is the foundation of any economic evaluation of health interventions and programmes. It involves enumerating the resources consumed due to health issues and the resources used in the programme to address the issue. It is a partial economic evaluation as it does not include assessment of the programme effectiveness. It serves as a first step or first half of a full economic evaluation approach such as CEA. The approach uses the total value of the resources used and not just the money spent on the programme. Cost analysis contributes to informed decision making with regards to the resource (budgetary) allocations by comparing the cost of services and sites, assessment of the cost in case of changes in programme and understanding of the resource requirement. Cost analysis is mainly of two types –

(i). **Programme cost analysis**—This is used to estimate the total cost of resources required for implementing and running an intervention or programme. It provides an estimate of actual expenditure. This includes the cost incurred on human resource, capacity building, training, equipment, supplies, and other budget items. The treatment cost is also included in case it is the part of the programme. This is mainly used for preparing the budget.

(ii). **Cost-of-illness analysis—**There are costs associated with the illness. This includes the cost incurred by the patient towards getting diagnosed and treated as well as from loss of wages due to absence from work. Costs are also incurred on testing equipment, training of health staff, overhead for running clinics etc. This approach is used to estimate the economic burden of diseases and is reported as the average cost or annual cost over the entire lifetime of the patient. This is mainly used to determine the economic benefits of avoiding the health problems using the intervention.

11.2.2 Types of Cost

In a costing exercise, there can be numerous cost elements that need to be considered such as capital costs of infrastructure, human resources, equipment, management and administrative costs, overhead costs, and other costs including loss of working time and wages, cost of volunteer time. These cost elements are further categorized for the purpose of the analysis depending on the source of the costs. Table 11.2 provides the description with examples for the different types of cost used in the analysis. The choice of the type of cost to be used is mainly determined based on the research questions and the objective of the study. The most preferred choice is the fixed and variable cost as it distinctly covers the cost elements needed for the cost analysis.

Table 11.2 Types of cost

Type of cost		Description	Examples
Direct and Indirect costs	Direct cost	Costs directly associated with output	Health care services, tests, medical personnel
	Indirect cost	Costs linked to supporting activities; loss of income/productivity due to illness	Administrative cost, space for office/clinic, training, premature death, wage loss of patient/family member
Recurrent and Capital costs	Recurrent cost	Costs incurred on providing and maintaining the day-to-day services	Premise rent, transportation, electricity, fuel
	Capital cost	Investment expenses different from operating costs having long-term benefits with depreciation over time	Durable goods, equipment, pre-service/one-time in-service training
Fixed and Variable costs	Fixed cost	Costs remain unchanged irrespective of the output quantity. Both recurrent and capital costs included for resources with constant value over the analysis period.	Equipment, building rent, R&D, media campaign, overheads
	Variable costs	Costs that change depending on the quantity of the output such as the number of participants served.	Personal allowances, supplies (contraceptives, drugs, syringes, vaccines), ad-runs (pamphlets)
Joint and non-joint costs	Joint cost	Cost shared by multiple patients, or service	Time value of personnel, administrative costs, equipment
	Non-joint	Costs incurred only on the allocated service or activity.	One-time use (disposable) medical supplies

Steps involved in cost assessment [[1], 20]

1. **Resource Identification:**

   The first step is to identify the resources required for the interventions. This depends on the objective of the analysis. The resources required are mostly linked to the administration and the outcome of the health effect being investigated. For instance, if two surgical interventions are being considered for the same health problem, the resources related only to the outcome is considered, while those related to diagnosis are considered irrelevant.
2. **Quantification:**

   Once the resources to be included in the analysis have been identified, the next step is to quantify the identified resources for the interventions. This involves determining what to measure based on the outcome of the intervention such as in case of outcome being reduced, hospital days, length of hospital stay will be required. Likewise, if the outcome is reduced hospital admission, discharge or admission data will be required for quantification.
3. **Resource Allocation:**

   Assigning costs to the quantified resources is carried out in this step. This is achieved using the unit cost and the quantified resources. Different approaches have been used to reach the unit cost.

- The most used approach is the use of opportunity cost or the cost of the foregone benefit. For example, lost value of physician consultation fees in case of inability to undertake another consultation at the time used for one consultation. In most of the countries, the market prices are a good choice for representing the opportunity cost of resources.
- Tariffs or the price set for the health care system by the government or by insurers is used as cost. This may, however, not always represent the opportunity cost as in countries where separate payments are made for each service, tariffs are used to regulate supply of resources.
- Provider billing serves as the easiest source of unit cost. These charges are usually

Table 11.3 Approaches for estimation of indirect costs

Human capital theory	Friction cost method
The "market price" of the individual represented by the earning is used as the basis for estimating the indirect cost. The value of the "loss of work time" attributable to illness, premature death or retirement is used to represent the indirect cost. This is estimated either from the collected data or using the age and gender adjusted national average salary.	This is based on the notion that production loss due to premature death or early retirement is limited as they are replaced in short period, assuming easy availability of equally skilled workers. Production losses due to absence from work are far less and is achieved by temporary redistribution of work, assuming availability of spare workers and willingness to pay more for overtime.
Estimation of the production losses considers the entire period during which the person was unemployed.	Estimation of the production losses considers only the period before the replacement is made available.
Ex: The caregiver giving care by absence from work.	**Ex**: If one of the workers is absent from his duties, the work is distributed among the present employees.

higher than the actual opportunity cost as they might also include the charges to be used for subsidizing other related activities.

- 'Replacement cost' or loss of leisure is applied to attain the opportunity cost in cases where the market prices for health care services are not available.
- Estimating the indirect cost depends mainly on the type of health effect being considered. Different approaches have been used to estimate the indirect cost. The two commonly used approaches include the estimations based on human capital theory and the friction cost method as detailed out in Table 11.3:

4. **Discounting and Annualizing cost:**

This step involves adjustment in cost of resources to accommodate the cost of such resources that have usage at different point in time of the programme. Usually, capital cost incurred on capital assets such as infrastructure, equipment, vehicles, etc. provides benefits and services for a long period of time beyond the year of purchase. This calls for spreading out the value of such resources over more than a year of purchase. Their values need to be included while estimating the costs for each year of the programme. This is achieved by a process called annualization which provides the average value over the lifetime of the programme indicating the annual value to be added to the annual recurrent estimate representing the value-in-use of the capital item rather than value at the time it was purchased. While discounting is used to incorporate the time preference to the initial capital cost that may provide benefits over a period.

11.3 Cost-Effectiveness Analysis (CEA)

- Cost-effectiveness analysis compares the net costs and the health outcome or effect of an intervention or programmes with an alternative intervention or baseline situation. It is a full economic evaluation approach as it involves both the cost as well as effect.
- Common natural health units are used to represent the health outcomes such as deaths averted, cases of breast cancer, life years gained, received vaccination, intermediate outcomes such as reduction in blood pressure, cholesterol.
- CEA serves as an excellent approach when it comes to decision making on the most appropriate interventions with the same health outcome at the programme level.
- The decision on the interventions is facilitated by the incremental cost-effectiveness ratio (ICER) which is the ratio of the additional cost (difference in net costs of the options) to the gain or loss in outcome (difference in health outcomes or effectiveness) when the comparison is made between the programme and next least effective programme.

- It essentially represents the costs incurred in purchasing one additional unit of health.
- ICER is expressed as cost (monetary term) per unit heath outcome such as dollars per averted outcome.

11.4 Cost-Utility Analysis (CUA)

- Cost-utility analysis is a specialized version of CEA which uses utility measures in place of natural health units for health outcomes.
- Utility measures used for health outcomes include Quality-Adjusted Life Years (QALYs) or Disability-Adjusted Life Years (DALYs).

DALY is a measure of total burden of disease = morbidity + mortality.
DALY = YLL + YLD.

Years lost due to disability (YLD)—refers to the weighted count of years lived with disability.

Years of life lost due to mortality (YLL)—refers to years of life lost.

QALY is a measure of health GAIN due to increased survival or quality of life.

- The major benefit of transforming health outcomes in utility measures is that it allows the flexibility to compare interventions with different natural health outcomes.
- CUA is best suited for interventions where quality of life is a prominent determinant of effectiveness.
- Just like CEA, the decision making is facilitated using incremental cost-utility ratio (ICUR) represented by difference in costs and utility outcomes.
- ICUR is expressed as cost (monetary term) per unit heath outcome (utility measures) such as dollars per QALY gained or DALY averted.

11.5 Cost-Benefit Analysis (CBA)

- Cost-benefit analysis is used to compare the interventions based on the ratio of the cost incurred and benefits of the interventions. Unlike CEA and CUA, the health outcome in CBA is expressed in monetary terms.
- Costs include the monetary values of resources used for implementing the interventions, productivity loss, and health losses. Benefits include the monetary value of the avoided medical expenses, gain in productivity, and health improvements.
- The decision is based on the net benefits calculated as difference in the benefits and costs, and net present value (NPV) after *discounting*.
- Discounting is needed as health gains achieved now is valued more than future health gains.

NPV = \$ present value of all benefits—\$ present value of all costs

$$\text{Net Present Value}(\text{NPV}) = \sum_{t=0}^{n} \frac{(\text{Benefits} - \text{Costs})_t}{(1+r)^t}$$

Where:

r = discount rate.
t = year.
n = analytic horizon (in years)

- The intervention is preferred if the benefits outweigh the cost which is expressed as positive net benefits (i.e., NPV is positive).

11.6 Steps in Conducting Economic Evaluation

The purpose of conducting economic evaluation is to provide a comparative analysis of the cost and effectiveness of alternative health interventions or programmes for informed decision making. This section provides step wise guidance on conducting an economic evaluation of the interventions using the methodological approaches discussed earlier. Figure 11.3 depicts the steps that one needs to follow while performing an economic evaluation of health intervention for decision making.

11.6.1 Setting up Economic Evaluation

- The first step of an economic evaluation exercise is to identify the most appropriate intervention that is to be evaluated, alternative intervention, and the base case or the existing practice, if any.
- This is followed by defining the perspective of the evaluation as it determines for whom the evaluation is being done and accordingly the cost and benefits is to be considered—patient, health ministry, or society in general.

11.6.2 Health Outcome Assessment

- The health outcome of an intervention can be in natural health terms (avoided deaths) or utility (QALYs gained or DALYs averted) terms.
- This step involves assessing the health outcome of the interventions being compared. This is achieved using models as they help understand the magnitude of health issues, the impact of interventions on the outcome, and the cost of interventions.
- The most used model is a decision tree which enables visual representation of decisions, the processes involved and the outcome of the intervention. It is used to estimate the outcome of the competing interventions in the presence of uncertain chance events that may influence the outcome.
- The magnitude of the impact on the outcome is estimated using the expected values.

11.6.3 Cost Analysis

- This is the most crucial step of the economic evaluation as it is the first half of any full economic evaluation approaches—CEA, CUA, and CBA.
- It involves enumeration of all the costs (direct and indirect or fixed and variable) associated with the health issue and the interventions. Steps involved in cost analysis have been discussed in detail in the methodological approach section.

11.6.4 Economic Evaluation Approaches

- Once the costs and the health outcomes of the interventions being compared are known, a

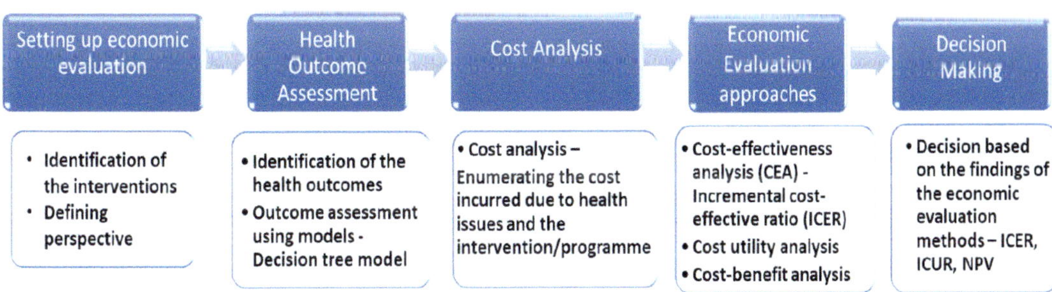

Fig. 11.3 Steps followed for economic evaluation of health interventions

full economic evaluation approach (CEA, CUA, CBA) is used to determine the cost-effectiveness of the interventions.

- CEA and ICER are the most used approaches for economic evaluation. While CUA and ICUR are also used mainly in evaluating the bigger health care programmes. Steps for evaluation using these approaches have been discussed in detail in the methodological approach section.

11.6.5 Decision-Making

- This is the final step in economic evaluation of an intervention. The findings of the economic evaluation approaches in terms of ICER, ICUR, or NPV are used to make decisions on the most cost-effective intervention from among the interventions being compared.
- The intervention with the lowest ICER or ICUR is the most preferred intervention. In case, CBA has been carried out, the intervention with the positive NPV is the preferred intervention.

11.7 Conducting an Economic Evaluation of Public Health Intervention

Based on the approach for the economic evaluation discussed in this chapter, Ray et al. [2] have evaluated the cost-effectiveness of an intervention for addressing the issue of severe anaemia during pregnancy. A comparison of administering IV iron sucrose to oral intake of iron has been carried out using ICER. The impact of the health outcome of the competing interventions has been estimated using a decision tree model that is explained using an example in Fig. 11.4. The cost and the effects of the competing interventions are obtained from the decision tree (for detailed economic evaluation see Ray et al. [2].

> **Q.11.1** *In reference to case study on IV iron sucrose and Ekjut trial describe the type of economic evaluation undertaken and what are the outcomes of those economic evaluation? Justify your response.*

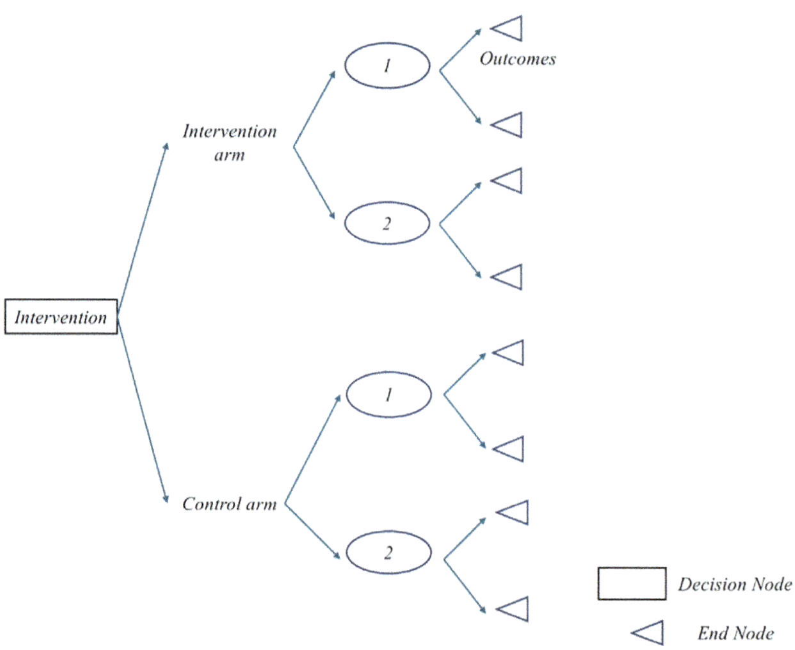

Fig. 11.4 *Decision analysis model example. (For detail read decision analysis model used for cost-effectiveness analysis from Ray* et al. [2]

11.7.1 Measuring Cost-Effectiveness

The cost and the effects of the competing interventions from the decision tree are used to determine the cost-effectiveness. This is mainly estimated using ICER or ICUR which compares the costs and effects of intervention and control groups using the following formula:

$$ICER / ICUR = {(Ca - Cb)}/{(Ea - Eb)}.$$

where

Ca = Cost of the intervention *a*
Cb = Cost of the control *b*
Ea = Effectiveness/Utility of the intervention *a*:
Eb = Effectiveness/Utility of the control/alternative intervention *b*

11.7.2 The Cost-Effectiveness Plane

Figure 11.5 represents the quadrants of cost-effective planes. The difference in the effect and the cost of the intervention being evaluated (A) and the alternative (O) are represented by the horizontal and the vertical axes, respectively. Quadrant II represents the acceptable zone as the intervention is both more effective and less costly, whereas in Quadrant IV, it is unacceptable as it is less effective and more costly. In I & III, acceptance is subject to willingness to accept the highest CE ratio. The CE ratio is represented by the slope of the line OA.

11.8 Critical Assessment of Economic Evaluation

There is a process in an economic evaluation to find whether it is near perfect for decision-making. However, it is important to note that not every study satisfies all these relevant questions, but the application of these points helps readers to assess the strengths and weaknesses of studies.

11.8.1 Checklist for Assessing Economic Evaluation

The economic evaluation study should satisfy the following criteria -

- A well-defined question or the goal for evaluation.
- Evidence for effectiveness of intervention or programmes.
- All relevant costs and outcomes for each alternative are well identified.
- All relevant costs and outcome are accurately measured in physical units.
- All relevant costs and outcome are accurately valued.

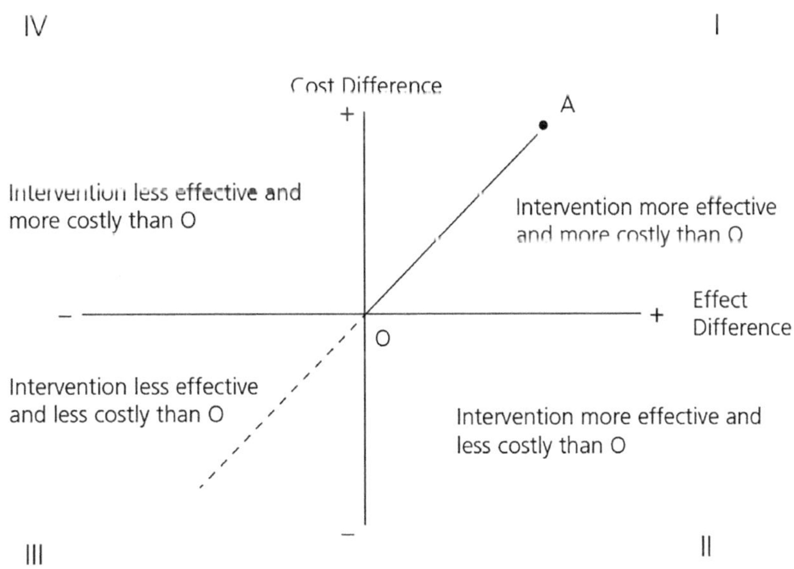

Fig. 11.5 Cost effectiveness plane (Adapted from Drummond et al. [3])

- All relevant costs and outcome are adjusted for the future—properly discounted or annualized.
- The study specifically includes incremental analysis for alternatives.
- The study should address the uncertainty in the estimates of costs and outcomes.
- The discussion of the findings of the study results should address all concerns of the users.

Q.11.2 *Develop a plan to undertake an economic evaluation of JSY case study. Explain the essential points to keep in mind while designing and undertaking such evaluation.*

References

1. Kobelt G. Health economics: an introduction to economic evaluation. 3rd ed. London: Office of the Health Economics; 2013.
2. Ray S, Neogi SB, Singh R, Devasenapathy N, Zodpey S. Is IV iron sucrose a cost-effective option for treatment of severe anaemia in pregnancy as compared with oral iron? Health Policy Plan. 2020;35(10):1339–46.
3. Drummond MF, Sculpher MJ, Claxton K, Stoddart GL, Torrance GW. Methods for the economic evaluation of health care programmes. 4th ed. Oxford University Press; 2015. p. 54–5.

12 Ethical Consideration in Research and Registration of Interventional Studies, Informed Consent

Anuj Kumar Pandey and Vinay Tripathi

Learning Objectives
After going through this section, participants will be able to

- Describe the principles of ethics in relation to public health interventions.
- Explain the importance of ethics in implementation research.
- Explain the ethical issues arising in different phases of implementation research.
- Appreciate the conflicts, dilemmas, and challenges involved in addressing the ethical issues of implementation research; and.
- Outline the roles and responsibilities of regulatory bodies and ethics committees in reviewing the implementation of research-related studies.
- Describe what registration of intervention studies means and its significance.
- Identify the relevant National and International registration platforms.
- Describe the Informed consent, its utility in interventional studies and key points to remember in respect to informed consent.

12.1 An Overview to the Ethical Consideration in Research

The nature of implementation research, which has been discussed in the previous chapters, highlights the significance of ethical principles and their associated complexities. The fact that implementation research is carried out in real settings, the likelihood of overlapping of ethical considerations pertaining to medical ethics, research ethics, bioethics, and public health ethics is quite plausible. The medical ethics which focuses on individual patients, doctor–patient relationship, duties of doctors/nurses, etc., is more individual centric. The research ethics talks about protection of study participants, informed consent, cost-benefit analysis, etc., and is more participant oriented. The emerging public health ethics, which is highly relevant to the implementation research, focuses on population health, health programs and policy issues, scientific evidence, etc., and is more of health system oriented. Sometimes and particularly in the context of implementation research, it becomes difficult to have or establish clear cut demarcation among them. Therefore, in implementation research, the ethical considerations cut across these frame-

A. K. Pandey
Department of Health Systems and Implementation Research, International Institute of Health Management Research (IIHMR), New Delhi, India
e-mail: anuj@iihmrdelhi.edu.in

V. Tripathi (✉)
International Institute of Health Management Research, New Delhi, India
e-mail: vinay@iihmrdelhi.edu.in

S. Bandyopadhyay Neogi, A. K. Pandey (eds.), *Designing and Evaluating Public Health Interventions*, https://doi.org/10.1007/978-981-97-9574-1_12

works. Nevertheless, the implementation research, like any other research, is expected to adhere to the following four basic principles of ethics [1]:

a) **Autonomy** with respect to the individual's thought, intent, and action while making decision so that the decision-making process remains free from any coercion or persuasion. This requires that we understand all risks and benefits and the likelihood of success of intervention.
b) **Justice** with regard to benefits and impacts being distributed equally among all sections of the society implying fair selection of individuals or communities, equal resource allocation, consideration of contending needs, rights and obligations, and potential conflicts, if any.
c) **Beneficence** involves the intention of doing good to the individuals.
d) **Non-maleficence** means no harm (or minimum harm) to individuals or groups in society.

These basic principles of ethics have been further categorized in following 12 "general principles" in the ICMR National Ethical Guidelines for Biomedical and Health Research involving Human Participants (2017) [1–3]:

- Principle of Essentiality
- Principle of Professional Competence
- Principle of Voluntariness
- Principle of Maximization of Benefit
- Principle of non-exploitation
- Principle of Institutional Arrangements
- Principle of Social Responsibility
- Principle of Transparency and Accountability
- Principle of Ensuring Privacy and Confidentiality
- Principle of Totality of Responsibility
- Principle of Risk Minimization
- Principle of Environmental Protection

Since the public health ethics is closely related to the implementation research, it would be worthy to review and get appraised with some of the ethical questions and concerns which guides the public health ethics. For instance,

- What is that extent of risk which is acceptable at the individual or community level?
- Is coercion justifiable and if yes, how much coercion is justifiable?
- How to weigh individual interest versus the common or public good?
- In relation to health promotion, how much influence from the government is allowed which can influence or interfere with personal choices on health?
- How can be the fair participation of the study participants ensured in decision-making?
- Priority setting and allocation, i.e., who will get what if resources are scarce or short?

Based upon these questions, the WHO (2019) [1] has put forward two broad categories of ethical principles in context of public health (which can also apply to implementation research). These categories include "substantive" ethical principles and "procedural" ethical principles, which are briefly elaborated below:

- Substantive ethical principles
  - These principles define "what is right and wrong, and the right and wrong actions in public health" and facilitate "ethical conduct in public health, producing benefits and minimizing harms."
  - These principles include aspects pertaining to the benefit, potential harm, individual autonomy, equity, trust, solidarity, and stewardship.
- Procedural ethical principles
  - These principles define "rules by which public health should be practiced and decision made and are concerned with the process of delivery of public health services."
  - These rules include aspects pertaining to transparency, relevance, inclusivity, responsiveness, accountability, participation, and sustainability.

In some situations, these substantive principles may conflict with each other. For instance, selecting a quarantine routine during pandemics may raise the dilemma between ethical considerations like "autonomy" and "common good" or "autonomy" versus "solidarity." Similarly, targeted interventions, which are found to improve efficiency and generate common good, may not be equitable in terms of distribution of gains thus raise the conflicting concerns among the ethical principles of "equity" and "common good." Keeping above-mentioned questions and ethical principles in perspective, few instances are being presented below for the readers to think upon and reflect on conflicting or non-conflicting ethical issues which may arise in such scenarios [4]:

- With respect to universal health coverage, the effectiveness of social insurance schemes has been known. Think of potentially conflicting ethical principles which may arise due to implementation of such schemes *(for instance, risks involved in social insurance, principle of justice in terms of selecting the participants, solidarity principle, etc.).*
- Evidence has indicated the critical role which mobile-based technology can play in timely collection of health data by community health workers. Think of some of the ethical issues which may arise due to implementation of mobile technology-based health interventions *(for instance, data protection and confidentiality, data ownership, obtaining consent mandatory or not, etc.).*

A case study, which has been reproduced from the work of Gopichandran et al. [3] is presented below to further detail out some of the key ethical issues which may arise in implementation research.

Case Study: Implementation Research of Strategies to Improve Vaccine Coverage in Children in Nomadic Populations [3]

Study Description

An unknown country had a poor vaccine coverage as a sub-section of the population, i.e., nomadic population were not able to reach by the routine vaccination program of the country. A need assessment study was carried out among this sub-section of the population, and it was found that the vaccination coverage is very low among them. The assessment also pointed out other factors such as low community engagement, inadequate logistic support and difficulty in finding the location of the nomads also contributed toward poor vaccination coverage.

Implementation research was designed to address the issue. As part of intervention, Special Outreach Teams (SOTs) were constituted. These teams were given extensive training on the topics related to immunization as well as on the community engagement aspects. They were also equipped with necessary and required logistics arrangements like vehicles, vaccine stocks, ice boxes, and temperature logs. The SOTs were then deployed on the field. The SOTs got in touch with the routine health workers of those communities where the nomadic population were stationed and established contact with the nomads. Further, as part of sub-study within this implementation research, a small number of nomadic groups were also given mobile phone-based GPS trackers to locate the group on real-time basis. The group was also given solar powered battery packs that ensured that the phone remains active. This helped the research team to pass on their locations to the SOTs which in turn helped the team to provide the services to the nomadic population.

12.2 Ethical Issues

This implementation research study raises several significant ethical concerns. Ethical responsibility demands active engagement and collaboration with this unique marginalized group to enhance vaccination coverage. The health system is mandated to protect and safeguard the rights of the nomadic population while improving their health. The justification for conducting the study is rooted in equipoise, primarily arising from uncertainty about how the intervention will be adopted and its effectiveness within this specific context, despite knowledge of the effectiveness of vaccinations in other populations.

Nevertheless, it is important that potential confounders like nutritional status should be considered while monitoring the vaccine effectiveness in the new population. The study outcomes will provide insights into the feasibility and acceptability of the intervention within nomadic communities, thereby supporting the implementation of the vaccination coverage campaign. Ethical considerations include active community engagement, particularly in marginalized communities where inherent mistrust in health systems exists. In this context, involvement of identified and selected gatekeepers helps not only in the process of obtaining informed consent but also the long-term involvement of the community.

The use of mobile-based GPS trackers is certainly an intrusion into community privacy and an issue from an ethical perspective. Therefore, ethical consideration should weigh in this intrusion viz.-a-viz. potential benefits and reduced child mortality due to improved vaccination coverage in this population. It is imperative to uphold the confidentiality of GPS tracking data, with careful deliberation on issues such as sharing the tracking information with the local health system and other entities that may have interests but not related to vaccination. Additionally, the study may identify various health needs within these communities, giving rise to ethical concerns related to ancillary care responsibilities.

It is important to note that the ethical issues pertaining to the implementation of research can arise either during planning or implementation or post-implementation phase or during all the phases of the research. Some of the key ethical consideration arising in these different phases are presented below:

Planning Phase	Sensitivity to community needs and priorities, Equipoise, Research design, Involvement of stakeholders and the community, Balancing risks, and benefits, resources available, permission from relevant authorities.
Implementation Phase	Individual autonomy and informed consent, Confidentiality and privacy, Standard of care, Ancillary care, Empowerment of community/health system
Post-implementation Phase	Sharing research results, Ownership of data, transforming findings into public health measures, Scalability and sustainability, Sharing benefits.

Source: Gopichandran et al. [3]

The conflicting dilemmas, emerging nature of ethical dimensions, and challenges regarding ethical considerations in implementation research necessitates a strong facilitative role of regulatory bodies and ethics committees. The role of the ethical committees in implementation research is more critical. The ethical committees are not only responsible to ensure that the research adheres to the general ethical principles, as outlined in the beginning, but also ensures that research is undertaken following ethical principles across different stages of the implementation research. Given the scale and issues which implementation research addresses, it is very important that ethical committees ensure that the studies focusing on implementation research are trustworthy, have minimal risks with sustainable and impactful outcomes as well as are valued by the communities.

It is essential that the ethical committees are sensitized upon and be updated with the emerging ethical principles of public health as well as implementation research in order to provide appropriate and useful insights to the study team. In Indian setting, the Indian Council of Medical Research (ICMR) [2] plays a pivotal role in guiding the ethics committees via setting and establishing the biomedical and health research ethics. The ICMR came out with the first ethical policy document way back in 1980s ("Policy Statement on Ethical Considerations involved in Research on Human Subjects") and revised it in 2000 and 2006 (Ethical Guidelines for Biomedical Research on Human Subjects). The latest revised policy document which is titled as "National Ethical Guidelines for Biomedical and Health Research involving Human Participants" came out in 2017 (hereafter, ICMR-2017 guidelines) and provides important insights to the ethical committees. The policy document elaborates and highlights on the responsible way of conducting research, informed consent process, etc. The policy document details the ethical principles, considerations and issues involved in public health research, which can guide and aid the ethical committees to review the implementation of research protocols. A sub-section (titled Implementation Research) specifically discusses on the implementation research and delineates the following roles of the ethics committee:

- Since implementation research is "adaptive in its essence, this approach diverges from protocols that demand exact pre-definition of interventions, delivery methods, outcome measurement, and the role of study participants. Hence, ethical committees should recognize the necessity for flexibility or adaptability when reviewing Implementation Research (IR) projects."
- The process of implementation research strives to allocate roles and responsibilities among researchers and various stakeholders, including those being researched, to a certain extent. Ethical committees should recognize these elements of good participatory practice in implementation research and delivery sciences—both formally, through training, and informally, by fostering discussion and debate.
- "The theoretical foundation of a complex intervention should remain consistent while acknowledging and embracing the inherent flexibility and adaptability of the study design. The ethics of implementation research is a developing field and will continue to evolve with increasing experience."
- "The importance of governance and accountability for all stakeholders is crucial, given the asymmetry in knowledge and power relationships, and this factor should be taken into consideration" by the ethics committees.

Apart from above roles, the ICMR-2017 guidelines [2] highlight following roles of ethics committee in public health research (*which is also applicable in implementation research*):

- Ethical committees "ethical committees should verify that researchers have implemented sufficient measures for data security, confidentiality, disclosure permissions, and have clearly outlined the appropriate use of the accessed data."
- Ethical committee members "The ethical committees should recognize the significance of social benefit, public good, and the potential public health impact addressed by these studies. Decisions regarding consent should be made on a case-by-case basis."
- Ethical committee membership should have experts from diverse backgrounds or should seek advice from experts in a pertaining subject.
- Ethical committees should deliberate "standards of care, ancillary care, stakeholder engagement and obligation to scale-up, or sustain the public health intervention."

Regulatory bodies and ethics committees play an important role in implementation research. However, their role is more challenging particularly considering the nature of implementation research studies, ethical implication involved in designing and conducting implementation research, evolving ethical considerations in public health research, and the impacts which these studies can have on people's health. Time to time release and updating of ethical guidelines facilitates ethics committees in dovetailing their roles and responsibilities. The ICMR-2017 guidelines also highlight the registration of Ethics Committee, need of registering intervention studies with concerned authorities and roles of investigators. The same is being discussed briefly in subsequent paragraphs.

The guidelines [2] states that the ethics committees "The researchers should comply with regulatory requirements by registering with the relevant authority. Additionally, they should strive to obtain recognition, certification, or accreditation from reputable national or international bodies, including but not limited to Strategic Initiative for Developing Capacity in Ethical Review (SIDCER), Association for the Accreditation of Human Research Protection Programmes (AAHRPP), CDSCO, and Quality Council of India through the National Accreditation Board for Hospitals and Healthcare Providers (NABH) or any other recognized entities. It is essential to maintain and update such certification or accreditation continuously." It should be noted that the Department of Health Research (DHR), Ministry of Health and Family Welfare, Government of India, has been designated as the sole regulatory authority of Ethics Committees (ECs) for Biomedical and Health Research in India. All Ethics Committees reviewing biomedical and health research should register with DHR.

Likewise, the ICMR guidelines [2] also emphasize on registration of "all clinical research including intervention studies should get registered with the Clinical Trials Registry of India (CTRI) [5]. The registry, connected to the WHO registry, offers a complimentary and internet-based public record platform for enlisting clinical trials, theses, and another biomedical research. All clinical trials falling under the purview of the Drugs and Cosmetics Act, and its Rules are obligated to register with CTRI. Registering research in CTRI guarantees the availability of more comprehensive, verified, and easily accessible data on research to the public, thereby enhancing transparency, accountability, and accessibility of research.

The role of investigators/researchers has been highlighted in different sections of the ICMR guidelines. It starts with the researcher and team ensuring that general ethical principles are followed up and is responsible for "protecting the dignity, rights, safety, and well-being of the participants enrolled in the study." Researchers and the research team are obligated to adhere to high standards and uphold the fundamental values of research. They are responsible for securing the written, informed consent of prospective participants or their legally acceptable/authorized representatives (LARs). In cases where an individual is incapable of providing informed consent, the consent of the LAR should be obtained. If a participant or LAR is illiterate, a literate impartial witness should be present during the informed consent process. Researchers must also ensure the confidentiality of research-related data for both participants and the community. Reporting all serious adverse events to the Ethics Committee within 24 hours of awareness is another responsibility of researchers. In the event of any changes to study protocols, researchers must promptly inform the ethics committee. Regular updates on the study's progress are also required to be provided to the ethics committee by the researchers.

Q.12.1
Refer to the case study HBNC and Solidarity trial. Discuss the ethical issues raised pertaining to the intervention.

12.3 Introduction to Registration of Interventional Studies

Every trial or interventional study aims to compare a novel intervention with a standard intervention, a placebo intervention, or no intervention. These types of studies are undertaken to benefit the patients and the society as a whole, and also to generate new evidence and knowledge in the public health/medical field.

A meta-analysis by Dickersin et al. (decades ago) highlighted selective reporting and publication bias amongst the published literatures in the past three decades. The authors noted distinctions in the conclusions drawn from trials that proactively registered their protocols in a registry compared to those that did not register [6]. In most cases owing to the busy schedule of the researcher, the research is either abandoned, or the manuscript is not prepared or not submitted for publication and the selective publication and outcome reporting impedes holistic interpretation of the information.

Another article reported that studies with "negative findings" are less likely to be published than those with positive findings [7]. Even in cases of registered or published protocols, there is evidence of selective reporting, where outcomes are only partially reported, primary outcomes are altered, or statistically significant outcomes are more likely to be disclosed. To address these limitations in the conduct and reporting of trials or any interventional studies, regulatory bodies have implemented guidelines mandating the prospective registration of trial/study protocols.

As per the World Health Organization (WHO), the registration of all interventional trials is a scientific, ethical, and moral responsibility [8]. Thus currently, it is mandatory to prospectively register a trial or any interventional study in a publicly accessible registry and provide relevant details about the study [8–10].

12.4 What Is Registration of Interventional Studies

World Health Organization (WHO) defines trial registration as the "*publication of an internationally agreed set of information about the design, conduct and administration of an interventional study or a clinical trial*" [11].

It is essential to understand certain aspects of registration of any trial or any interventional study and they are as follows -

- Why is registration important?
- What are the different trial registration platforms?
- How to register for a trial?
- Types of clinical trials for registration?
- What is Universal Trial Number (UTN)?

12.5 Why Is Registration Important?

The main objective of the International Clinical Registry Platform is to provide a comprehensive overview of research accessible to all individuals involved in healthcare decision-making. This is intended to enhance transparency in the research domain, thereby strengthening the validity and value of the scientific evidence base.

12.6 Different Trail (or Trial) Registration Platforms

The National Institute of Health (NIH) USA has defined Trial [12] as- "a research study in which one or more human subjects are prospectively assigned to one or more interventions (which may include placebo or other control) to evaluate the effects of those interventions on health-related biomedical or behavioral outcomes." Thus, studies in compliance with the present definition are required to be prospectively registered in a publicly accessible registry.

The International Clinical Trials Registry Platform (ICTRP) is a global initiative with an objective to make information about all clinical trials publicly available. The ICTRP Secretariat is hosted by WHO in its headquarters in Geneva [8, 11]. These platforms serve as a space for sharing information and collaborating to establish optimal practices for the registration of trials.

The ICTRP Registry Network is composed of:

a) **<u>Primary Registries</u>**: Primary Registries within the WHO Registry Network adhere to specific criteria related to content, quality, validity, accessibility, unique identification, technical capacity, and administration, aligning with the standards set by the ICMJE [13].
b) **<u>Partner Registries</u>**: This registry meets the same criteria for content, quality, and validity, etc. as that of Primary registries [14] in WHO Registry Network except that they:

- Do not need to have a national or regional support of the government,
- Be open to all prospective registrants.
- Be managed by a non-for-profit agency.
- They should also have an affiliation with either a Primary Registry in the WHO Registry Network or a registry approved by the ICMJE.

12.7 How to Register a Trial and What Are the Advantages?

A set of information like the title of the study, details about the principal investigator and other co-investigators, objective of the study, study duration, methodologies adopted, outcomes, analytical steps involved, and ethical considerations need to be shared.

In India, Clinical Trials Registry – India (CTRI) [15], made it a mandate for prospective registration of trials as stated by Drugs Controller General India (DCGI) [16]. As per the guidelines laid by DCGI on trial registration, "even multinational clinical trials in which participants from India are recruited needs to be prospectively registered in CTRI."

As mandated, all public health interventional studies are supposed to be registered with CTRI.

Registration has numerous advantages like [10]:

- Subsequent publication of registration could later be used to assess if the trial followed the protocols and enhances the liability of the investigators.
- Reduces publication bias or selective reporting of the results.
- Provides information about any ongoing trial; thus, helps researchers identify similar work.
- This also minimizes the chance of duplication of research therefore aids in cautious use of funds.

12.8 Trial/Universal Trial Number

The aim of the Universal Trial Number or a Trial registration number is to facilitate the explicit identification of clinical trials [17].

12.9 Informed Consent

Informed consent is defined as [18] "...permission given by an individual or someone acting on behalf of another individual for a procedure or set of procedures in clinical medicine or in clinical research" (Fig. 12.1).

This concept came way back in the twentieth-century as a legal concept that has now been integrated into medical and medical research practice. This process enables for an open discussion between the provider and the patient and may theoretically help reduce medical inaccuracies, improve patient outcomes, and increase patient empowerment [19].

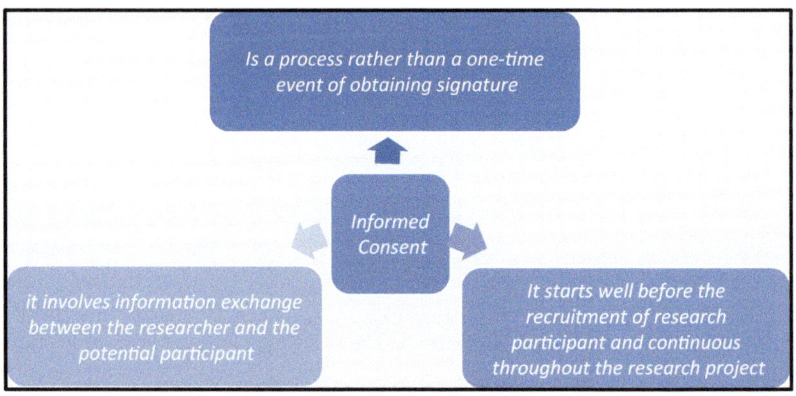

Fig. 12.1 Essential components of the Informed Consent process

12.9.1 Steps Involved in Informed Consent

Steps include [20]:

i. **How?**
   - It should be done in a language that is easy to comprehend by the research participants.
   - It should be clear and non-technical.
   - It should be delivered in the most effective way.

ii. **By Whom?**
   - Detailed information needs to be provided by the investigator or researchers having full knowledge of the study.

iii. **The participants must be able to.**
   - Understand the issue and retain the information long enough to make a decision based on that information.
   - The participant should believe that the information is true, and they should be able to consider the information appropriately before making a decision.
     – To check if the participants understood, the researchers/Investigators must ask open-ended questions to assess if the participants understood everything actually.

iv. **Who can give Consent:**
   - By a person who is legally and factually capable of consenting to the person.
   - In case of incompetent/incapable person, consent should be obtained from parents/legal guardian/legal representative.
   - **In case of research on vulnerable population** like children, diseased, institutionalized individuals (mentally ill, old, prisoners, etc.), tribals, uneducated ethnic minorities or refugees should not be included in the study unless study demands and benefits special groups.
   - Those below the age of 18 years require a parent or a guardian who can take the decision for them in addition to the legally required consent from the parent or guardian. The potential participant may also be asked for their agreement to participate in the research which is called **Assent** [20]. Assent is not legally binding, however favored by many ethics' committees.

12.9.2 Other Types of Informed Consent

i. **What is an impartial witness?**
   - An impartial witness is required when the participant or representatives are illiterate. This is essential to ensure that the investigator or the researchers don't unfairly influence the participants.
   - Signing of the witness along with investigators/researcher is mandatory to assess if the consent is deliberate without any force.

ii. **Verbal Consent.**
   - This is used in Minimal risk studies and depends upon the data collection methodology like telephonic survey or quick face to face survey.
   - It is essential for the investigators to document such consent and prior approval of ethics committee is mandatory.

iii. **Staged Consent.**
   - Such consent is necessary when the deception/covert data collection is necessary due to HAWTHORNE EFFECT[1].
   - This is done in two steps. First step consent is given to the research procedures, or a waiver is obtained in the second stage; that is after data collection the participants are then briefed about the situation and consent is obtained to use the data that has already been collected.
   - This form of consent requires IRB approval and should be explicitly stated in the protocol.

iv. **Community consent.**
   - This is the agreement of the local community leadership and often this is a good

[1]The Hawthorne effect is a type of reactivity in which individuals modify their behavior in response to their awareness of being observed.

research practice or even mandatory in some communities.

- However, obtaining agreement from community leadership does not serve as a substitute for the consent or assent of individual participants, especially when collecting data at the individual level.

12.9.3 Elements of Informed Consent Process

The process of Informed consent consists of following elements:

- Describing the entire protocol, its strengths, and limitations to the participant.
- Talk over the role of participant in decision-making process. Also make them understand the associated risks and benefits.
- Inquiring about related concerns.
- Evaluating if the patient understood the information provided or not and.
- Decision-Making: Not trying to convince or undue force the participants and thus obtaining the patient's preference (the consent).

These elements represent the informed consent process as a whole. However, there are some core components of Informed Consent process and include:

1. Disclosure: Could be addressed by providing adequate information.
2. Comprehension: By Understanding and seeking clarification.
3. Decision-Making: Participation should be volunteer and should be free from coercion.

12.9.4 Waiver of Consent

This can only happen with the approval of the ethics committee. This may also happen in emergency studies where the patient is incapacitated and incapable of providing consent wherever possible. The documentation of any discussion regarding the approval of the consent of the participant could be recorded. A waiver may also be obtained for the use of secondary data or retrospective studies that are based entirely on previous medical or lab records.

In some cases, consent may also be waived in the process of data collection. For example, in the case of self-administered questionnaires such as online surveys where there are no researchers or data collectors and the process of agreeing to participate in the survey itself voluntary.

Q.12.2
Refer to the case study on HBNC and IV-iron sucrose. Discuss the process of registration of the trial.

References

1. World Health Organization. UNICEF/UNDP/World Bank/WHO special programme for research and training in tropical diseases. In: Ethics in implementation research: facilitator's guide [Internet]. Geneva: World Health Organization; 2019. p. 167. [cited 2022 Nov 5]. Available from: https://apps.who.int/iris/handle/10665/325608.
2. National ethical guidelines for biomedical and health research involving human participants. 2017 [Internet]. [cited 2022 Nov 5]. Available from: https://ethics.ncdirindia.org/asset/pdf/ICMR_National_Ethical_Guidelines.pdf.
3. Gopichandran V, Luyckx VA, Biller-Andorno N, Fairchild A, Singh J, Tran N, et al. Developing the ethics of implementation research in health. Implement Sci. 2016;11(1):161.
4. Luyckx VA, Reis A, Maher D, Vahedi M. Highlighting the ethics of implementation research. Lancet Glob Health. 2019;7(9):e1170–1.
5. Clinical trials registry - India (CTRI) [Internet]. [cited 2024 Jan 1]. Available from: https://ctri.nic.in/Clinicaltrials/login.php.
6. NIH clinical trials and publication bias - PubMed [Internet]. [cited 2022 Mar 9]. Available from: https://pubmed.ncbi.nlm.nih.gov/8306005/.
7. Harriman SL, Patel J. When are clinical trials registered? An analysis of prospective versus retrospective registration. Trials. 2016;17(1):187.

8. World Health Organization. International standards for clinical trial registries: the registration of all interventional trials is a scientific, ethical and moral responsibility [Internet]. World Health Organization; 2018. [cited 2022 Mar 9]. 48 p. Available from: https://apps.who.int/iris/handle/10665/274994.
9. Veluswamy S, Babu A. Clinical trial registration: what do we need to know? Indian J Respiratory Care. 2015;4:618–23.
10. Why should i register and submit results? - ClinicalTrials.gov [Internet]. [cited 2022 Mar 9]. Available from: https://clinicaltrials.gov/ct2/manage-recs/background.
11. International clinical trials registry platform (ICTRP) [Internet]. [cited 2022 Mar 11]. Available from: https://www.who.int/clinical-trials-registry-platform.
12. Admin. Clinical trials [Internet]. Office of science policy. [cited 2022 Mar 11]. Available from: https://osp.od.nih.gov/clinical-research/clinical-trials/.
13. Primary registries [Internet]. [cited 2022 Mar 11]. Available from: https://www.who.int/clinical-trials-registry-platform/network/primary-registries.
14. Partner registries [Internet]. [cited 2022 Mar 11]. Available from: https://www.who.int/clinical-trials-registry-platform/network/partner-registries.
15. Clinical trials registry - India (CTRI) [Internet]. [cited 2022 Mar 11]. Available from: http://ctri.nic.in/Clinicaltrials/login.php.
16. CDSCO India- clinical trials [Internet]. [cited 2022 Mar 11]. Available from: https://cdsco.gov.in/opencms/opencms/en/Clinical-Trial/clinical-trials/.
17. The Universal trial number (UTN) [Internet]. [cited 2022 Mar 11]. Available from: https://www.who.int/clinical-trials-registry-platform/unambiguous-trial-identification/the-universal-trial-number-(utn).
18. Informed consent - an overview | ScienceDirect Topics [Internet]. [cited 2022 Mar 14]. Available from: https://www.sciencedirect.com/topics/medicine-and-dentistry/informed-consent.
19. Cordasco KM. Obtaining informed consent from patients: brief update review [Internet]. [cited 2022 Mar 14]. Available from: https://europepmc.org/books/n/erta211/ch39/?extid=24423049&src=med.
20. Shah P, Thornton I, Turrin D, Hipskind JE. Informed consent. In: StatPearls [Internet]. Treasure Island, FL: StatPearls Publishing; 2022. [cited 2022 Mar 14]. Available from: http://www.ncbi.nlm.nih.gov/books/NBK430827/.

13 Scalability Assessments of a Public Health Intervention

Sutapa Bandyopadhyay Neogi

Learning Objectives
After going through this section, participants will be able to:

- Describe the factors influencing policy-maker's decisions to scale up any intervention.
- Describe factors that need to be explored to increase the probability for interventions to be implemented or scaled up in a new geographic area.
- Develop a scaling up strategy.

13.1 Scaling-up an Intervention

Implementation science (IS) is the "systematic study of strategies and methods that enable the uptake of evidences from research into use by practitioners and policymakers or adapt and utilize the evidence-based intervention" [1]. There are various objectives of IS, one being to increase the use of evidences being generated from high quality researches for greater public health impact [2].

This aspect of generalizing the evidence-based intervention was explained and introduced by Campbell in his theory on external validity. External validity affects the representativeness or generalizability of the outcome of an intervention [3]. Thus, it is necessary to understand the concept of generalizability or scaling up of an intervention to attain population-wide benefits and to encourage sustainable policy and program development.

An evidence-based intervention is executed in a similar setting identical to where the intervention was tested and was found effective and thus it is expected that the intervention would provide a similar benefit. However, the effectiveness of the same intervention depends upon various factors [4] which is explained in the definition of scalability by Milat et al. [5] as-

- "the ability of a health intervention shown to be efficacious on a small scale and/or under controlled conditions to be expanded under real world conditions to reach a greater proportion of the eligible population while retaining effectiveness" [5]

S. Bandyopadhyay Neogi (✉)
Department of Health Systems and Implementation Research, International Institute of Health Management Research (IIHMR), New Delhi, India
e-mail: sutapa@iihmrdelhi.edu.in

S. Bandyopadhyay Neogi, A. K. Pandey (eds.), *Designing and Evaluating Public Health Interventions*, https://doi.org/10.1007/978-981-97-9574-1_13

WHO ExpandNet has defined scalability [6] as-

- the "Deliberate efforts to increase the impact of successfully tested health innovations so as to benefit more people and to foster policy and programme development on a lasting basis."
- Scaling up refers to the expansion of an interventions already tested as part of a research project and found effective in terms of effectiveness of intervention to avert disease condition and cost effectiveness [7].

Definitions of scaling up varies, but it is important to note that the model should not get changed; however, in the case where new services are added or if the mode of implementation changes, then the model itself changes.

13.2 Creating a Vision for Scaling up

To achieve greater benefit, effective health intervention should be rolled out, thus planning for scaling-up should start during the design phase of a pilot project. Figure 13.1 depicts a range of parameters that need attention during planning for scaling-up an intervention.

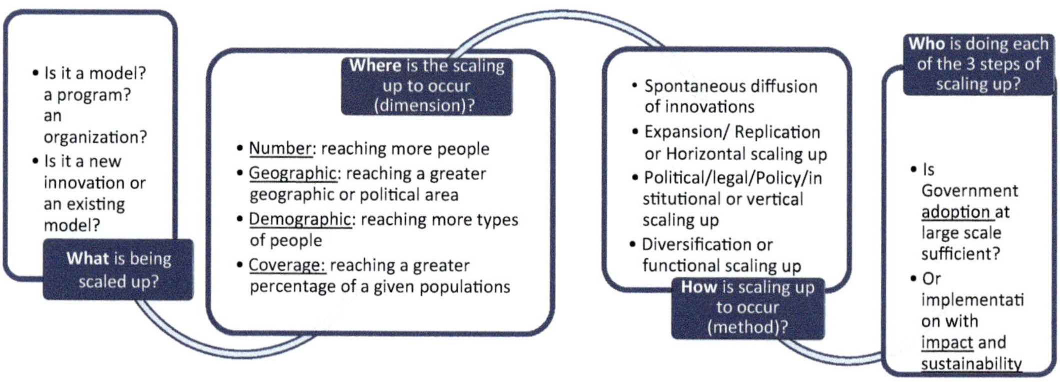

Fig. 13.1 Showing parameters that need attention during planning for scaling-up an intervention

13.3 Methods of Scaling-up

There are four methods of scaling up process [6, 8–10].

1. **Spontaneous diffusion of innovations**. This happens when the intervention addresses a clear gap or need in an ongoing program. Although this is very rare to happen, it usually requires purposeful attention.
2. **Expansion/Replication or horizontal scaling up** occurs when successful interventions are replicated in different geographical locations or to a new population category. Intervention's effectiveness becomes a priority. Figure 13.2 explains the vertical and horizontal dimensions of diffusion.
3. **Political/legal/Policy/institutional or vertical scaling up** happens when government's decisions are made to adopt an intervention at national and subnational level. It usually gets established through national planning mechanism, policy change, etc. Vertical scaling up requires strong advocacy.
4. **Diversification or functional scaling up** comprises analyzing and adding up an intervention to some existing, ongoing package.

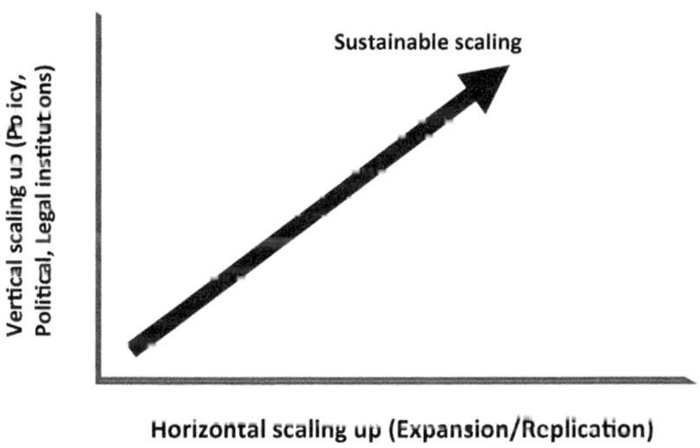

Fig. 13.2 Horizontal and vertical scaling up [6]

13.4 Conceptual Framework for Scaling up an Intervention (as Given by WHO)

The framework as developed by WHO [7, 11] (Fig. 13.3) provides a basis for systematic and strategic planning and management about scaling up process. The framework comprises five components of scaling up and strategic choice areas that interact with each other: the innovation, the user organization, the environment, the resource team, or organization, and the strategy for scaling.

The scaling-up elements interact with each other and modifications in the status of one component affect another component. Thus, this change in status of elements will have consequences for scaling process. Effective strategy might maximize prospects for success.

13.4.1 The Elements of Scaling up

(i) **The Environment**: Scaling-up task does not only include the technical and managerial undertaking. This gets heavily influenced and affected by various environmental factors like gender inequality, poverty in the country, health system capacity, political factors, etc. [10]. Associated opportunities and obstacles that must be recognized and addressed at the planning stage.

(ii) **The User organization:** This refers to the firm/organization. Here the user organization could be an NGO, any public or private sector service provider institution, any combination of institutions, etc. The prime goal of the user organization is to scaleup the intervention wherein the members could be from the resource team or new members may join as per the need.

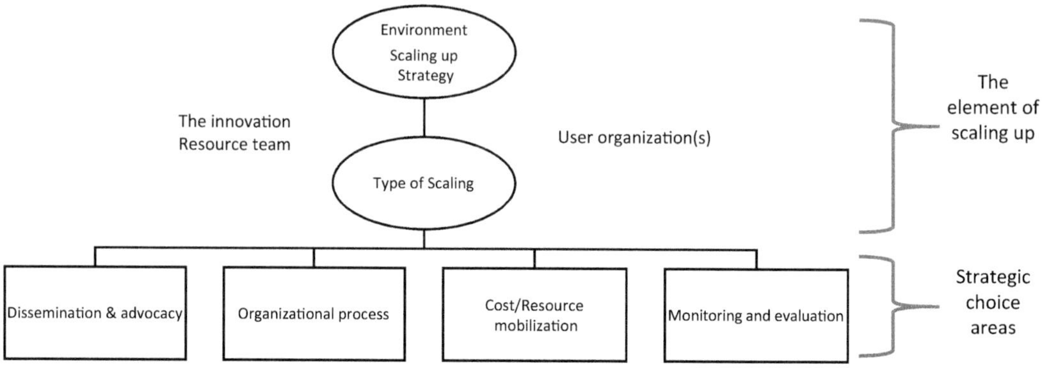

Fig. 13.3 The ExpandNet framework for scaling up

(iii) **Resource team: (**Individuals and organizations). This team provides technical assistance in scaling up the intervention on a large scale. Team members of various organizations like NGOs, private organizations, government bodies having researchers, trainers, program managers, community representatives, etc. could be the member of resource team.

(iv) **Innovation:** Refers to a combination of interventions that is to be scaled up.

The Strategic choice areas: The major elements of scaling-up have many implications for the scaling-up strategy referring to the plans and actions necessary to determine the policies for better rolling-out of the intervention on a larger scale. Planning and implementing a scaling-up strategy also involves making a number of strategic choices related to-

(i) **The type of scaling up process** needs to be identified at the planning phase: Various approaches can be undertaken for scaling up activity as there are four types of scaling up process: <u>*expansion, replication, collaboration.*</u>

- Extending organizational structures and/or service offerings is referred to as **<u>expansion</u>** (geographical expansion, expansion of population reached). ***Replication*** refers to implementing new, innovative, or good practices in other, more, or less independent organizations and setting. The two poles of a continuum or ideal type can be thought of as expansion and replication. In reality, they frequently overlap, and promoting and inhibiting forces are somewhat similar.

(ii) **Dissemination and advocacy approaches** are the methods by which the intervention is communicated to the user organization. Approaches could include training, orientation sessions, peer exchange, utilizing mass media or any other channels.

(iii) **User organization** Critical component is identification of new partners or organizations for expansion of the intervention.

(iv) **Costs of scaling up and resource utilization** include ensuring availability of adequate funds or resources for scaling process.

13.5 Scalability Assessment

The fundamental step in the process of scaling up is assessing if the intervention will have an impact similar to where the intervention was tested [6, 7, 12] and to avoid unwanted resource wastage and efforts to scaleup any intervention [13]. Successful scale-up requires a comprehensive analysis and strategic planning of the system to which the intervention will be implemented [14]. Evidence shows that there is need to identify the key barriers and facilitators for successful scaleup. Figure 13.4 explains various factors that

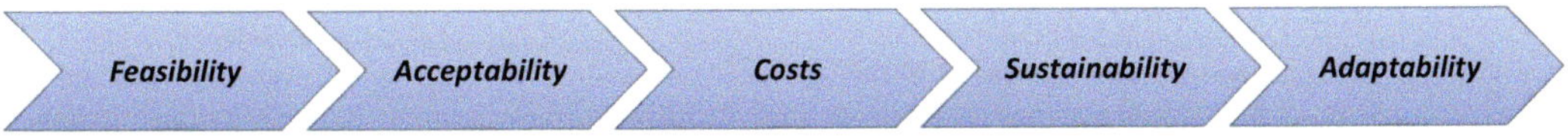

Fig. 13.4 Explaining factors influencing scalability

need to be assessed before scaling up an intervention [5].

The international health field has identified some key points to consider while planning for a scale-up [14]:

1. ***Scaling-up is a complex process and must be handled strategically*** by including key stakeholders including researchers', policymakers, beneficiaries, etc. during planning as well as implementation stages to address the barriers comprehensively.
2. Pilot projects need to be planned to keep in mind the sustainability, large-scale implementation, financial resources, and political commitments; thus, the planning for scale-up should happen during the planning phase of an intervention design.
3. ***Financial resources in support of scale-up should be given adequate attention*** to understanding the costs of scale-up and set financial commitments before the start of the project.
4. ***Robust Monitoring and Evaluation framework*** to understand the phasewise events that are happening and to take corrective measures during the process of scaling up.
5. ***"One size fit all" approach does not suit to scaling up strategy***. Every situation or intervention is unique and thus the strategy should be tailored independently.

13.6 A Three-Step, Ten Task Process for Effective Scaling up [15]

The "scaling up" concept has gradually become more popular as with time it has been observed that on extending the reach of an intervention the possibility of the intervention not showing similar result has increased. Thus, the scaling up management (SUM) have developed a framework for effective scaling up [15]-

A. ***Step 1: Develop a Scaling Up Plan.***
   1. Task 1: Create a Vision.
      (i) The Model: What Is Being Scaled Up?
      (ii) The Methods: How Will Scaling Up Be Accomplished?
      (iii) Organizational Roles: Who Performs the Key Functions?
      (iv) Dimensions of Scaling Up: Where and For Whom Does Scaling Up Occur?
   2. Task 2: Assess Scalability.
      (i) Determining the Viability of the Model for Scaling Up.
      (ii) Analyzing the Organizational and Social Context.
   3. Task 3: Fill Information Gaps.
   4. Task 4: Prepare a Scaling Up Plan.

B. ***Step 2: Establish the Pre-Conditions for Scaling Up.***
   1. Task 5: Legitimize Change.
   2. Task 6: Build a Constituency.
   3. Task 7: Realign and Mobilize Resources.

C. **Step 3: Implement the Scaling Up Process.**
   1. Task 8: Modify Organizational Structures.
   2. Task 9: Coordinate Action.
   3. Task 10: Track Performance and Maintain Momentum.

Scaling Up Management framework evolved from "strategic management" field, i.e., all the three broad steps cover theoretical and practical aspects of strategic planning and execution of an intervention.

Step 1 is centered on best practices associated with planning strategically whereas **step 2** emphasizes the political and change management aspect associated with policy change, agreement building etc. At the end of the process, the operational aspects of complex and multifactorial reform are emphasized.

13.7 Intervention Scalability Assessment Tool

The tool [13, 16] was developed to assist policymakers to systematically assess the suitability of intervention for scale-up. A scalability assessment checklist (Table 13.1) is referred for further reference.

The tool consists of three sections.

- PART A: Includes information on the existing public health issue, the context in which it is planned, the intervention will be scaled up.
- PART B: Examines the execution and feasibility factors relating to all potential scale-up aspects.
- PART C: Summarize information collected to aid the scalability process.

Table 13.1 Scalability assessment category (adapted from Scaling Up—From Vision to Large-Scale Change: Tools for Practitioners) for details read—Scaling Up—From Vision to Large-Scale Change: Tools for Practitioners

Assessment category
How convincing is the scaling strategy?
Is the intervention credible?
How strong is the support for change?
Does the intervention have relative advantage over existing practice?
How easy is the intervention to transfer and adopt?
How good is the fit between the intervention and adopting organization?
Is there a sustainable source of financing?

13.8 Barriers to Scale-up

Researchers have identified many barriers that can inhibit the acceptance of best practices even when known merits of the intervention exists, these barriers may exist at many levels of health system [17–19].

Developing countries like India have very limited resources and these are often inequitably distributed amongst various regions and urban/rural areas. Thus scaling-up requires effective policies to be in place at all levels of a health system to overcome barriers such as-

Resource mobilization challenges.

Weaknesses in infrastructure and support systems.

Lack of qualified managers and staff.

Conflict with Laws, policies, and regulations and Lack of clear implementation policies.

Cultural sensitivity or endurance to a new policy or practice.

Q.13.1

Refer to the case study on Raipur rani project and Bellary model. Discuss the scalability of the intervention.

References

1. Lobb R, Colditz GA. Implementation science and its application to population health. Annu Rev Public Health. 2013;34:235–51.
2. Aarons GA, Sklar M, Mustanski B, Benbow N, Brown CH. "Scaling-out" evidence-based interventions to new populations or new health care delivery systems. Implement Sci. 2017;12(1):111.

3. Campbell DT. Factors relevant to the validity of experiments in social settings. Psychol Bull. 1957;54(4):297–312.
4. Ben Charif A, Zomahoun HTV, LeBlanc A, Langlois L, Wolfenden L, Yoong SL, et al. Effective strategies for scaling up evidence-based practices in primary care: a systematic review. Implement Sci. 2017;12(1):139.
5. Milat AJ, King L, Bauman AE, Redman S. The concept of scalability: increasing the scale and potential adoption of health promotion interventions into policy and practice. Health Promot Int. 2013;28(3):285–98.
6. WHO Practical guidance for scaling up health service innovations [Internet]. 2009. [cited 2022 Jan 3]. Available from: https://www.who.int/reproductivehealth/publications/strategic_approach/9789241598521/en/.
7. Regions for Health Network, Euregio Meuse-Rhin/Maas-Rhein/Maas-Rijn, World Health Organization. Regional Office for Europe. Scaling up projects and initiatives for better health: from concepts to practice [Internet]. Copenhagen: World Health Organization. Regional Office for Europe; 2016. [cited 2022 Jan 3].Available from: https://apps.who.int/iris/handle/10665/343809.
8. Uvin P, Miller D. Paths to scaling-up: alternative strategies for local nongovernmental organizations. Hum Organ. 2008;55(3):344–54.
9. Hasan R, Reich M, Fink G. Agenda-setting of population in Bangladesh and West Bengal and impact on fertility. 40.
10. Kirkup B. Scaling up health service delivery—from pilot innovations to policies and programmes. Public Health. 2009;123(9):638–9.
11. WHO Nine steps for developing a scaling-up strategy [Internet]. 2010. [cited 2022 Jan 4]. Available from: https://www.who.int/reproductivehealth/publications/strategic_approach/9789241500319/en/.
12. [PDF] Scaling Up—A Conceptual and Operational Framework | Semantic Scholar [Internet]. [cited 2022 Jan 4]. Available from: https://www.semanticscholar.org/paper/Scaling-Up-%E2%80%93-A-Conceptual-and-Operational-Framework-Cooley-Tacher/90c8da014b6d0ea0465f2612d4491f908d42e57c.
13. Milat A, Lee K, Conte K, Grunseit A, Wolfenden L, van Nassau F, et al. Intervention scalability assessment tool: a decision support tool for health policy makers and implementers. Health Res Policy Syst. 2020;18(1):1.
14. Resource-scale-up-health-systems-strengthening.pdf [Internet]. [cited 2022 Jan 4]. Available from: https://www.fhi360.org/sites/default/files/media/documents/resource-scale-up-health-systems-strengthening.pdf.
15. Services C for E. CES. Scaling Up—From Vision to Large-Scale Change: A Management Framework for Practitioners. [cited 2022 Jan 5]. Available from: www.effectiveservices.org/.
16. The Australian Prevention Partnership Centre and the NSW Ministry of Health. The intervention scalability assessment tool: a guide for assessing the scalability of health interventions. The Australian Partnership Prevention Centre, NSW Ministry of Health, University of Sydney, University of Newcastle; 2019. p. 30.
17. Hardee K, Ashford L, Rottach E, Jolivet R, Kiesel R. The policy dimensions of scaling up health initiatives. Washington, DC: Futures Group, Health Policy Project; 2012. Available from: https://www.healthpolicyproject.com/index.cfm?ID=publications&get=pubID&pubID=83.
18. Mangham LJ, Hanson K. Scaling up in international health: what are the key issues? Health Policy Plan. 2010;25(2):85–96.
19. Mccannon CJ, Berwick DM, Massoud MR. The science of large-scale change in global health. JAMA. 2007;298(16):1937–9. https://doi.org/10.1001/jama.298.16.1937.

14 Quality Assurance and Dissemination of Findings

Sutapa Bandyopadhyay Neogi
and Anuj Kumar Pandey

Learning Objectives
After going through this section, participants will be able to:

- Describe the concept of quality assurance.
- Describe frameworks/components of quality assurance.
- Describes the sequential steps, for measuring, implementing, and assuring a quality public health intervention.
- Describe ways and means of dissemination of findings of a public health intervention.

14.1 Introduction to Quality Assurance

The importance of quality cannot be ignored. Despite its importance, there have been limited sustained QA efforts in the developing countries till date. Systematic efforts to improve the quality based on the study findings are required [1].

S. Bandyopadhyay Neogi (✉) · A. K. Pandey
Department of Health Systems and Implementation Research, International Institute of Health Management Research (IIHMR), New Delhi, India
e-mail: sutapa@iihmrdelhi.edu.in; anuj@iihmrdelhi.edu.in

Research is necessary to ascertain the safety and effectiveness of an intervention. Intervention studies form the foundation for "evidence-based medicine," but such research can only be relied upon only if it is conducted as per the principles and standards jointly referred to as "Good Clinical Research Practice" (GCP) [2]. These WHO's principles of GCP provide an overview and practical advice on the application and implementation of internationally accepted principles for GCP and one of the essential principles is to assure the quality of every aspect of an intervention.

14.1.1 Principle 14 of the GCP Guideline States

> *"…development of procedures to control, assure, and improve the quality of data and records and the quality and effectiveness of processes and activities related to the conduct and oversight of clinical research."*

The fundamentals to the success of an intervention involve researchers' compliance with the study protocols, informed consent process and quality of the generated data (accurate and reliable).

Thus, quality is defined as the measure of the ability of a product, process, or service to satisfy stated or implied needs. A high-quality product readily meets those needs [3].

S. Bandyopadhyay Neogi, A. K. Pandey (eds.), *Designing and Evaluating Public Health Interventions*, https://doi.org/10.1007/978-981-97-9574-1_14

14.2 Difference between "Quality Control," "Quality Assurance," and "Quality Improvement"

"**Quality control** [2]" implies to the steps taken during an intervention (e.g., supervision, monitoring, and any review authorities) to make sure that the intervention follows the guidelines laid down in the protocol.

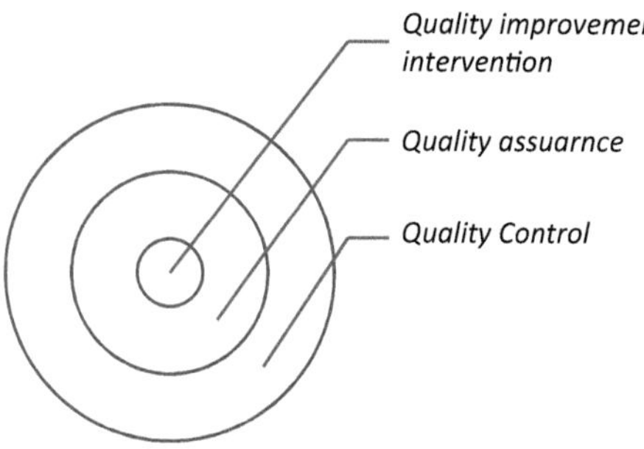

"**Quality assurance**" implies the systematic process which determines if the quality system is working and is effective or not.

- This is performed during the duration of an intervention or after the intervention.
- This is carried out through independent auditing of quality control activities or by some regulatory authorities through inspection of quality control systems and activities.
- The purpose of auditing is to examine the intervention for its conduct and compliance with the protocol, SOPs, and other applicable regulatory requirements.

"**Quality improvement**" means a systematic process of utilizing the insights gained through the quality assurance audits and activities and utilizing this knowledge to make changes in the intervention process in order to increase the ability to fulfill quality requirements.

14.3 How to Ensure Quality of an Intervention

Some of the steps that can be paid attention to ensure the quality of an intervention are enlisted below:

1. **Adherence to the study protocol**: Researchers should adhere to the design and approved protocols.
2. **Accordance with the ethical standards**: Along with strict adherence to the procedures laid down in the study protocol, it is also essential to implement them in accordance with the ethical standards.
3. **Thorough recording of all observations**: A meticulous recording of all observations, not only observations, but sometimes even the process of research itself is required. This may also include the field notes.
4. **Well versed with the literature:** Incorporates or considers what has worked and what has not worked while designing the intervention.
5. **Replication by other investigators.**

14.4 The Quality Assurance Process

Quality assurance [1] is a cyclic process that needs to be applied flexibly to meet the need of the intervention or any program. Quality assessment is a cyclical/continuous process and not a one-time effort. It is an incremental process, or an internal process driven by motivated staff where improvements are added with each cycle.

The entire process is explained in Fig. 14.1, which may begin with a comprehensive effort to define the plan, procedures for quality assurance, setting up the standards and also communicating the standards. This ten-step process can be discussed as:

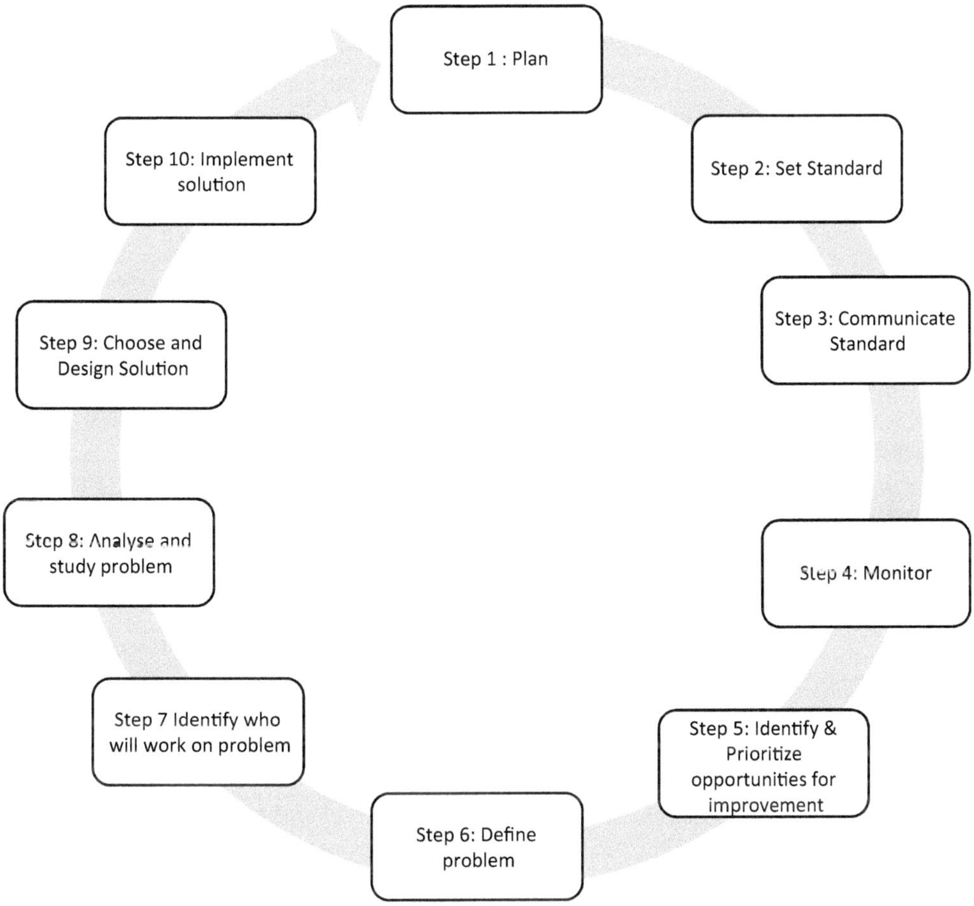

Fig. 14.1 Quality Assurance Cycle [4]

- Planning for Quality assurance
- Setting standards and specifications
- Communicating Guidelines and Standards
- Monitoring Quality
- Identifying Problems and Selecting Opportunities for Improvement
- Defining the Problem
- Choosing a Team
- Analyzing and Studying the Problem to Identify the Root Cause
- Developing Solutions and Actions for Quality Improvement
- Implementing and Evaluating Quality Improvement Efforts

QA makes use of the available guidelines and can be performed by members from the research committee called "***Internal quality assessment***" or by any third party named as "***external quality assessment.***"

The QA process has both advantages and disadvantages.

14.4.1 Advantages of Quality Assurance

- A major advantage includes **final costs reduction**—as the majority of the flaws can be

addressed at early stage of an intervention so that no time and effort is wasted on reworking and redoing to get the desired outcome.
- Enhanced motivation as the employees understands their value and also gets recognition for what they do.
- QA enhances collaborative approaches rather than supervisory thus decreasing the barriers between the workers and the managers.

14.4.2 Disadvantages

- Time-consuming — it requires a lot of time to train the staff to perform QA.
- High initial costs

14.5 Dissemination of Findings

The last objective after completing a research study is the dissemination of the findings for the wider use. Dissemination is the ***intended distribution of information and intervention materials to a particular public health or clinical practice audience.*** The intent or the evidence of dissemination has various goals like [5]-

- Spread Knowledge and associated outcome based on the intervention.
- Increase the extent of evidence on a large scale within or across multiple geographic areas.
- Increase people's enthusiasm for using and applying evidence.
- Increase people's ability to use evidence.
- Share with the researchers the lessons that were learned or to share what impact the intervention had on the community/target audience due the intervention.

Lessons learned [6]: This may be identified throughout the implementation of the intervention activities and may later-on be formally discussed with the funding agencies/researchers. This may help others develop and implement appropriate health intervention for their communities. This may include information related to:

- Challenges that the intervention addressed throughout the study like any factors that may hamper the success of an intervention.
- Best practices and strategies that the intervention utilized to address the identified challenges.
- Any new findings or new information evolved after the intervention that may be replicated in other similar study settings.
- Essential resources like human resources, funding requirements and supporting hands, etc. while implementing such intervention.

Dissemination strategies could be Active or Passive dissemination strategies.

1. **Active Dissemination strategies** [7]: This involves active efforts to spread the study findings or the generated evidence from the study.
    - This includes the "Traditional methods" of disseminating the research findings by *scientific peer-reviewed journal publications, presentation at scientific conferences, and scientific reports.*
    - *Scientific peer review* of the findings provides an assessment of the quality of the study design and study findings prior to dissemination.
    - These methods provide a wider dissemination of the research findings to the research audience.
    - This may also involve the policy and practice professionals with the responsibility, interest, and time to search and review articles for translation purposes.
    - This also facilitates the inclusion of the study into forthcoming published systematic reviews of the field, which is a "gold standard" of evidence-based or proof-of-impact research.
    - Along with publication, presentation of the findings at a scientific conferences and scientific reports is another essential step of dissemination.
2. **Passive Dissemination strategies**: This is the usual care or practice for findings dissemination. This includes uncontrolled spread of the information.

14.5.1 Common Methods of Dissemination Include

- Research findings in peer-reviewed journals and state-wide publications.
- Presenting the findings at any national/international conferences and meetings of professional associations.
- Presenting the intervention results to local community groups/stakeholders.
- Creating and distributing intervention outcome materials, such as guides, pamphlets, etc.
- Creating toolkits based on the findings of training materials and training curriculum.
- Sharing information related to the intervention through social media or disseminating the findings on the organization's website.
- Preparing and submitting progress reports with summary findings for the funders.
- Discussing interventions activities on local audio or audio-visual media.
- Advertising information in the local newspaper or issuing a press release.
- Hosting events for health promotion activities related to the study at health fairs or at any events as per the target audience.

Q.14.1
Refer to the case study on SSD. What were the different methods adopted to disseminate the study findings to the policy makers and to the community.

References

1. Brown LD, Franco LM, Rafeh N, Hatzell TA. Quality assurance of health care in developing countries. 2nd ed. Quality Assurance Project: Bethesda, MD; 1993. p. 33.
2. World Health Organization. (2005). Handbook for good clinical research practice (GCP): guidance for implementation. World Health Organization. https://iris.who.int/handle/10665/43392.
3. Quality assurance framework | National health systems resource centre | Technical Support Institute with National Health Mission [Internet]. [cited 2022 Apr 5]. Available from: http://qi.nhsrcindia.org/quality-assurance-framework.
4. JaypeeDigital | Quality assurance [Internet]. [cited 2024 Jan 4]. Available from: https://www.jaypeedigital.com/book/9789351529538/chapter/ch42.
5. Communication and dissemination strategies to facilitate the use of health-related evidence | Effective health care (EHC) Program [Internet]. [cited 2022 Apr 6]. Available from: https://effectivehealthcare.ahrq.gov/products/medical-evidence-communication/research-protocol.
6. Module 6: disseminating best practices [Internet]. [cited 2022 Apr 7]. Available from: https://www.ruralhealthinfo.org/toolkits/rural-toolkit/6/disseminating-best-practices.
7. McBride N. Dissemination phase of the intervention research framework: presentation and dissemination of results. In: McBride N, editor. Intervention research: a practical guide for developing evidence-based school prevention programmes [internet]. Singapore: Springer; 2016. p. 149–64. https://doi.org/10.1007/978-981-10-1011-8_11.

Case Study 1: Janani Suraksha Yojna (JSY)

15

Anuj Kumar Pandey
and Sutapa Bandyopadhyay Neogi

> "An intervention aimed at reducing maternal mortality."

This case study pertains to an intervention focused at reducing the maternal mortality in India. High incidence of maternal mortality has always been a concern to the program managers, researchers, and the policymakers. Several global initiatives have been implemented aimed at decreasing the maternal mortality, starting with the Safe Motherhood Initiative in 1987 [1].

It was observed that there existed an inverse correlation between institutional deliveries and maternal mortality. An inference was drawn that any intervention to increase institutional deliveries would result in a reduction in maternal mortality ratio (MMR). The probability of mortality is maximum in the first 48 hours after deliveries. Hence it was presumed that increased institutional deliveries would reduce maternal and neonatal mortality. National programs advocating for institutional deliveries in India, however, did not have any significant impact on the institutional delivery rates.

A. K. Pandey · S. Bandyopadhyay Neogi (✉)
Department of Health Systems and Implementation Research, International Institute of Health Management Research (IIHMR), New Delhi, India
e-mail: anuj@iihmrdelhi.edu.in; sutapa@iihmrdelhi.edu.in

Step 1: Is there enough evidence to say that a particular disease (maternal mortality in this case) is a substantial public health concern?

Response: Yes.—Supported by following facts. The proportion of the institutional delivery was around 40.8% during 2005–06 [2], i.e., before the launch of JSY. Indian Government focused on increasing the institutional delivery as a means to increase the maternal survival which was as high as 254 deaths per 100,000 live births as per the SRS report of 2004–05 [3].

India's National Health Policy (NHP) was introduced in year 2002, while the National Population Policy (NPP) was introduced in 2000. In order to meet its targets by 2010, the NPP planned to lower MMR to 100 per 100,000 live births. Additionally, NPP proposed a new target of increasing the institutional delivery by 80% [4]. Later, the National Rural Health Mission (NRHM) was founded in 2005 to meet the unachieved targets laid down by NPP and NHP. This indicated the need for new guidance for health policies and initiatives [5].

Step 2: Are there potential solutions/interventions to tackle the problem?

Response: Yes. It was thought that providing cash incentives to mothers would result in increased motivation for institutional deliveries. Some past experiences from India for providing cash incentives providing supported this viewpoint. **National Social Assistance Programme (NSAP**: *started 15th August 1995*) was initiated

S. Bandyopadhyay Neogi, A. K. Pandey (eds.), *Designing and Evaluating Public Health Interventions*, https://doi.org/10.1007/978-981-97-9574-1_15

as a social assistance program for the householders belonging to non-wealthier section [6]. This NSAP program has three broad sections with *National Maternity Benefit Scheme (NMBS)*" being one of them. Under NMBS, pregnant women received a cash support of Rs. 500/-per birth, and up to two live births who met the other eligibility criteria of age ≥ 19 years and were from below poverty line (BPL) households. The Maternal mortality in India before launch of JSY scheme was incongruously high and failed to meet MDG5. Thus with a broad goal of reducing the maternal deaths, Government of India (GOI) launched the Conditional cash transfer (CCT) program named Janani Suraksha Yojana (JSY) to encourage more institutional deliveries and thus reducing mortalities [5]. It was suggested to change the NMBS in order to implement the JSY, which falls under the National Rural Health Mission (NRHM) program. While NMBS has been associated with providing pregnant women from Below Poverty Line (BPL) families with a better diet, the Janani Suraksha Yojana established coordinated care systems by field level health workers to integrate cash assistance with all the intrapartum, delivery, and postpartum care in a healthcare facility [7].

Step 3: What is the level of evidence?

Response: A Cochrane review [8] conducted between November 2005 and May 2009 assessed the effectiveness of CCT. The objective was to assess if CCT was effective to improve access to healthcare facilities and later improve the health outcomes. Of 29 included studies, ten (four randomized controlled trials) met the inclusion criteria and were pooled for the study result synthesis.

Study findings suggest that CCT schemes have numerous benefits on overall health and wellbeing. The study reported that CCT scheme led to an overall uptake of preventive health seeking behavior and health outcomes. Although the study reported an improvement in the health outcomes, it is still unclear to attribute this improvement to which component of the scheme.

A randomized control trial [9] was conducted to see effectiveness of CCT on Child Health, under a national program in Mexico named "PROGRESA" which began in year 1997. The program was devised to address immediate population needs for those living below poverty. The eligible families received a cash transfer, which was around 20–30% of total household income.

During first 3 years, "PROGRESA" provided case transfer benefits to 10% of the families in Mexico which was close to 2.6 million families in 50,000 villages. As a part of the trial—320 treatment and 185 control villages were randomly selected across seven states (505 experimental villages) in Mexico during 1998. The study reported that the newborns in the treatment arm are 25.3% less likely to be unhealthy and fall sick. It was worth noting that in the treatment group, after 6 months of the program benefit, the illness rate was 39.5% less as compared to the control arm.

It is well documented that in LMICs, institutional delivery might reduce the neonatal mortality risk by 29% [10].

Step 4: Is it cost effective?

Response: There were no cost effectiveness studies done.

Step 5: Can the intervention be scaled up?

Response: The intervention was later scaled up.

15.1 Janani Suraksha Yojana (JSY)

Also named as "A safe motherhood intervention".

JSY was launched in India in April 2005 under the flagship program of the Government of India named as National Rural Health Mission (NRHM). This flagship program—JSY was centrally sponsored, implemented with an objective to reduce the maternal and infant mortality by increasing the institutional deliveries [11, 12]. Under this program-

- Cash assistance is provided to eligible women. If women deliver in a government accredited health center, they are entitled for the benefit of the scheme.
- The program primarily targets low-income pregnant women and provides a special bene-

fit for regions with less than 25% institutional delivery rates. These states are referred to as low-performing states (LPS) under the program, while the others are termed as high performing states (HPSs).

- Under the scheme, the women health volunteers named as ASHAs (accredited social health activist) also receive incentives. These incentives are usually performance based. ASHAs promote and encourage pregnant women for institutional delivery.

In JSY, the financial assistance was different based on the place of residence (urban/rural) of the women and states which they belonged to.

1. **Is JSY successful in increasing institutional deliveries?**

A study representing a nationally representative sample for the year 2015–16, aimed at understanding the coverage of JSY at district levels. It found a difference in the regional coverage of the scheme. The study reported that JSY coverage was 36.4% with geographical variability and clustering in its coverage. These clustering were significant across regions, districts, and socioeconomic groups [13].

An evaluation [5] was done in large states (Bihar, Madhya Pradesh, Rajasthan, Odisha, and Uttar Pradesh), which constitutes 39% of the total population of India. Assessment was done using both quantitative and qualitative research methods to check for surge in institutional deliveries (among low-income categories population) and barriers and facilitators in the implementation of the scheme. Findings indicate that there was a significant increase in the institutional deliveries amongst the low performing states in India. This increase could be attributed to immense popularity of the JSY scheme as 81% of the mothers had knowledge of JSY scheme and the associated benefits. With the exception of Jharkhand and Chhattisgarh, where the sample's representation of BPL and SC/ST was larger than that of the population, the study also demonstrated an equity in excess of women to institutional deliveries.

2. **Did a rise in institutional deliveries result in a reduction of maternal and neonatal mortality rates?**

Evaluations to this effect has demonstrated that JSY did not bring about any reduction in MMR and NMR [14].

Although JSY has increased the coverage of interventions, the program's main objective is to enhance health outcomes. The author noted that the number of neonatal and perinatal mortality linked to JSY has decreased, but JSY did not, however, appear to have a discernible impact on the quantity of perinatal or neonatal fatalities.

Discussion Points

- Effectiveness of Janani Suraksha Yojana and its comparison with other Conditional cash transfer benefits.
- What are the learnings from the trial?

References

1. Starrs AM. Safe motherhood initiative: 20 years and counting. Lancet. 2006;368(9542):1130–2. https://doi.org/10.1016/S0140-6736(06)69385-9.
2. National family health survey. [cited 2022 Jul 18]. Available from: http://rchiips.org/nfhs/.
3. SRS—maternal mortality bulletin | Government of India. [cited 2022 Jul 18]. Available from: https://censusindia.gov.in/census.website/data/SRSMMB.
4. Rai RK, Tulchinsky TH. Addressing the sluggish Progress in reducing maternal mortality in India. Asia Pac J Public Health. 2015;27(2):NP1161–9.
5. Lim SS, Dandona L, Hoisington JA, James SL, Hogan MC, Gakidou E. India's Janani Suraksha Yojana, a conditional cash transfer programme to increase births in health facilities: an impact evaluation. Lancet. 2010;375(9730):2009–23.
6. NSAP.pdf [Internet]. [cited 2022 Feb 28]. Available from: https://megcnrd.gov.in/forms/NSAP.pdf.
7. Rai RK, Singh PK. Janani Suraksha Yojana: the conditional cash transfer scheme to reduce maternal mortality in India—a need for reassessment. WHO South-East Asia J Public Health. 2012;1(4):362.
8. Lagarde M, Haines A, Palmer N. The impact of conditional cash transfers on health outcomes and use of health services in low and middle

income countries. Cochrane Database Syst Rev [Internet]. 2009;2009(4):CD008137. https://doi.org/10.1002/14651858.CD008137.
9. Gertler P. Do conditional cash transfers improve child health? Evidence from PROGRESA's control randomized experiment. Am Econ Rev. 2004;94(2):336–41.
10. Tura G, Fantahun M, Worku A. The effect of health facility delivery on neonatal mortality: systematic review and meta-analysis. BMC Pregnancy Childbirth. 2013;13(1):18.
11. Yojana JS. Janani Suraksha Yojana (JSY). 28.
12. Janani Suraksha Yojana: National Health Mission. [cited 2022 Feb 28]. Available from: https://www.nhp.gov.in/janani-suraksha-yojana-jsy-_pg.
13. Mishra PS, Kumar P, Srivastava S. Regional inequality in the Janani Suraksha Yojana coverage in India: a geo-spatial analysis. Int J Equity Health. 2021;20(1):24.
14. Randive B, Diwan V, Costa AD. India's conditional cash transfer Programme (the JSY) to promote institutional birth: is there an association between institutional birth proportion and maternal mortality? PLoS One. 2013;8(6):e67452.

16 Case Study 2: Home-Based Newborn Care (HBNC)

Anuj Kumar Pandey
and Sutapa Bandyopadhyay Neogi

"An intervention aimed at addressing high neonatal mortality in India."

This case study is related to a public health intervention aimed at addressing high neonatal mortality in India. The intervention revolves around providing Home-Based Newborn Care in communities. Let us understand the case study and examine the details.

Step 1: Is there enough evidence to say that a particular disease (neonatal mortality in this case) is a public health problem?

Response: Yes. This is supported by the following facts. Globally, 2.6 million neonatal deaths have been estimated of which 0.76 million occur in India [1]. About 7.6 lakh infants die within the first 4 weeks of births in India catering to a neonatal mortality rate (NMR) of 26/1000 live births. Looking at the mortality within 1 year of life, i.e., the infant mortality rate, it is 39/1000 live births [2, 3]. Home deliveries accounts for 63% of all deliveries in the developing nations, whereas 83% of the births in the rural India were home deliveries [4].

Step 2: Are there potential solutions/interventions to tackle the problem?

Response: **Yes**. We have ample evidence to imply that home/community-based newborn care is crucial for reduction in neonatal mortality.

- ***The Lancet Every Newborn Study Group*** has evaluated a set of interventions focusing on the continuum of care and other intra and post-partum services. The objective was to model the result of such interventions and assess the cost effectiveness for wider scaling in other 75 high burden countries. It has been reported that an increase in the overall coverage of interventions at all the stages since preconception, until delivery and post-partum care might avert 71% of the neonatal deaths (1·9 million [range 1·6–2·1 million]), 33% of stillbirths (0·82 million [0·60–0·93 million]), and 54% of maternal deaths (0·16 million [0·14–0·17 million]) per year [5].
- In countries, where coverage of services are poor and neonatal mortality rates are high (more than 40/1000 livebirths), home-based newborn care can be a strategy to reduce neonatal deaths [6].
- The ***Cochrane review*** on community-based interventions including 18 cluster randomized/quasi-randomized trials, recorded a significant

A. K. Pandey · S. Bandyopadhyay Neogi (✉)
Department of Health Systems and Implementation Research, International Institute of Health Management Research (IIHMR), New Delhi, India
e-mail: anuj@iihmrdelhi.edu.in; sutapa@iihmrdelhi.edu.in

S. Bandyopadhyay Neogi, A. K. Pandey (eds.), *Designing and Evaluating Public Health Interventions*, https://doi.org/10.1007/978-981-97-9574-1_16

reduction in neonatal mortality (RR 0.76; 95% CI 0.68 to 0.84), stillbirths (RR 0.84; 95% CI 0.74 to 0.97) and perinatal mortality (RR 0.80; 95% CI 0.71 to 0.91). This reduction was attributed to the robust implementation of community focused interventions [7]. This qualifies as Level 1 evidence.

Step 3: What is the level of evidence?

Response: Although there was emerging evidence that home-based newborn care was effective in bringing down the mortality, such evidence from India was not available in 1990s. Community-based interventions should be context specific as these are influenced by socio cultural factors. Hence it was mandatory to have some evidence from India to understand whether it would work or not. The study yielded level 1 evidence.

16.1 Gadchiroli Model: Home-Based Neonatal Care (HBNC)

A field trial of HBNC, during 1990s in a tribal district of Gadchiroli, Maharashtra aimed to design and evaluate an effective intervention for reducing the neonatal mortality in India and other developing nations. The overall aim was also to enhance delivery of primary neonatal care by volunteers available in select villages who were later trained to provide healthcare services to the newborns. The study assessed the effectiveness of this low-cost approach of identifying and training community members for reducing the neonatal mortality [8]. This study trial was undertaken in 39 intervention and 47 control villages of Gadchiroli district.

Discussion points: Study Design, Sampling strategy, Sample size, Quality control parameters, Consent, and ethics.

16.1.1 Effectiveness of Intervention

There was a net percentage reduction of 25.5 (62.2%) in the neonatal mortality in the intervention arm as compared to the control. However, Infant mortality showed a decline by 38.8 (45.7%) and perinatal mortality showed a decline by 47.8(71%) in the intervention arm as compared to the control ($p < 0.001$). The study also reported a significant ($p < 0.001$) decline in the overall case fatality due to neonatal sepsis from 16.6% (163 cases) to 2.8% (71 cases) implying the effectiveness of the treatment intervention by the trained health workers in the villages.

16.2 Are There Any Ethical Issues Involved?

- **Ethical consideration:** The Gadchiroli Model has undergone a debate on the ethical aspects of the study [9]. Researchers identified various questions owing to the study design. Questions were raised for not offering treatment in the control arm, even when treatment option was well known and established [10].

Step 4: Is it cost effective?

Response: Economic evaluation was not conducted as part of this study. However, a detailed costing analysis showed that the cost of per neonate care was around US$ 5.3. This cost of care was considerably lower than that of the hospital based neonatal care which ranged between $17.3–$44.2/day in a metropolitan city of India with a mean hospitalization of 8·8 days. This was around $17/neonate in Vellore during 1992 for providing interventions similar to the study. Researchers have noted that HBNC care averted one death/18 neonates who received the HBNC intervention [4].

Step 5: Can the intervention be scaled up?

Response: Scalability of the intervention was considered in phases. The Gadchiroli trial was undertaken in a tribal district of Maharashtra (a state in India). Due to the absence of multiple geographies and type of population, the intervention lacked external validity. Therefore, the decision to scale up could not be taken immediately. Owing to the robust evidence, two similar projects were proposed in order to replicate the study in other geographies and population of India.

16.3 The ANKUR Project (2001–2005) [11, 12]

Post success of HBNC trial, another study named Child mortality study was conducted by 13 NGOs to assess the replicability of the trial activities.

Later, "The Child Deaths Study and Action Group" (CDSAG), Maharashtra team decided to initiate another intervention trial named as "Ankur" (meaning The Sprout) as one of the largest evaluations of HBNC trials. Timeline of HBNC trial from evidence generation to replication study to HBNC program rollout in India is shown in Fig. 16.1. The overall aim was to assess if the trial activities can be replicated to other geographies with diverse populations.

Study Design: Multi-site intervention trial with pre–post comparison.

Project Findings: At replication study ANKUR, study reported 85% coverage of HBNC with 51% decline in NMR and 47% decline in IMR.

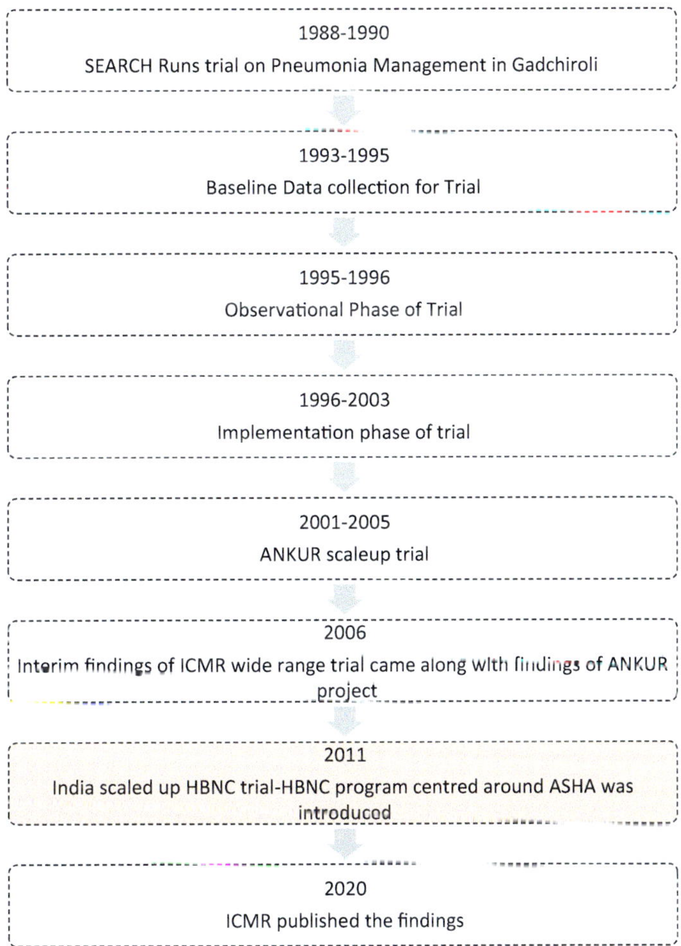

Fig. 16.1 Timeline of HBNC trial from evidence generation to replication study to HBNC program rollout in India

16.4 Indian Council of Medical Research (ICMR) Study [13]

Study Design: A multi-centric study, three-armed, community-based cluster randomized trial.

Study site: Five districts representing diverse geographies in India. Unit of randomization being the primary health centers.

Intervention: As this was three arm cluster randomized trial, thus in two arms, the intervention package was delivered by special recruited community level health workers or by the Shishu Rakshak (SR). In the other one arm, intervention was delivered by existing front-line workers named as Anganwadi workers (AWW). The control arm newborns received routine care being provided by the nearest healthcare facilities.

Trial registration: It was registered as a Cluster Randomized Trial on December 11, 2011 [14].

Project Findings: The study found that the risk of mortality among the neonates were 25% lower in the Shishu Rakshak arm with an aOR of 0.75, 95% CI 0.57 to 0.99. The study reported a significant decline in early neonatal mortality of 32%, infant mortality of 33% and young infant mortality of 27%. It was worth noting that in the AWW arm there was no significant difference in the mortality change when compared with that of the control arm neonates.

The project concluded that there is a significant reduction in NMR when the neonatal care is being delivered at home by a dedicated worker even in settings with low NMR.

Step 6: Can the intervention be a part of the national program?

Response: Yes. The national HBNC program positioned around Accredited Social Health Activists (ASHAs) who are the front-line workers was introduced as a national policy in 2011. HBNC is now one of the community level programs for improving neonatal health outcomes.

Discussion Points

- Evidence on effectiveness of intervention by ASHAs.
- Evidence on cost effectiveness of intervention.
- Scalability of HBNC program.
- Current program impact.

References

1. Wang H, Bhutta ZA, Coates MM, Coggeshall M, Dandona L, Diallo K, et al. Global, regional, national, and selected subnational levels of stillbirths, neonatal, infant, and under-5 mortality, 1980–2015: a systematic analysis for the global burden of disease study 2015. Lancet. 2016;388(10053):1725–74.
2. Revised HBNC operational guidelines 2014 English.pdf [Internet]. [cited 2021 Dec 15]. Available from: https://nhsrcindia.org/sites/default/files/2021-03/Revised%20HBNC%20Operational%20Guidelines%202014%20English.pdf.
3. Census of India: Sample Registration System (SRS)-statistical report 2016.
4. Bang AT, Bang RA, Baitule SB, Reddy MH, Deshmukh MD. Effect of home-based neonatal care and management of sepsis on neonatal mortality: field trial in rural India. Lancet. 1999;354(9194):1955–61.
5. Bhutta ZA, Das JK, Bahl R, Lawn JE, Salam RA, Paul VK, et al. Can available interventions end preventable deaths in mothers, newborn babies, and stillbirths, and at what cost? Lancet. 2014;384(9940):347–70.
6. Newborn mortality [Internet]. [cited 2022 Jul 18]. Available from: https://www.who.int/news-room/fact-sheets/detail/levels-and-trends-in-child-mortality-report-2021.
7. Lassi ZS, Haider BA, Bhutta ZA. Community-based intervention packages for reducing maternal and neonatal morbidity and mortality and improving neonatal outcomes. Cochrane Database Syst Rev. 2010;(11):CD007754. https://doi.org/10.1002/14651858.CD007754.pub2. Update in: Cochrane Database Syst Rev. 2015 Mar 23;(3):CD007754. https://doi.org/10.1002/14651858.CD007754.pub3.
8. Bang AT, Bang RA, Reddy HM. Home-based neonatal care: summary and applications of the field trial in rural Gadchiroli, India (1993 to 2003). J Perinatol. 2005;25(1):S108–22.
9. Bang A. Was the Gadchiroli trial ethical? Response from the principal investigator. Indian J Med Ethics

[Internet]. 2010;7(1):12–4. https://doi.org/10.20529/IJME.2010.004.
10. Bandewar SV, John TA. SEARCH's HBNC trial: towards a broader debate on the ethics of social intervention research. Indian J Med Ethics. 2011;8(2):78–85. https://doi.org/10.20529/IJME.2011.032.
11. vdocument.in [Internet]. [cited 2021 Dec 15]. Process documentation-ANKUR project | PDF | Non Governmental Organization | Leadership.
12. Mavalankar DDV, Raman P. ANKUR Project: a case study of replication of home based newborn care. Ahmedabad: Centre for Management Health Services, Indian Institute of Management. p. 25.
13. Rasaily R, Saxena N, Pandey S, On behalf of the ICMR-HBMYI Study Group, et al. Effect of home-based newborn care on neonatal and infant mortality: a cluster randomised trial in India. BMJ Glob Health. 2020;5:e000680. Available from: https://gh.bmj.com/content/5/9/e000680.
14. ICMR clinical trial registration details [Internet]. [cited 2021 Dec 16]. Available from: https://www.ctri.nic.in/.

Case Study 3: IV Iron Sucrose

17

Anuj Kumar Pandey
and Sutapa Bandyopadhyay Neogi

"An intervention on management of anemia in pregnancy"

This case study is regarding management of anemia in pregnancy. The intervention is around parenteral therapy for management of moderate and severe anemia during pregnancy.

Step 1: Is there enough evidence to say that a particular disease (anemia in pregnancy in this case) is a significant public health problem?

Response: Anemia at the time of pregnancy is a known risk factor for perinatal and maternal mortality. It is well known that it increases the chances of having low birth weight babies (i.e., babies ≤2500 g) with poor health status in later life and thus chances of morbidity and mortality increases. Literature suggests that such babies are more inclined to develop heart and other metabolic diseases in life. SDG target 2.2 reiterates to end all form of malnutrition by addressing the nutritional demands of all age group individuals, especially adolescent girls, pregnant, and lactating women [1]. Literatures suggest that anemia affects more than half, i.e., 50% of pregnant women in India. Thus, WHO global target aims to reduce the global burden of anemia among the women of reproductive age by 50% by 2025 relative to 2010 prevalence [2].

Step 2: Are there potential solutions/interventions to tackle the problem?

Response: There are various treatment options for anemia during pregnancy. Among various other treatment modalities, oral iron is well-established treatment option in India, which has been a part of national program since decades. However, compliance to oral regimen has remained a big challenge. To meet the requirement of rapid replenishment of iron in women during pregnancy, parental iron therapy came into practice as an alternative. IV iron sucrose is one such example, which was widely used in pregnant women in public and private sectors [3, 4]. Its efficacy for increasing hemoglobin (Hb) had been studied through numerous small studies. However, its safety and effectiveness for improving clinical outcomes had not been established through well controlled robust studies [5]. Hence, it was not being considered by the Ministry for inclusion in the national program.

Step 3: What is the level of evidence?

Response: Dearth of evidence on safety and efficacy of intravenous iron therapy over oral iron led to the conceptualization of a randomized controlled trial. The objective was to assess the effectiveness of intravenous iron sucrose as compared

A. K. Pandey · S. Bandyopadhyay Neogi (✉)
Department of Health Systems and Implementation Research, International Institute of Health Management Research (IIHMR), New Delhi, India
e-mail: anuj@iihmrdelhi.edu.in; sutapa@iihmrdelhi.edu.in

S. Bandyopadhyay Neogi, A. K. Pandey (eds.), *Designing and Evaluating Public Health Interventions*, https://doi.org/10.1007/978-981-97-9574-1_17

to oral iron during pregnancy. The study was funded by WHO India, in collaboration with Ministry of Health and Family Welfare, Government of India. With a sample size of more than 2000 pregnant women, it was one of the largest ever trial on anemia which was undertaken in a pragmatic care setting.

17.1 Findings of the FeSPAW (Ferrous Sucrose in Pregnant Anemic Women in India) Trial [6]

Study Design: Open label, randomized control trial. The study had two arms of equal size.

Study setting: Hospital based, undertaken at four Government Medical colleges in India. Women with hemoglobin level between 5–9 gm/dl were randomized either to the intervention iron sucrose or to the control arm keeping in mind other inclusion and exclusion criteria [6].

Study results were not sufficient to conclude the superiority of intravenous iron as compared to the oral iron in reducing the adverse maternal outcomes (aOR 0·95, 95% CI 0·70–1·29). The Hb (mean difference ranging from 0·45 to 0·95 g/dl) was significantly higher and faster after the therapy (6 wks. Post-randomization, delivery, and 6 wks. postpartum) in the IV arm. The likelihood of a woman to have Hb $\geq$ 11 mg/dl at 6 weeks postpartum was more (AOR 2·48, 95% CI 1·98, 3·10) in IV arm. IV iron sucrose was safe with 13·4% women reporting minor self-limiting adverse effects at the time of infusion and 24% experiencing late minor adverse effects.

Comparing the adverse outcome—Blood transfusion (BT) among women in intravenous iron arm was less as compared to the standard therapy arm group women. Number needed to treat was 27 which indicated that for every 27 women who received intravenous iron therapy instead of standard therapy, i.e., oral iron, one BT could be avoided [7].

Step 4: Is it cost effective?

Response: Alongside the trial, a well-planned economic evaluation [8] was also undertaken to inform policy makers about the relative cost and benefits associated with intravenous iron as compared to the standard therapy, i.e., oral iron. The study considered safe delivery outcome as the outcome for cost-effectiveness. Incremental cost-effectiveness ratio (ICER) represented the incremental cost for every additional safe delivery outcome analyzed from a societal perspective. Intravenous iron therapy was regarded as more effective whereas it was more costly also when compared with the standard therapy, i.e., oral iron. Calculated ICER was Rs.31,951 (445.2 USD) per safe delivery.

At a limit of half GNI (INR 57,230, 797.4 USD), intervention arm group continued to be cost effective in 67% of the iterations in the model. At the available ICER, for every 32 severely anemic pregnant woman treated with intravenous iron sucrose, one additional pregnant woman will have safe delivery.

Step 5: Can the intervention be scaled up?

Response: IV iron sucrose was already being administered in public and private hospitals. But, it was not included in the policy guidelines for want of robust evidence. Based on the trial results and cost-effectiveness findings, the same has now been included in the policy guidelines under the flagship program Anemia Mukt Bharat or Anemia Free India [4].

Discussion Points

- Evidence on impact of anemia or deranged Hb level amongst pregnant women. Impact on the outcome of pregnancy.
- Effectiveness of intervention.
- Evidence on cost-effectiveness of intervention.
- Scalability of the program.

References

1. SDG Indicators — SDG indicators [Internet]. [cited 2022 Aug 3]. Available from: https://unstats.un.org/sdgs/metadata/?Text=&Goal=2&Target=2.2.
2. Global nutrition targets 2025: anaemia policy brief [Internet]. [cited 2022 Aug 3]. Available from: https://www.who.int/publications-detail-redirect/WHO-NMH-NHD-14.4.
3. Devasenapathy N, Singh R, Moodbidri P, Bhushan H, Gupta S, Zodpey SP, et al. An observational study on the use of IV iron sucrose among anaemic pregnant women in government healthcare facilities from two states of India. J Obstet Gynaecol India. 2015;65(4):230–5.
4. Anemia Mukt Bharat (AMB) | National Health Mission Tamil Nadu, Department of Health & Family Welfare Govt. of Tamil Nadu, India [Internet]. [cited 2022 Jul 12]. Available from: https://www.nhm.tn.gov.in/en/nhm-programsrmncha/anemia-mukt-bharat-amb.
5. Abhilashini GD, Sagili H, Reddi R. Intravenous iron sucrose and oral iron for the treatment of iron deficiency anaemia in pregnancy. J Clin Diagn Res JCDR. 2014;8(5):OC04–7.
6. Neogi SB, Devasenapathy N, Singh R, Bhushan H, Shah D, Divakar H, et al. Safety and effectiveness of intravenous iron sucrose versus standard oral iron therapy in pregnant women with moderate-to-severe anaemia in India: a multicentre, open-label, phase 3, randomised, controlled trial. Lancet Glob Health. 2019;7(12):e1706–16.
7. Pandey AK, Gautam D, Tolani H, Neogi SB. Clinical outcome post treatment of anemia in pregnancy with intravenous versus oral iron therapy: a systematic review and meta-analysis. Sci Rep. 2024;14(1):179. https://doi.org/10.1038/s41598-023-50234-w. PMID: 38167523; PMCID: PMC10761955.
8. Ray S, Neogi SB, Singh R, Devasenapathy N, Zodpey S. Is IV iron sucrose a cost-effective option for treatment of severe anaemia in pregnancy as compared with oral iron? Health Policy Plan. 2021;35(10):1339–46.

18 Case Study 4: The Raipur Rani Project and the Bellary Model

Anuj Kumar Pandey
and Sutapa Bandyopadhyay Neogi

"A case study to address growing Mental health disease burden in India."

This case study pertains to an intervention to address growing mental health disease burden in India.

Step 1: Is there enough evidence to say that a particular disease (psychiatric problems in this case) is a substantial public health problem?

Approximately, 2–3% of Indians suffered from severely disabling mental illnesses, according to epidemiological surveys carried out in the 1970s [1–3]. A meta-analysis of 15 epidemiological studies reported a high prevalence rate of 73/1000 population at the national level. Study also reported that the urban morbidity was 3.5% higher than the rural morbidity [4].

Looking at the services availability, the majority of the patients during 1970s did not have easy access to the mental health care facilities. With an estimate of one psychiatric bed and five trained healthcare professional/million population [5], condition demanded more trained professionals and healthcare facilities. Although the magnitude of the disease was very high, unfortunately no clear plans were available to meet the needs of the majority of mentally unwell individuals.

Step 2: Are there potential solutions/interventions to tackle the problem?

Acknowledging the complexity of mental health seeking behavior pattern and health service delivery, various health models were proposed by the policy makers/researchers across globe. Some of these models in Australia [6] and South Africa [7] offer some of the best examples for community level psychiatric models. Further some researchers have also suggested decentralizing and integrating primary mental health care with general health care services [2, 5, 8, 9].

The recommendation of World Health Organization's expert consultation committee, published in 1975 highlighted an urgent need for establishing national mental health program (NMHP) & provided major motivation for organization of mental health services [8].

Step 3: What is the level of evidence?

The Raipur Rani project followed by the Bellary Model has been a key influential project that led to the establishment of India's mental health services.

A. K. Pandey · S. Bandyopadhyay Neogi (✉)
Department of Health Systems and Implementation Research, International Institute of Health Management Research (IIHMR), New Delhi, India
e-mail: anuj@iihmrdelhi.edu.in; sutapa@iihmrdelhi.edu.in

S. Bandyopadhyay Neogi, A. K. Pandey (eds.), *Designing and Evaluating Public Health Interventions*, https://doi.org/10.1007/978-981-97-9574-1_18

18.1 Raipur Rani Project [10]

This study was undertaken as part of one of the WHO's collaborative study on extending mental healthcare in India. The study was undertaken in an agricultural area named Raipur Rani in Ambala District, in one of the northern states in India.

- The primary focus was on evaluating if mental health care can be integrated with the general health care services. The district with a population of 60,000, served by four doctors and some paraprofessionals was selected for study.
- Baseline data of the deceased were gathered. Selected disorders with priority for intervention were included during the baseline survey. After almost a year, around 4000 individuals started accessing the mental healthcare facility.
- ***Effectiveness of the project:*** Interviews with a subset population revealed a positive change in the behavior of the general population and thus an increase in identification and mental health seeking behavior. The project ensured an overall acceptance of primary health care team. The project also facilitated the development and piloting of various mental health-related research instruments.
  - The project identified means to study the community attitude.
  - The development of manual and simple training program was another significant contribution of the project.
  - Gaps related to supervision and smooth functioning of the services by peripheral health workers were identified and necessary steps to cater to those issues were also formulated.
  - The creation of the "Mental Health Association" by village leaders. This association ensured an overall community awareness.
- ***Project's Limitation*** [1]: The work was criticized for not being inclusive as patient's identification was not being done by the trained healthcare professionals, care being provided, and overall impact.

Step 4: Is it cost effective?

The studies were conducted to assess the feasibility of including it in national programs; however, no separate economic evaluation was carried out.

Step 5: Can the intervention be scaled up?

Recognizing that the NMHP would not likely be operationalized in a district under the name "**The Bellary District Project**," the NIMHANS-Bangalore in 1985 established a program to operationalize and implement the NMHP in a district without first demonstrating its viability in bigger populations.

To initiate the development of a mental health program at the district level, the project took place in Bellary District, located in the southern part of Karnataka, India. The initiative focused on a healthcare unit at the district level, catering to a population of 2 million residents.

- The initiative comprised the decentralized training of primary healthcare professionals, the delivery of mental healthcare across all facilities, engagement of diverse health and welfare personnel, supply of necessary medications, documentation tasks, and the establishment of a system to monitor work activities.

  Project Effectiveness: The project demonstrated the feasibility of integrating basic mental health care into primary health services. Additionally, findings indicated a restricted participation of specialist professionals in both planning and service delivery. Consequently, the project underscored the necessity to establish a mental health care.
- Between 1985 and 1990, the feasibility of providing fundamental mental health services at the district, taluk, and primary health center levels through trained primary health center personnel was illustrated throughout the entire Bellary district in the state of Karnataka [11, 12].
- Bellary project continued till 1995 and concluded that mental health services can effectively be provided at PHC settings.

The "Bellary Model" resulted in the formulation of District Mental Health Programme

(DMHP), a core for NMHP. This is a fully centrally sponsored scheme for 5 years [13]. The program was implemented in two phases during 1996–1997 and 1997–2002. During initial stage it got scaled in 27 districts and later-on got rolled out across the country in all the districts in phased manner [14].

Is This a Successful Model?

India with 1 in 20 population currently suffering from depression and nearly 10% of the population suffering from some mental health illness with high prevalence of substance use, researchers are critically evaluating the success of the DMHP [15]. Researchers have pointed the inadequacy of DMHP in successfully delivering the services to the community due to inadequacy of trained human resources, infrastructure, and service delivery component, political consciousness toward the program's objective [16].

Discussion Points

- Evidence on effectiveness of intervention by DMHP.
- Evidence on cost-effectiveness of intervention.
- Scalability of DMHP program.
- Current program impact and quality control aspect of the program.

References

1. Murthy RS. Rural psychiatry in developing countries. Psychiatr Serv. 1998;49(7):967–9.
2. Verghese A, Beig A, Senseman LA, Rao SS, Benjamin V. A social and psychiatric study of a representative group of families in Vellore town. Indian J Med Res. 1973;61(4):608–20.
3. Dube KG. A study of prevalence and biosocial variables in mental illness in a rural and an urban community in Uttar Pradesh—India. Acta Psychiatr Scand. 1970;46(4):327–59.
4. Ganguli HC. Epidemiological findings on prevalence of mental disorders in India. Indian J Psychiatry. 2000;42(1):14–20.
5. Waraich BK, Raj L, Chavan BS, Badhan R, Panda S. Decentralisation of mental health services under DMHP. Indian J Psychiatry. 2003;45(3):161–5.
6. Kelly BJ, Perkins DA, Fuller JD, Parker SM. Shared care in mental illness: a rapid review to inform implementation. Int J Ment Health Syst. 2011;5:31.
7. Sokhela NE, Uys LR. The integration of comprehensive psychiatric/mental health care into the primary health system: diagnosis and treatment. J Adv Nurs. 1999;30(1):229–37.
8. WHO Expert Committee on Mental Health & World Health Organization. Organization of mental health services in developing countries : sixteenth report of the WHO expert committee on mental health [meeting held in Geneva from 22 to 28 October 1974]. World Health Organization; 1975. Available from: https://apps.who.int/iris/handle/10665/38212.
9. Kapur RL. Mental health care in rural India: a study of existing patterns and their implications for future policy. Br J Psychiatry J Ment Sci. 1975;127:286–93.
10. Wig NN, Murthy RS, Harding TW. A model for rural psychiatric services—Raipur Rani experience. Indian J Psychiatry. 1981;23(4):275–90.
11. Nagarajaiah RK, Chandrashekar CR, Isaac MK, Srinivasamurthy R. Evaluation of short term training in mental health for multipurpose workers. Indian J Psychiatry. 1994;36(1):12–7.
12. Naik AN, Parthasarathy R, Isaac MK. Brief report: families of rural mentally ill and treatment adherence in district mental health programme. Int J Soc Psychiatry. 1996;42(1):68–72.
13. National Mental Health Programme (NMHP) | Ministry of Health and Family Welfare | GOI [Internet]. [cited 2022 Aug 3]. Available from: https://mohfw.gov.in/sites/default/files/9903463892NMHP%20detail_0_2.pdf.
14. Issue-brief-DMHP-IV.pdf [Internet]. [cited 2022 Mar 8]. Available from: https://cmhlp.org/wp-content/uploads/2021/08/Issue-Brief-DMHP-IV.pdf.
15. Chakraborty K. District mental health program—moving beyond Bellary model. Indian J Psychiatry. 2018;60(4):510–1.
16. Singh OP. District mental health program—need to look into strategies in the era of mental health care act, 2017 and moving beyond Bellary model. Indian J Psychiatry. 2018;60(2):163–4.

Case Study 5: Sex Selection Drugs (SSD)

19

Anuj Kumar Pandey
and Sutapa Bandyopadhyay Neogi

"An intervention to combat increasing birth defects."

This case study is pertaining to an intervention aimed at reducing the birth defects due to community malpractices of sex selection. Later it has led to stricter enforcement of PCPNDT act (Pre-Conception and Pre-Natal Diagnostic Techniques Act) in India.

Step 1: Is there enough evidence to say that a particular disease (sex-selective drug consumption during pregnancy in this case) is a substantial public health problem?

Response: Yes. Supported by the following facts.

In many communities, there is a significant preference for male child due to certain social factors. To fulfill the demands, people use a range of techniques to have male child [1]. An incidental finding by a public health researcher during a meeting led to the investigation regarding use of indigenous preparations, referred to as sex selection drugs (SSD) in northern India.

The usage of various SSD among general population for conceiving a boy has also been documented in one of the literatures explaining traditional practices on sex selection in the northern part of India [1, 2]. It emphasized that 0.5% of pregnant women consume the traditional drugs for a male child. It is worth noting that this proportion of consuming such drugs increase substantially to 10% and 40% if the first child is female and if family has two girl children, respectively [1, 3].

Step 2: Are there potential solutions/interventions to tackle the problem?

Response: Yes.

Concerns about the sex ratio date back many years; surveys have revealed a skewed trend, favoring the males. There have been instances for use of a variety of methods to conceive boys, such as going through several pregnancies until a son is born, sex-selective abortions, and even drug use after conception for a boy child. A study entitled "**history of son preference and sex selection in India and in the west** [4]" explains various approaches adopted by population for a male child. It was typical for people to follow stringent rituals such as consuming a special diet both before and after conception, time, and date of sexual activity (including specific dates like the second, fourth, or sixth of the month for male children or full/no moon) and recite mantras(prayers).

A. K. Pandey · S. Bandyopadhyay Neogi (✉)
Department of Health Systems and Implementation Research, International Institute of Health Management Research (IIHMR), New Delhi, India
e-mail: anuj@iihmrdelhi.edu.in; sutapa@iihmrdelhi.edu.in

S. Bandyopadhyay Neogi, A. K. Pandey (eds.), *Designing and Evaluating Public Health Interventions*, https://doi.org/10.1007/978-981-97-9574-1_19

Apart from these approaches, intake of various indigenous preparations during the first trimester of pregnancy is also a common practice in certain part of India [4–6]. Various research findings and also anecdotal narratives revealed usage of such drug in India leading to banning of production of such drugs by the Government of Gujarat during 1991 [7]. There were no study or evidence suggesting deleterious effects due to consumption of such drugs.

Step 3: What is the level of evidence?

Response: There was evidence that SSD use is quite prevalent. However, there was no documented evidence about the harms that could be associated with SSDs. The research gap paved the way for designing two population-based case control studies for generating evidence on its association with congenital malformations and stillbirths.

Studies conducted in a State in the northern part of India—Haryana, demonstrated that intake of such medicines/drugs named as SSDs is linked to negative consequences like birth abnormalities and stillbirths. The percentage of live-born infants who consumed them ranged from 7.3% to 10% and had no obvious birth abnormalities. However, 25% for infants born with abnormalities had a history of use of such drug, whereas it was about 16% for stillbirths. According to these study findings, such medications increase the risk of having any noticeable birth defect by three times and 2.5 times higher risk of stillbirths [8].

A biochemical examination of these drugs to look for phytoestrogens and testosterone revealed very high levels—nearly ten times the maximum permitted limits [9].

Step 4: Is it cost effective?

Response: Not applicable as the intervention results were negative.

Step 5: Can the intervention be scaled up?

Response: Evidence of this nature that directly impacts mankind warrants immediate action and intervention. In order to translate the findings into real action, the Government of Haryana took a strong stand to curb the practice. They enforced the implementation of PCPNDT Act (Pre-Conception and Pre-Natal Diagnostic Techniques Act) with a special focus on SSDs. They set up a strong mechanism to identify SSD sellers and conduct raids on them. The entire state Government machinery right from the topmost level till the front-line workers got involved in the process.

First Information Reports (FIRs) were filed under the PCPNDT Act's provisions, and individuals found selling these fake medications or gender selection kits with the aim of promoting the birth of male children were the targets of searches. In Haryana in 2015–2016, 124 of these raids were carried out effectively in a single year, 24 of which targeted individuals offering gender selection kits or SSDs in exchange for the ability to facilitate the birth of a male kid. Additionally, they pursued punitive measures against two sex selection websites. Sex ratios had been gradually but steadily reversing in numerous areas as a result of the Act's tight enforcement.

The gender ratio in Haryana had surpassed 900 for the first time in recorded history is a testimony of the fact that the act of Sex selection is gradually declining. The nation's leaders, from the prime minister at the top to the chief ministers at the state and district magistrates at the district levels, demonstrated a clear dedication to the cause, which accelerated the movement down to the local level. The genuine spirit and meaning of "Beti Bachao Beti Padhao," as embodied by Haryana, gradually became apparent to the nation.

The second intervention was to generate awareness among common people. A short film of 50 seconds duration highlighting the harmful effects of SSDs was developed and was uploaded by Department of Science and Technology (DST) onto their website and subsequently by India Bioscience and the Wire.

Discussion Points

- What was the level of evidence generated?
- Why was cost-effectiveness not required?
- Ways to scaling up

References

1. Bandyopadhyay S, Singh AJ. Sex selection through traditional drugs in rural North India. Indian J Community Med. 2007;32(1):32.
2. Neogi SB. Gender Before Birth in India. Springer Singapore; 2021 Sep 18.
3. Neogi SB, Zodpey S, Negandhi P, Gupta R. Use of sex selection techniques for social reasons: a menace. Indian Pediatr. 2017;54(2):99–101.
4. Bandyopadhyay S, Singh A. History of son preference and sex selection in India and in the west. Bull Indian Inst Hist Med Hyderabad. 2003;33(2):149–67.
5. Bhagat N, Laskar AR, Sharma N. Women's perception about sex selection in an urban slum in Delhi. J Reprod Infant Psychol. 2012;30(1):92–104. https://doi.org/10.1080/02646838.2011.635297.
6. Manchanda S, Saikia B, Gupta N, Chowdhary S, Puliyel JM. Sex ratio at birth in India, its relation to birth order, sex of previous children and use of indigenous medicine. PLoS One. 2011;6(6):e20097.
7. Unnikrishnan PV. Banned — select: "a drug to alter the sex of the foetus.". Health Millions. 1993;1(2):29–30.
8. Neogi SB, Negandhi PH, Ganguli A, Chopra S, Sandhu N, Gupta RK, et al. Consumption of indigenous medicines by pregnant women in North India for selecting sex of the foetus: what can it lead to? BMC Pregnancy Childbirth. 2015;15:208.
9. Neogi SB, Negandhi PH, Sandhu N, Gupta RK, Ganguli A, Zodpey S, et al. Indigenous medicine use for sex selection during pregnancy and risk of congenital malformations: a population-based case-control study in Haryana. India Drug Saf. 2015;38(9):789–97.

20 Case Study 6: Solidarity Trial

Anuj Kumar Pandey
and Sutapa Bandyopadhyay Neogi

"An intervention for generating evidence on treatment regimens for COVID-19."

Since the COVID-19 got declared as a pandemic [1], healthcare systems across the globe has focused on containing the spread of the disease and also management of the cases [2]. Despite all the efforts to limit morbidity and mortality, the massive rise in cases has exhausted the entire health system. Beyond any public health interventions, based on very limited understanding, several drugs have been considered as treatment modality for SARS-CoV-2 infection [2, 3]. The present case study deals with generating evidence on treatment regimens and their contribution in changing global policy.

Step 1: Is there enough evidence to say that a particular disease (COVID in this case) is a significant public health problem?

Response: Yes.

Step 2: Are there potential solutions/ interventions to tackle the problem?

Response: 2914 trials as on 23rd February 2021 were completed or underway for identifying an effective intervention to manage, treat, and contain the spread of COVID-19 virus [4]. Despite these efforts put forth globally, knowledge regarding the treatment options for COVID-19 infection was minimal [3].

During early pandemic, no known treatment (Therapeutic) option existed, thus supportive care was the only way forward for the recovery [5]. In order to provide evidence-based recommendations, one of the largest randomized control trials (RCT) on SARS-nCOV2 therapeutics was initiated. The objective was to provide insight on the effectiveness of drugs as a treatment modality for COVID-19 [6].

Step 3: What is the level of evidence?

Response: "Solidarity Trial"—a trial with international collaborations in order to identify effective treatment for the fatal COVID-19 infection was initiated. FDA, i.e., Food and Drug administration, authorized a set of drugs for use amongst COVID-19 infected patients, under Emergency Use authority (EUA). The approved drugs were-**Remdesivir** [7], **Hydroxychloroquine** [8], **Ritonavir or lopinavir** [9], and **lopinavir/ ritonavir/ interferon beta 1a** [10]. Thus, this trial aimed to provide insights on whether these approved drugs is effective in saving lives of those infected with COVID-19. One of the primary objectives was to

A. K. Pandey · S. Bandyopadhyay Neogi (✉)
Department of Health Systems and Implementation Research, International Institute of Health Management Research (IIHMR), New Delhi, India
e-mail: anuj@iihmrdelhi.edu.in; sutapa@iihmrdelhi.edu.in

S. Bandyopadhyay Neogi, A. K. Pandey (eds.), *Designing and Evaluating Public Health Interventions*, https://doi.org/10.1007/978-981-97-9574-1_20

identify effectiveness of these drugs in severely infected COVID-19 patients. Other objectives were to assess effectiveness of these drugs on overall mortality, ventilatory support requirement, and hospitalization rate/duration [11].

- **Type of Study**: Randomized, open, or blinded clinical trial.
- **Duration of the trial**: 22 March to fourth October 2020.
- **Sample enrolment**: 11,330 COVID-19 positive patients (405 hospitals- 30 countries).
- **Trial registration:** This trial was registered prospectively (ISRCTN83971151) as an open-label, randomized trial [12].
- **Randomization**: Unstratified 1:1 randomization between the drug and control. Sampling flowchart explains the trial entry with follow-up and intention to treat analysis, available elsewhere [13].
- **Treatment allocation:**

Sr. No.	Number of patients assigned under each medicine heads
1.	2750 patients—Remdesivir
2.	954 patients—Hydroxychloroquine (HCQ)
3.	1411 patients—Lopinavir (without interferon)
4.	2063 patients—interferon (651—interferon plus lopinavir)
5.	4088—no trial-drug
So, 94 to 96%—adherence through treatment, 2 to 6% crossover.	

- **Trial Findings** [13]:
  - 1253 deaths were stated (IQR: 4–14, Median: 8 days). The Kaplan–Meier 28-day mortality was 11.8%.
  - In Remdesivir intervention arm, 301 mortalities happened (from 2743 received the drug), whereas 303 people died (from 2708) in its control arm (rate ratio, 0.95; 95% confidence interval [CI], 0.81 to 1.11; P = 0.50).
  - In HCQ arm, 104 mortalities (from total sample of 947) happened as compared to 84(from 906) in its control arm (rate ratio, 1.19; 95% CI, 0.89 to 1.59; P = 0.23).
  - In Lopinavir arm, 148 people died (from 1399) as compared to 146 (from 1372) in the control arm in (rate ratio, 1.00; 95% CI, 0.79 to 1.25; P = 0.97).
  - In the interferon group, 243 mortalities were reported from 2050 patients as compared to 216 mortality (from 2050) in its control arm (rate ratio, 1.16; 95% CI, 0.96 to 1.39; P = 0.11).
- **Trial Conclusion** [13]:
  - The trial concluded that from the list of approved drugs, none was effective in reducing the mortality effectively. Neither of the drug showed positive effect on the ventilation or hospitalization status or even for decreasing any major secondary clinical outcomes.

Step 4: Is it cost effective?

Response: Not required as the intervention results were negative.

Step 5: Can the intervention be scaled up?

Response: Not applicable.

Step 6: Can the intervention be a part of the national program?

Response: Yes. It became a part of global policy.

Discussion Points

- **Ethical considerations of the trial.**
- **Effectiveness of the trial:** Change in the Treatment protocol for COVID-19 case management.
- **What are the learnings from the trial?**

References

1. WHO announces COVID-19 outbreak a pandemic [Internet]. [cited 2022 Feb 22]. Available from: https://www.euro.who.int/en/health-topics/health-emergencies/coronavirus-covid-19/news/news/2020/3/who-announces-covid-19-outbreak-a-pandemic.
2. Garegnani LI, Madrid E, Meza N. Misleading clinical evidence and systematic reviews on ivermectin for COVID-19. BMJ Evid Based Med. 2022;27(3):156–8. https://doi.org/10.1136/bmjebm-2021-111678.

3. Siemieniuk RA, Bartoszko JJ, Ge L, Zeraatkar D, Izcovich A, Kum E, et al. Drug treatments for COVID-19: living systematic review and network meta-analysis. BMJ. 2020;370:m2980.
4. COVID-19 clinical trials [Internet]. [cited 2022 Feb 23]. Available from: https://www.covid19-trials.org/.
5. Dagens A, Sigfrid L, Cai E, Lipworth S, Cheng V, Harris E, et al. Scope, quality, and inclusivity of clinical guidelines produced early in the COVID-19 pandemic: rapid review. BMJ. 2020;369:m1936.
6. UN News [Internet]. 2020. UN health chief announces global 'solidarity trial' to jumpstart search for COVID-19 treatment. [cited 2022 Feb 23]. Available from: https://news.un.org/en/story/2020/03/1059722.
7. Bose D, Gogtay NJ, Rajan SK. Placing the results of the SOLIDARITY trial with regards to remdesivir in perspective. Lung India. 2021;38(4):382–6.
8. Thomson K, Nachlis H. Emergency use authorizations during the COVID-19 pandemic: lessons from hydroxychloroquine for vaccine authorization and approval. JAMA. 2020;324(13):1282–3.
9. Magro P, Zanella I, Pescarolo M, Castelli F, Quiros-Roldan E. Lopinavir/ritonavir: repurposing an old drug for HIV infection in COVID-19 treatment. Biom J. 2021;44(1):43–53.
10. Researcher SSNI MD, MPH, MBA, Senior. An Investigation Into Beneficial Effects of Interferon Beta 1a, Compared to The Base Therapeutic Regiment in Moderate to Severe COVID-19: A Randomized, Double-Blind, Placebo-Controlled, Clinical Trial [Internet]. clinicaltrials.gov; 2020 Apr [cited 2022 Feb 21]. Report No.: NCT04350671. Available from: https://clinicaltrials.gov/ct2/show/NCT04350671.
11. An international randomised trial of additional treatments for COVID-19 in hospitalised patients who are all receiving the local standard of care [Internet]. [cited 2022 Feb 23]. Available from: https://www.who.int/publications/m/item/an-international-randomised-trial-of-additional-treatments-for-covid-19-in-hospitalised-patients-who-are-all-receiving-the-local-standard-of-care.
12. ISRCTN—ISRCTN83971151: Public health emergency SOLIDARITY trial of treatments for COVID-19 infection in hospitalized patients [Internet]. [cited 2022 Feb 23]. Available from: https://www.isrctn.com/ISRCTN83971151.
13. WHO Solidarity Trial Consortium, Pan H, Peto R, Henao-Restrepo AM, Preziosi MP, Sathiyamoorthy V, Abdool Karim Q, Alejandria MM, Hernández García C, Kieny MP, Malekzadeh R, Murthy S, Reddy KS, Roses Periago M, Abi Hanna P, Ader F, Al-Bader AM, Alhasawi A, Allum E, Alotaibi A, Alvarez-Moreno CA, Appadoo S, Asiri A, Aukrust P, Barratt-Due A, Bellani S, Branca M, Cappel-Porter HBC, Cerrato N, Chow TS, Como N, Eustace J, García PJ, Godbole S, Gotuzzo E, Griskevicius L, Hamra R, Hassan M, Hassany M, Hutton D, Irmansyah I, Jancoriene L, Kirwan J, Kumar S, Lennon P, Lopardo G, Lydon P, Magrini N, Maguire T, Manevska S, Manuel O, McGinty S, Medina MT, Mesa Rubio ML, Miranda-Montoya MC, Nel J, Nunes EP, Perola M, Portolés A, Rasmin MR, Raza A, Rees H, Reges PPS, Rogers CA, Salami K, Salvadori MI, Sinani N, JAC S, Stevanovikj M, Tacconelli E, Tikkinen KAO, Trelle S, Zaid H, Røttingen JA, Swaminathan S. Repurposed antiviral drugs for Covid-19 — interim WHO solidarity trial results. N Engl J Med. 2021;384(6):497–511.

21 Case Study 7: Polio Eradication Program

Anuj Kumar Pandey
and Sutapa Bandyopadhyay Neogi

> "An intervention regarding India's success story in eliminating polio."

This case study is regarding India's success story in eliminating polio, challenging the prediction that it is non-eradicable owing to poor sanitation and hygiene in the country. It presents how India could overcome its low priority and high eradication cost, polio was not considered worth eradicating [1].

Step 1: Is there enough evidence to say that a particular disease (Polio in this case) is a substantial public health problem?

Response: Yes, supported by following facts. Polio was hyperendemic in India during the 1970s to the early 1990s, with 200,000–400,000 cases each year which was equal to approximate 500 cases/day [2]. India being one of the developing countries was among most affected with polio prior to its decline in 1990s.

Step 2: Are there potential solutions/ interventions to tackle the problem?

Response: Yes. In the context of polio, India contributed to pioneering research to understand the epidemiological and vaccination component to stop the spread of this capricious disease [3].

- First study on low immunogenic efficacy of oral polio vaccine with accepted dosage was published in 1972 which corroborated with the development of polio disease amongst children who have received all the recommended doses of OPV [4, 5]. Studies from India also reported low immunogenic efficacy [6, 7]. In contrary to this, IPV had showed significant vaccine efficacy in some clinical studies; unfortunately, this couldn't be used due to licensing issues [8].
- Sabin's oral polio vaccine (OPV) received approval in the USA as monovalent and trivalent vaccines in 1961 and 1963, respectively. Consequently, Sabin contributed these vaccine strains to India (Pasteur Institute—Tamil Nadu) and provided direct training to the personnel for OPV production. However, between 1968 and 1974, only six batches were released, and rather than expanding the production capacity, the OPV unit was ultimately shut down [9].

Step 3: What is the level of evidence?

Response: There is ample evidence that proved to be effective in controlling the spread and later in eradicating Polio.

A. K. Pandey · S. Bandyopadhyay Neogi (✉)
Department of Health Systems and Implementation Research, International Institute of Health Management Research (IIHMR), New Delhi, India
e-mail: anuj@iihmrdelhi.edu.in;
sutapa@iihmrdelhi.edu.in

S. Bandyopadhyay Neogi, A. K. Pandey (eds.), *Designing and Evaluating Public Health Interventions*, https://doi.org/10.1007/978-981-97-9574-1_21

Polio in India-Expanded Program on Immunization (EPI) Era and Phases of Polio Eradication

- In 1974, WHO's recommendation of OPV usage was launched and later 1978 India adopted it. India started importing OPV for use in EPI post its manufacturing discontinuation in 1974. India's public sector by then started large scale manufacture of DPT and BCG vaccine, thus EPI began in India.
- As the vaccine was being imported, it was initially given to urban residents (1978–1980) and later to the rural areas (1981–1982) [10].
- Despite OPV in EPI, there was no decline in the polio cases as there was no provision for robust surveillance activity and the sentinel surveillance system was reporting just 10% of the total cases [3].
- Status of polio (1974–1994) can be seen published elsewhere [3].
- During this period (1970s and 1980s) due to the low vaccine efficacy many cases of polio were getting reported from children having complete three dosage of OPV. Increase in vaccine failure increased from 10% in 1979 to 30% in 1985 and later 50% in 1989 [9].
- In response to low vaccine efficacy, several modifications were attempted and one of them was to give additional dosage, which have shown proportional increase in the vaccine efficacy [11]. Thus, five doses policy was recommended which was again not accepted by EPI [3]. In addition to this, **pulsing three doses** have also shown to increase the vaccine efficacy [12].
- Vellore in India became first city to be "Polio free" post-OPV immunization and thus the concept of pulse immunization was created and started [13].
- ICMR initiated a study during 1985 in North Arcot district having 5 million population with OPV dosage in one arm and IPV in another arm. Study reported a decline in the polio incidence in both the arms, with faster decline in IPV arm [14].

  "The Pulse Polio Initiative was implemented with the goal of attaining complete coverage with the Oral Polio Vaccine. The objective was to immunize children by enhancing social mobilization, strategizing mop-up operations in regions where the poliovirus was nearly eradicated and sustaining a high level of public morale."
- **Effectiveness of intervention**: Later in 1989, almost a decade after the launch of EPI, the number of cases of polio started declining showing a cumulative effect of increasing the vaccine coverage and thus a direct effect of vaccine efficacy and indirect effect of herd immunity.
- Thus 1995–2012 for India was considered as a phase of polio eradication.
- In line with the World Health Assembly's decision to eliminate polio in 1988, India began its implementation efforts at the national level in 1995–1996. The initiation of the National Polio Surveillance Project (NPSP), a collaborative venture between the World Health Organization and the Government of India, marked the commencement of polio eradication activities. Subsequently, these activities were concurrently organized with the Universal Immunization Program (UIP) as a distinct national initiative.

Step 4: Is it cost effective?

Response: An article by T J John on "**Cost and benefits of immunization in India** [15]" stated a detailed economic burden of Polio. The article discusses the annual productivity loss which accounts to almost 50% per capita gross national product. Considering an estimated 2–4 lakhs polio cases annually during 1987–1988, it translated to almost a loss of 15 lakhs INR/ paralyzed child extending to over 30 years of productivity for almost 3,00,000 victims of polio thus concluding to almost loss of 45,000 crores which is excluding other expenses. Thus, the authors have stated that this intervention was not only necessary on humanitarian grounds but rather for socio-economic growth of the country also.

Step 5: Can the intervention be scaled up?

Response: The intervention was scaled up across the country [16].

- In 1994, an initial polio immunization campaign was launched in Delhi, targeting approximately 1 million children aged up to 3 years. This effort expanded nationwide in 1995, ultimately immunizing 88 million children within the 3-year age range. The campaign was further extended to include children under 5 years, leading to a significant reduction in polio incidences.
- Active surveillance of acute flaccid paralysis (AFP) began in October 1997 under the National Polio Surveillance Project (NPSP). In 1999, the Government of India established the India Expert Advisory Group for polio (IEAG).
- By the years 2000 and 2001, there were only 265 and 268 cases attributed to Wild Polio Virus (WPV) 1 and 3, marking a remarkable decline of over 99% in India from the 1980s. While effective control of polio was achieved by 2000, complete interruption of WPV transmission had not occurred.
- In 2012, a single case of Vaccine-Derived Polio Virus (VDPV) was reported. Importantly, this occurrence did not negate the status of the absence of WPV in human infection over the 2 years leading up to January 2013.
- India successfully attained polio-free status in January 2011 and has maintained this status to the present day.

Step 6: Can the intervention be a part of the national program?

Response: Yes. Pulse polio was one of the biggest vertical programs in India.

Discussion Points

- Evidence on Success of Pulse polio.
- Economic aspect of Pulse polio and Scalability of Pulse polio.

References

1. Kew O. Reaching the last one per cent: progress and challenges in global polio eradication. Curr Opin Virol. 2012;2(2):188–98.
2. John TJ. Poliomyelitis in India: prospects and problems of control. Rev Infect Dis. 1984;6(Suppl 2):S438–41.
3. Eradicating poliomyelitis: India's journey from hyperendemic to polio-free status [Internet]. [cited 2022 Jul 15]. Available from: https://main.icmr.nic.in/sites/default/files/icmr_bulletins/January_December_2013.pdf.
4. John TJ, Jayabal P. Oral polio vaccination of children in the tropics. I. The poor seroconversion rates and the absence of viral interference. Am J Epidemiol. 1972;96(4):263–9.
5. John TJ. Problems with oral poliovaccine in India. Indian Pediatr. 1972;9(5):252–6.
6. Ghosh S, Kumari S, Balaya S, Bhargava SK. Antibody response to oral polio vaccine in infancy. Indian Pediatr. 1970;7(2):78–81.
7. Pangi NS, Master JM, Dave KH. Efficacy of oral poliovaccine in infancy. Indian Pediatr. 1977;14(7):523–8.
8. John TJ. The golden jubilee of vaccination against poliomyelitis. Indian J Med Res. 2004;119(1):1–17.
9. John TJ. Understanding the scientific basis of preventing polio by immunization. Pioneering contributions from India. Proc Indian Natl Sci Acad B, Rev Tracts Biol Sci. 2003;69(4):393–422. Available from: https://scholar.google.com/scholar_lookup?journal=Proc+Indian+Natl+Sci+Acad&title=Understanding+the+scientific+basis+of+preventing+polio+by+immunization.+Pioneering+contributions+from+India&author=TJ+John&volume=B69&publication_year=2003&pages=393-422&
10. Basu RN. Expanded programme on immunization in India: progress report. Indian J Pediatr. 1980;47(5):361–5.
11. John TJ. Immunisation against polioviruses in developing countries. Rev Med Virol. 1993;3(3):149–60.
12. John TJ, Joseph A, Vijayarathnam P. A better system for polio vaccination in developing countries? Br Med J. 1980;281(6239):542. https://doi.org/10.1136/bmj.281.6239.542.
13. John TJ, Pandian R, Gadomski A, Steinhoff M, John M, Ray M. Control of poliomyelitis by pulse immunisation in Vellore, India. Br Med J Clin Res Ed. 1983;286(6358):31–2.
14. John TJ, Samuel R, Balraj V, John R. Disease surveillance at district level: a model for developing countries. Lancet Lond Engl. 1998;352(9121):58–61.
15. John TJ. Cost and benefits of immunization in India. Indian Pediatr. 1981;18(8):513–6.
16. John TJ, Dharmapalan D. Challenges en route to polio eradication. Lancet. 2022;400(10350):428–9. https://doi.org/10.1016/S0140-6736(22)01274-0.

22 Case Study 8: Ekjut Trial

Anuj Kumar Pandey
and Sutapa Bandyopadhyay Neogi

> "An intervention regarding improving birth outcomes by improving community mobilization through participatory women's group."

This case study is regarding improving birth outcomes by improving community mobilization through participatory women's group in the rural, underdeveloped communities. The evaluation of this approach primarily took place in a predominantly tribal and rural population across three districts in the eastern part of India.

Step 1: Is there enough evidence to say that a particular disease (neonatal mortality and maternal depression) is a substantial public health problem?

Response: Yes, supported by following facts. Globally approximately 3.7 million children die per year during the first month of life [1, 2]. The advancement in reducing maternal and child mortality rates was inadequate, with fewer than 25% (16 out of 68 countries) making sufficient strides to meet the national targets. This goal aimed to achieve a two-thirds reduction in mortality rates among children under the age of five between 1990 and 2015 [3]. The situation among India reported that India accounted for around 20% of maternal deaths, 21% of all the mortality among children less than 5 years and one fourth of all the neonatal mortalities globally [4].

Depression among mothers is a matter of concern due to its high prevalence and wide range of health implications in low-income countries [5]. Due to this demand collaborative effort to reduce the mortality through cost-effective and scalable interventions.

Step 2: Are there potential solutions/ interventions to tackle the problem?

Response: Yes. There is abundant evidence indicating the efficacy of participatory interventions engaging women's groups in enhancing birth outcomes.

A cluster-randomized controlled trial was conducted in Nepal [6] to determine the impact of community-based participatory intervention on neonatal mortality rates. The study, spanning from 2001 to 2003, revealed a lower neonatal mortality in the intervention group (26.2 per 1000) compared to the control arm (36.9 per 1000) (adjusted odds ratio 0.70 [95% CI 0.53–0.94]). Additionally, the study observed a reduction in the maternal mortality ratio in the intervention cluster (69 per 100,000) in contrast to the control cluster (341 per 100,000) (0.22 [0.05–0.90]). No significant changes in stillbirth rates were noted in either group. This yielded Level 1 evidence.

A. K. Pandey · S. Bandyopadhyay Neogi (✉)
Department of Health Systems and Implementation Research, International Institute of Health Management Research (IIHMR), New Delhi, India
e-mail: anuj@iihmrdelhi.edu.in; sutapa@iihmrdelhi.edu.in

S. Bandyopadhyay Neogi, A. K. Pandey (eds.), *Designing and Evaluating Public Health Interventions*, https://doi.org/10.1007/978-981-97-9574-1_22

In addressing the community's needs, an additional study [5] incorporated participatory health education into the intervention to address issues related to maternal and newborn care. This approach has demonstrated effectiveness in enhancing the health conditions of both mothers and newborns.

There was limited understanding, if such interventions could be expanded with frontline workers (FLWs) from the government in settings with high mortality rates.

Step 3: What is the level of evidence?

Response: Although there was emerging evidence that participatory health education was effective in improving the maternal and newborn's health condition, such evidence from India was not available in 1990s and early 2000s. If important intervention attributes are kept and modified to local circumstances, participatory intervention might affect mother and child health outcomes. Hence, it was mandatory to have some evidence from India to understand whether it would work or not [7].

About Ekjut Trial

Researchers of Ekjut trial hypothesized a reduction in the neonatal mortality by at least 25% and reduction in maternal depression by 30% in underdeveloped tribal areas of the eastern part of India. The study planned to improve health seeking behaviors by a participatory intervention.

Thus, Cluster randomized controlled trial was initiated from a total of 36 clusters in two eastern States of India namely—Jharkhand and Orissa. Using a stratified randomization technique 18 clusters were designated to intervention arm and other to control arm as explained in randomization process published elsewhere [7].

Effectiveness of Intervention [7]

The study documented neonatal mortality rates (NMRs) of 55.6, 37.1, and 36.3 per 1000 live births in the intervention arm during the first three consecutive years, in contrast to 53.4, 59.6, and 64.3 in the control clusters per 100,000 live births. Additionally, it highlighted a 32% reduction in NMR in the intervention cluster when adjusted for sampling parameters (odds ratio 0.68, 95% CI 0.59–0.78) over the 3 years, with a 45% lower rate in years 2 and 3 (0.55, 0.46–0.66). While there was a 57% reduction in maternal depression in the third year of the study (0.43, 0.23–0.80), the overall findings did not indicate any significant impact on maternal depression.

Are there any Ethical Issues Involved?

Ethical consideration [8]**:** No ethical concerns were documented in the trial; instead, a separate group of researchers observed that such interventions can notably diminish socioeconomic disparities in newborn mortality, contributing to a more unbiased accomplishment the sustainable development goal (SDG).

Step 4: Is it cost-effective?

Response: Economic evaluation [7, 9, 10] was not conducted as a component under this study. However, a detailed costing analysis showed that cost of women's group intervention and the activities for enhancing the health system (estimated at 2007 prices) were the monetary and economic expenses for organizing the intervention and maintaining expenses throughout the trial. When health service strengthening efforts were added, the incremental rose to $1308 (in 2007 prices) for each baby life saved. The women's group intervention had an incremental cost per life year saved of $33 ($48 including health service strengthening measures). Thus, authors determined that the women's group intervention in this context proved to be a more economically efficient approach.

Step 5: Can the intervention be scaled up?

Response: Scalability of the intervention was considered in phases. Although the intervention has shown to be a sustainable and effective intervention on improving the overall quality of lives of individuals, in the absence of multiple geographies and type of population, the intervention lacked external validity. Thus, the decision to scale up this intervention was not taken up immediately.

An important aspect that goes in favor of scalability is its impact on equity. An analysis of data obtained through prospective surveillance showed that the most marginalized benefitted the most. Among them, the NMR was 59% lower in year 2 (70%, year 3). This is compared to 36% reduction in NMR among less marginalized.

(*P*-value for difference = 0.028, years 2–3; *P*-value for difference = 0.009, year 3) [8].

Once the trial was over, from 2008 to 2011, women's groups in the intervention clusters independently continued participating in a new cycle of participatory learning and action (Zone 1). Simultaneously, the original control group initiated a series of meetings focusing on maternal and neonatal health (Zone 2). The impact of the intervention persisted in Zone 1, with a decrease in neonatal mortality rate (NMR) from 41.3 to 34.2. In Zone 2, there was also a reduction in NMR from 57.0 to 41.0. The researchers concluded that the influence of participatory women's groups on neonatal survival was both sustainable and replicable [11].

A government-led initiative in Jharkhand implemented a pragmatic cluster non-randomized controlled trial, expanding women's groups engaged in participatory learning and action (PLA). Across 24 months of the intervention, the neonatal mortality rate (NMR) was 29.1 in the early implementation group and 39.2 in the delayed implementation group. This resulted in a 24% reduction in neonatal mortality (adjusted odds ratio (AOR) 0.76, 95% CI 0.59 to 0.98), including a 26% reduction among the most deprived (AOR 0.74, 95% CI 0.57 to 0.95). In 20 out of Jharkhand's 24 districts where the intervention achieved sufficient meeting coverage and quality, an estimated 11,803 newborn lives were saved over 42 months, costing 41 international dollars per life year saved [10].

Owing to the impact of this intervention, this has resulted in their extension to additional Indian states like **Bihar, West Bengal, and Madhya Pradesh**.

Step 6: Can the intervention be a part of the national program?

Response: Yes. Scaling up is being done in a phased manner in high priority areas.

Discussion Points

- Evidence on effectiveness of such intervention.
- How this trial got scaled globally.
- Evidence on cost-effectiveness of intervention.

References

1. Lawn JE, Cousens S, Zupan J. Lancet neonatal survival steering team. 4 million neonatal deaths: when? Where? Why? Lancet Lond Engl. 2005;365(9462):891–900.
2. UNIGME-2023-Child-Mortality-Report.pdf. Available from: https://main.mohfw.gov.in/sites/default/files/26953755641410949469%20%281%29.pdf.
3. Countdown Coverage Writing Group, Countdown to 2015 Core Group, Bryce J, Daelmans B, Dwivedi A, Fauveau V, et al. Countdown to 2015 for maternal, newborn, and child survival: the 2008 report on tracking coverage of interventions. Lancet Lond Engl. 2008;(371, 9620):1247–58.
4. The state of the world's children 2008 [Internet]. [cited 2022 Jul 12]. Available from: https://www.unicef.org/reports/state-worlds-children-2008.
5. Morrison J, Tamang S, Mesko N, Osrin D, Shrestha B, Manandhar M, et al. Women's health groups to improve perinatal care in rural Nepal. BMC Pregnancy Childbirth. 2005;5(1):6.
6. Manandhar DS, Osrin D, Shrestha BP, Mesko N, Morrison J, Tumbahangphe KM, et al. Effect of a participatory intervention with women's groups on birth outcomes in Nepal: cluster-randomised controlled trial. Lancet Lond Engl. 2004;364(9438):970–9.
7. Rath S, Nair N, Tripathy PK, Barnett S, Rath S, Mahapatra R, et al. Explaining the impact of a women's group led community mobilisation intervention on maternal and newborn health outcomes: the Ekjut trial process evaluation. BMC Int Health Hum Rights. 2010;10(1):25.
8. Houweling TA, Tripathy P, Nair N, Rath S, Rath S, Gope R, et al. The equity impact of participatory women's groups to reduce neonatal mortality in India: secondary analysis of a cluster-randomised trial. Int J Epidemiol. 2013;42(2):520–32.
9. Tripathy P, Nair N, Barnett S, Mahapatra R, Borghi J, Rath S, et al. Effect of a participatory intervention with women's groups on birth outcomes and maternal depression in Jharkhand and Orissa, India: a cluster-randomised controlled trial. Lancet. 2010;375(9721):1182–92.
10. Nair N, Tripathy PK, Gope R, Rath S, Pradhan H, Rath S, et al. Effectiveness of participatory women's groups scaled up by the public health system to improve birth outcomes in Jharkhand, eastern India: a pragmatic cluster non-randomised controlled trial. BMJ Glob Health. 2021;6(11):e005066.
11. Roy SS, Mahapatra R, Rath S, Bajpai A, Singh V, Rath S, et al. Improved neonatal survival after participatory learning and action with women's groups: a prospective study in rural eastern India. Bull World Health Organ. 2013;91(6):426–433B.

Case Study 9: Banning of Vape in India

23

Anuj Kumar Pandey
and Sutapa Bandyopadhyay Neogi

"An initiative to ban ENDS or e-cigarettes in India"

"**Vape**" or an "**electronic cigarette**" is a battery-powered device that attempts to create the sensation of tobacco smoking. They heat up the nicotine and other components or flavoring substances to form an aerosol which then is used as a smoking substance as this facilitates the delivery of these products to the lungs and their absorption into bloodstream. It is a type of ENDS (Electronic Nicotine Delivery System). Vapes are different from cigarettes in their contents.

These products were manufactured mainly in China initially in year 2007 [1]. This was introduced ***as an alternative method or device for quitting smoking.*** E-cigarettes are categorized as not reusable, and rechargeable which can be refilled. More than over 466 brands of e-cigarettes are available in the market [2].

Step 1: Is there enough evidence to say that a particular disease (tobacco smoking in this case) is a significant public health problem?

Response: Yes.

Step 2: Are there potential solutions/ interventions to tackle the problem?

As of now, FDA has not granted approval for e-cigarettes to be used as a smoking cessation aid [3]. Nevertheless, limited studies available on this matter present varied findings.

- A ***Cochrane Review*** [4] examined studies investigating the effectiveness of e-cigarettes in aiding smoking cessation. The review incorporated a total of 61 randomized controlled trials. It revealed that individuals were likely to quit smoking for a duration of at least 6 months when using nicotine e-cigarettes compared to those using nicotine replacement therapy (4 studies, 1924 people), nicotine-free e-cigarettes (5 studies, 1447 people), or receiving no support/behavioral support only (6 studies, 2886 people).

  However, the review also noted that there is ***insufficient evidence to confidently assess the effects of e-cigarettes***, particularly the impact of newer varieties with enhanced nicotine delivery compared to older models of e-cigarettes.
- A survey conducted by the Center for Disease Control (CDC) [5] aimed at determining the prevalence of ten commonly employed smoking cessation methods among adult cigarette smokers was carried out between 2014 and 2016. The findings revealed that approxi-

A. K. Pandey · S. Bandyopadhyay Neogi (✉)
Department of Health Systems and Implementation Research, International Institute of Health Management Research (IIHMR), New Delhi, India
e-mail: anuj@iihmrdelhi.edu.in; sutapa@iihmrdelhi.edu.in

S. Bandyopadhyay Neogi, A. K. Pandey (eds.), *Designing and Evaluating Public Health Interventions*, https://doi.org/10.1007/978-981-97-9574-1_23

mately 74% of adults are utilizing e-cigarettes in their efforts to quit smoking. However, these individuals are unable to completely cease smoking cigarettes and often engage in the simultaneous use of both products, referred to as "Dual use." The study noted that a higher percentage of smokers turned to e-cigarettes, but due to a lack of conclusive evidence, further research is warranted.

- An additional investigation conducted in the United States in 2017, titled "The PATH Cohort Study," aimed to assess the "Efficacy of e-cigarettes as aids for smoking cessation." This study was undertaken on 3578 individuals who attempted to quit smoking and 1323 recent former smokers. The study found that in 2017, 12.6% (95% CI 11.3% to 13.9%) of recent quit attempters used e-cigarettes to assist in their cessation efforts, marking a decrease from prior years. The cigarette abstinence rate for e-cigarette users (9.9%, 95% CI 6.6% to 13.2%) was lower than for those who did not use any product (18.6%, 95% CI 16.0% to 21.2%). The absolute risk difference (aRD) for e-cigarettes versus pharmaceutical aids was −7.3% (95% CI −14.4 to −0.4), and for e-cigarettes versus any other method was −7.7% (95% CI −12.2 to −3.2). Only 2.2% (95% CI 0.0% to 4.4%) of recent former smokers switched to a high-nicotine e-cigarette.

  Higher relapse rate was reported amongst individuals who switched to e-cigarettes than others who have not switched to e-cigarettes or other tobacco (Not significant finding).

Step 3: What is the level of evidence?

A committee having members from various government and non-governmental organizations had reviewed various aspects of e-cigarettes usage and have put forth their views as a **White Paper on Electronic Nicotine Delivery System** [6]. The report suggested that-

- The use of nicotine is banned under the Food Safety and Standards Regulation, 2011 of the Food Safety and Standards Act, 2006.
- Such products are registered as hazardous chemicals under the Environment (Protection) Act, 1986 and in the Manufacture, Storage, and Import of Hazardous Chemical Rules, 1989.
- Committee members have also stated that there has been a decline in tobacco consumption in the past few years, in response to the various initiatives by Government.
- Members have emphasized that promoting a product such as ENDS, which lacks proven benefits and poses significant risks of addiction and health harm, is unwarranted as a tobacco control strategy.
- "Hence, the committee proposed a total ban on ENDS or e-cigarettes in India to safeguard public health comprehensively."
- Studies have reported that about 21% students in high school and 5% students in middle school reported to have used e-cigarettes in the last 30 days in 2018 [7, 8].
- An increasing trend in usage of ENDS was reported by the Global Youth Tobacco Survey and by a WHO report [9, 10].

Step 4: Is it cost effective?

Response: Not required as the intervention recommended to ban e-cigarettes.

Step 5: Can the intervention be scaled up?

Response: Yes.

Step 6: Can the intervention be a part of the national program?

Response: Yes; **E-cigarettes have been banned in India** [11].

In view of the concerns being raised by researchers worldwide regarding the use of electronic cigarettes, Government of India **imposed a ban on electronic cigarettes** in September 2019. The ban was imposed taking into consideration the recommendations given by the Indian Council of Medical Research, through its white paper on e-cigarettes. The white paper stated that the use of e-cigarettes is harmful to the health of the individual.

Discussion Points

- Impact of vaping on general population's health
- Evidence on the Effectiveness of banning of vaping.
- Evidence on Cost-effectiveness of banning of vaping.

References

1. Abuse NI on D. National Institute on Drug Abuse. 2020 [cited 2022 Mar 23]. Vaping devices (Electronic Cigarettes) DrugFacts. Available from: https://nida.nih.gov/publications/drugfacts/vaping-devices-electronic-cigarettes.
2. E-Cigarettes | Circulation [Internet]. [cited 2022 Mar 23]. Available from: https://www.ahajournals.org/doi/full/10.1161/CIRCULATIONAHA.114.007667?url_ver=Z39.88-2003&rfr_id=ori:rid:crossref.org&rfr_dat=cr_pub%3dpubmed.
3. Health CO on S and. Centers for Disease Control and Prevention. 2022 [cited 2022 Mar 23]. Smoking and Tobacco Use; Electronic Cigarettes. Available from: https://www.cdc.gov/tobacco/basic_information/e--cigarettes/about-e-cigarettes.html.
4. Can electronic cigarettes help people stop smoking, and do they have any unwanted effects when used for this purpose? | Cochrane [Internet]. [cited 2022 Mar 23]. Available from: https://www.cochrane.org/CD010216/TOBACCO_can-electronic-cigarettes-help-people-stop-smoking-and-do-they-have-any-unwanted-effects-when-used.
5. Caraballo RS, Shafer PR, Patel D, Davis KC, McAfee TA. Quit methods used by US adult cigarette smokers, 2014–2016. Prev Chronic Dis. 2017;14:160600.
6. Chakma JK, Dhaliwal RS, Mehrotra R. White paper on electronic nicotine delivery system. Indian J Med Res. 2019;149(5):574–83.
7. Cullen KA, Ambrose BK, Gentzke AS, Apelberg BJ, Jamal A, King BA. Notes from the field: use of electronic cigarettes and any tobacco product among middle and high school students—United States, 2011–2018. Morb Mortal Wkly Rep. 2018;67(45):1276–7.
8. Electronic cigarette use among middle and high school students—United States, 2011–2012. Morb Mortal Wkly Rep. 2013;62(35):729–30.
9. WHO Collaborating Centre on Tobacco Control \ textbar Center for Tobacco Control Research and Education [Internet]. Available from: https://tobacco.ucsf.edu/sites/tobacco.ucsf.edu/files/u9/Chan-letter-June16%20PST%20FINAL%20with%20129%20sigs.pdf.
10. National_Fact_Sheet_of_fourth_round_of_Global_Youth_Tobacco_Survey_GYTS-4.pdf [Internet]. Available from: https://escholarship.org/content/qt2f65f2j5/qt2f65f2j5.pdf.
11. Chakma JK, Kumar H, Bhargava S, Khanna T. The e-cigarettes ban in India: an important public health decision. Lancet Public Health. 2020;5(8):e426.

Case Study 10: Kangaroo Mother Care (KMC)

24

Anuj Kumar Pandey
and Sutapa Bandyopadhyay Neogi

"An initiative to assess effectiveness of community initiated KMC in LBW babies."

This case study is regarding "an implementation research" being undertaken to assess the if Kangaroo mother care, i.e., KMC is feasible, acceptable, and can be scaled in the community setting which later be called as cKMC, i.e., community-based Kangaroo mother care.

Step 1: Is there enough evidence to say that a particular disease (low birth weight in this case) is a substantial public health problem?

Response: **Yes**, supported by following facts.

Every year, approximately 15 million infants are born with a weight less than 2500 grams in low- and middle-income countries [1]. There are several studies suggesting that low birth weight increases the risk of various morbidities like, developmental delay due to infectious disease, and even death of infants and children also [2–5].

Step 2: Are there potential solutions/ interventions to tackle the problem?

Response: Yes. There is ample evidence to suggest the utility of Kangaroo Mother care (KMC) on improving outcomes.

- Kangaroo Mother Care (KMC) demonstrates positive effects compared to care provided in an incubator [6].
- Studies indicate that, in comparison to traditional care, Kangaroo Mother Care (KMC) is linked to a 40% relative decrease in the risk of mortality, a 65% reduction in the risk of acquiring hospital-acquired infections, and a 72% decrease in hypothermia at 40–41 weeks of postmenstrual age. Additional advantages encompass enhanced weight and height, cognitive development, strengthened mother-child bonding, and reduced stress levels in both mothers and infants [7–9].

Step 3: What is the level of evidence?

Response: There is substantial level I evidence supporting the efficacy of KMC, particularly in research studies conducted within hospitals and with KMC administered by trained healthcare professionals. However, there is a lack of adequate literature supporting the effectiveness of community-based KMC (cKMC) [10, 11]. Conducting formative research is essential in developing a delivery strategy for an intervention. Therefore, this formative research aimed to evaluate if cKMC is feasible, acceptable and can

A. K. Pandey · S. Bandyopadhyay Neogi (✉)
Department of Health Systems and Implementation Research, International Institute of Health Management Research (IIHMR), New Delhi, India
e-mail: anuj@iihmrdelhi.edu.in; sutapa@iihmrdelhi.edu.in

S. Bandyopadhyay Neogi, A. K. Pandey (eds.), *Designing and Evaluating Public Health Interventions*, https://doi.org/10.1007/978-981-97-9574-1_24

be scaled in community settings. The goal was to design an intervention package for a randomized controlled trial focusing on low-birth-weight infants.

As part of this research initiative, researchers conducted 40 in-depth interviews with recently delivered women and included six focus group discussions to gather insights from all family members and community health workers. Additionally, a prototype for an intervention package promoting cKMC was developed and tested. Study reported that -

- Mothers in the community were familiar that newborns with lower weight require special care. Despite being unaware of KMC practice, study participants believed that raising awareness of its advantages would encourage adoption of this practice. However, mothers have also expressed their concern about doing KMC just after delivery as they also need to take rest post-delivery. Some cultural practices like recently delivered women is not supposed to do any household chores was identified as an enabler to this practice.
- The study concluded that community-based KMC is acceptable to mothers with high adoption rates.

About the Trial [12]

This was a randomized controlled trial conducted amongst 552 stable low birth weight infants. Intervention involved promoting skin-to-skin contact and exclusive breast feeding. The intervention groups supported the study participants till 28 days postpartum until the baby started improving. These activities were undertaken by trained intervention delivery teams by visiting the homes of recently delivered women. Outcomes were measured and also a thorough assessment of infants using Bayley Scale of Infant Development (BSID-III) was also undertaken at infant-age 6 and 12.

Study reported that there is no significant impact of community initiated KMC on child developmental outcomes throughout infancy [13].

Step 4: Is it cost effective?

Response: The findings highlighted here are from the formative research done for developing a strategy for delivering an intervention; thus, economic evaluation was not undertaken.

Step 5: Can the intervention be scaled up?

Response: No, as the intervention results were negative.

Step 6: Can the intervention be a part of the national program?

Response: No.

Discussion Points

- How formative research can setup the base for an intervention.
- Negative results.

References

1. Lee ACC, Katz J, Blencowe H, Cousens S, Kozuki N, Vogel JP, et al. National and regional estimates of term and preterm babies born small for gestational age in 138 low-income and middle-income countries in 2010. Lancet Glob Health. 2013;1(1):e26–36.
2. Arifeen SE, Black RE, Caulfield LE, Antelman G, Baqui AH, Nahar Q, et al. Infant growth patterns in the slums of Dhaka in relation to birth weight, intrauterine growth retardation, and prematurity. Am J Clin Nutr. 2000;72(4):1010–7.
3. Ballot DE, Potterton J, Chirwa T, Hilburn N, Cooper PA. Developmental outcome of very low birth weight infants in a developing country. BMC Pediatr. 2012;12:11.
4. Soleimani F, Zaheri F, Abdi F. Long-term neurodevelopmental outcomes after preterm birth. Iran Red Crescent Med J. 2014;16(6):e17965.
5. Watkins WJ, Kotecha SJ, Kotecha S. All-cause mortality of low birthweight infants in infancy, childhood, and adolescence: population study of England and Wales. PLoS Med. 2016;13(5):e1002018.
6. WHO. Kangaroo mother care: a practical guide [Internet]. [cited 2022 Aug 23]. Report No.: 9241590351. Available from: https://www.who.int/publications-detail-redirect/9241590351.
7. Conde-Agudelo A, Belizán JM, Diaz-Rossello J. Kangaroo mother care to reduce morbidity and mortality in low birthweight infants. Cochrane Database Syst Rev. 2011;2011(3):CD002771. https://doi.org/10.1002/14651858.CD002771.pub2.
8. Conde-Agudelo A, Díaz-Rossello JL. Kangaroo mother care to reduce morbidity and mortality in low birthweight infants. Cochrane Database Syst Rev. 2016;2016(8):CD002771. https://doi.org/10.1002/14651858.CD002771.pub4.

9. Charpak N, Tessier R, Ruiz JG, Hernandez JT, Uriza F, Villegas J, et al. Twenty-year follow-up of kangaroo mother care versus traditional care. Pediatrics. 2017;139(1):e20162063.
10. Bazzano A, Hill Z, Tawiah-Agyemang C, Manu A, Ten Asbroek G, Kirkwood B. Introducing home based skin-to-skin care for low birth weight newborns: a pilot approach to education and counseling in Ghana. Glob Health Promot. 2012;19(3):42–9.
11. Chan GJ, Labar AS, Wall S, Atun R. Kangaroo mother care: a systematic review of barriers and enablers. Bull World Health Organ. 2016;94(2):130–141J.
12. Taneja S, Sinha B, Upadhyay RP, Mazumder S, Sommerfelt H, Martines J, et al. Community initiated kangaroo mother care and early child development in low birth weight infants in India-a randomized controlled trial. BMC Pediatr. 2020;20(1):150.
13. Mazumder S, Upadhyay RP, Hill Z, Taneja S, Dube B, Kaur J, et al. Kangaroo mother care: using formative research to design an acceptable community intervention. BMC Public Health. 2018;18(1):307.